Milton in the Age of Fish

Medieval & Renaissance Literary Studies

Milton
in the Age of
Fish

Essays on Authorship, Text, and Terrorism

edited by
Michael Lieb & Albert C. Labriola

DUQUESNE UNIVERSITY PRESS
Pittsburgh, Pennsylvania

Published in the United States of America by
DUQUESNE UNIVERSITY PRESS
600 Forbes Avenue
Pittsburgh, Pennsylvania 15282

Publication of this work was aided in part by a subvention from the University
of Illinois at Chicago.

Library of Congress Cataloging-in-Publication Data

Milton in the age of Fish : essays on authorship, text, and terrorism / edited
by Michael Lieb and Albert C. Labriola.
    p. cm. — (Medieval & Renaissance literary studies)
  A collection of essays that honors Stanley Fish, addresses wide range of issues
of Milton studies and the field of early modern culture.
  Includes bibliographical references (p.) and index.
  ISBN-13: 978-0-8207-0384-8 (acid-free paper)
  ISBN-10: 0-8207-0384-2 (acid-free paper)
  1. Milton, John, 1608–1674—Criticism and interpretation. 2. Milton, John,
1608–1674—Criticism, Textual. 3. Milton, John, 1608–1674—Authorship.
4. Milton, John, 1608–1674. Paradise lost. 5. Milton, John, 1608–1674. Samson
Agonistes. 6. Religion in literature. 7. Terrorism in literature. 8. Politics and
literature. 9. Fish, Stanley Eugene. I. Fish, Stanley Eugene. II. Lieb, Michael,
1940– III. Labriola, Albert C.
  PR3588.M487 2006
  821'.4—dc22
                                                                2006024411

∞ Printed on acid-free paper.

for *Stanley Fish*

Contents

Preface

This volume brings together a collection of essays that aims not only to honor Stanley Fish but also to address an entire range of issues of the first importance to Milton studies and the field of early modern culture. Whether directly or indirectly, these issues bear the mark of Fish's indelible imprint in matters both large and small. As such, the essays attest to his "presence" in all aspects of Milton studies, whether that be the matter of authorship, the "meaning" of the text, the various contexts through which Milton's works can be approached, or the way current readings (or misreadings) of Fish's stance provoke interpretations as incendiary as those they seek to disavow. Whatever else can be said about Stanley Fish, one fact endures: he is among our most provocative, as well as most eloquent, of critics. He is forever "closing up truth to truth" in a manner that challenges all comers to engage, if not grapple, with him, in the attempt to forge a way of understanding "how Milton works."[1]

Fish's *How Milton Works* (2001) has unleashed a storm of controversy that any author would be proud to claim as his or her own. We do not know of another book of its sort that has been as effective in demanding that we re-engage Milton's text so closely and with such care. *How Milton Works* argues that the truths advocated by Milton in his various writings, whether in the poetry or the prose, are clear and immutable. Adopting that viewpoint, the project takes issue with commentators determined to discover in Milton's works hidden subtleties and nuances that are nothing more than the means by which misguided critics divert attention from the urgent truths made evident in the Miltonic text. The premise of Fish's book is one that challenges anyone who seeks to understand Milton as poet and polemicist. Whether or not it wins adherents, it is a text that must be dealt with in the act of reading Milton's poetry and prose. *How Milton Works* rounds out a long and illustrious career given voice by Fish's earlier study, *Surprised by Sin: The Reader in "Paradise Lost"* (1967),[2] a book that has effectively shaped Milton criticism for almost 40 years. One might suggest that the earlier book is a harbinger of the later one, but however the relationship between the two is conceived, it is clear that Stanley Fish has emerged as one of the most important and engaging Miltonists of our time. Fish's critical commentary on Milton is always provocative, often controversial, and all-encompassing in its implications for those to whom Milton matters.

Preceded by an introduction to the volume as a whole, *Milton in the Age of Fish* is structured thematically in a manner that encompasses some of the most important concerns in Milton studies today. The volume is divided into three parts, the first of which addresses the issue of authorship and its bearing on authority. The second part addresses the issue of text, how it is construed, and the various contexts that define it, and the third part addresses the issue of terrorism and the charges that have been leveled at Fish for sanctioning the kinds of terror that have unfortunately become commonplace events in the world of today. The first and third sections frame the second in the sense that the essays there range widely among such subjects as the theology of the Son in *Paradise Lost* and the complex relationship between Milton and his contemporaries, as well as others whom his work has influenced. Anticipating the second part, the first part focuses upon authorship as a construction in Fish's self-reflexive sense of his role as critic and as a vital theme in Milton's view of himself as author. As a testament to Fish's practice of close readings, the first part concludes with a detailed examination of Milton's verbal practices. The final part is in a sense *sui generis* but at the same time in keeping with the goals of the volume as a whole. Stanley Fish is as much an "institution" as he is a literary critic. Because of his standing in the field of criticism in general and Milton studies in particular, he has found himself at the center of a storm of controversy that has arisen as the result of events that he could never have anticipated in producing his readings of Milton. Those events have provided the occasion for attacks on his most recent work that extend well beyond the boundaries of the text. The third part addresses these attacks and their implications for the future of Milton studies. In keeping with his sense of how he conceives himself in the context of the controversies his work has elicited, we have provided the occasion for Stanley Fish to have the final word. Given his paramount importance to the field, it is only proper that the final word should be his own, for who else can say it better than he?

Michael Lieb and Albert C. Labriola

Introduction

Lana Cable

While I was preparing to teach my first Milton course in the department that had just hired me, a colleague whom I had not met strode into my office, announced his name, and advised me that he, too, taught Milton. Then, pinning me behind my desk with a glare, he muttered, "I hear you were a student of Stanley Fish." I smiled: "Yes — do you know him?" "*Know* him?" the man bristled, "Not if I can help it!" He grabbed a chair, leaned toward me, and confided, "You realize, don't you, that Stanley Fish actually *is* the devil?" A joke, I thought, chuckling: "I expect a lot of people would agree with you." But my new colleague was not amused. He rose without another word and stomped out as abruptly as he had entered. To my genuine regret, he never gave me a chance to ask what lay behind his apparent conviction: had he felt seduced, or betrayed, by reading Fish? Perhaps both at once? And to which of countless provocative arguments was he responding? Did signs of cloven hoof and tongue appear to him only in *Surprised by Sin* and other literary critical works, or could he discern them as

1

well in Fish's theoretical interventions in jurisprudence, polit-ical culture, or academic institutional change? Whatever first induced my fierce new colleague to identify Fish with the Prince of Darkness, he may since have found an opportunity to check his hypothesis, having succumbed prematurely to a failed, outraged heart.

Reading Our Book

Unaware of this melodrama (though acquainted with variations on its script), Stanley Fish remains very much with us and, years later, still capable of sparking outrage. Readers of this volume will recall the April 2003 *Critical Inquiry* theory symposium, when a *New York Times* reporter culled from remarks of a stel-lar academic lineup a dozen sound bites that included Fish's devilish denial of the effectiveness of intellectual work. "The Latest Theory Is That Theory Doesn't Matter" trumpeted the headline, above a story itemizing reasons to conclude, "The era of big theory is over."[1] For some, this newsflash stirred indig-nant protest: since theory continues to sustain multiple schol-arly projects, its apparent trashing by a panel of experts seemed gratuitous. But for others in the academy — and certainly for students of Stanley Fish — the announcement of theory's demise was no news at all. Decades after leaving his seminars, our ears still ring with Miltonic precepts that "drive us from the letter, though we love ever to be sticking there."[2] Milton's "letter" became whatever our minds clung to as evidence of the truth, and that evidence included claims by, for, or in con-tradistinction to critical theory. We were riveted by extempore rhetorical performances during which, having switched on the little tape recorder behind a pile of books, Professor Fish's hands would rise and dart about like avid sparrows, pecking kernels of emphasis from the air to embellish one-liners such as: "If theory-talk is what they're buying in the market, then you'd better learn theory-talk"; or "Theory's nothing new, scholars have always done theory — they just keep wrapping it up in new packages"; or the wickedly gleeful "If you want to do [theory *XYZ*], then you'd better do it fast, because its shelf life is just about over!" To tune in to critical theory with Stanley Fish meant embracing intellectual inquiry as a vocation without ever granting to any particular theory deference or independent status: the pursuit-of-truth business was turning out to be much trickier than we had originally surmised.

That trickiness no doubt accounts for much of my colleague's outrage. Nothing so discomfits a hard-won sense of conviction — that rational focus on whatever we call "meaning" in professional life — than to have one's intellectual assumptions called into question. In his texts about reading (and in his readings of readers), Stanley Fish delights in exposing the complicities of will and word by which we all carry out our intellectual agendas. He forces us to think about the ways we think, and we do not like it. Yet we cannot refuse his challenge and still retain the integrity of our pursuit. Trickier still, we cannot refuse it without also turning our backs on the sheer zest of intellectual engagement with what the *Independent* has called "one of the greatest and most accessible minds in contemporary Western thought." Fish's challenge is delivered with such expressive clarity and exuberant wit, moving deftly from audacious propositions (*There's No Such Thing as Free Speech*) to even more audacious conclusions (*and it's a good thing too*), that while we may not feel betrayed, we are unquestionably seduced.

The brilliance that energizes this and every other challenge from Stanley Fish goes beyond common disdain for platitudes: it is a passion for intellectual architectonics. His fascination with the workings of intellect leads him ceaselessly to examine the thing itself, in a disciplinary exercise whose regenerative variety represents the vital essence of humanist inquiry.

In literary analysis he probes how words operate, what creative and analytical thinking is like, what technical maneuvers are required to put into place, and to track, linguistic nuance. His own rhetorical practice delivers a concrete, tactile appreciation of what it means to build an argument in poetry or prose, of precisely how it is that metaphors do their work of casting and elaborating otherwise amorphous conceptions, of bringing them to a state of accessibility on a page or in speech where they can be apprehended and perhaps recast. If we lose touch with this interpretive immediacy, or if what we call "the life of the mind" seems reduced to a cliché, reading Stanley Fish recollects us to the virtuosity of interpretive work by exploring how the mind functions when playing baseball, or choosing a Volvo, or deliberating a case in the Supreme Court. His analytic and persuasive genius takes the pursuit-of-truth enterprise out of the classroom and into public discourse seemingly without strain, because his disciplinary expertise — the discipline, that is, of interpreting what Milton in *Areopagitica* calls "our book" ("whatever thing we hear or see, sitting, walking, traveling, or conversing") — defines what Stanley Fish does regardless of where he does it. He interprets our all-encompassing book with scrupulous scholarly rigor and logical precision, yet he interprets it also with stylistic grace and clarity, delightful humor, genuine respect for differing viewpoints, percipient compassion, abundant generosity, endless curiosity, and spontaneous personal warmth uncompromised by sentimentality. For humanity and the humanities to be made the dedicated subject of such an interpreter is a credit — indeed a gift — to both, provided only that, as in Milton's *Sonnet VII*, both have the grace to use it so.

The Politics of Truth

The grace required to use that gift may not always emerge from circumstances conventionally associated with a gracious manner. Having created a renaissance in Milton studies and extended his humanities expertise into legal theory and beyond, having dedicated energy to building institutional support for the liberal arts through academic publishing and administration, Stanley Fish now finds higher education under siege. As he marshals his formidable powers of advocacy in the academy's defense, his venues grow ever more public. His arguments crop up in the *New York Times* and the *Chicago Tribune*, on MacNeil/Lehrer, CNN, CSPAN, and TV talk shows, on Pacifica Radio and National Public Radio, in *Harper's Magazine* and the *New Yorker*, in multiple speaking engagements, on platforms of public debate, and in his "All in the Game" columns for the *Chronicle of Higher Education*. Throughout, his interpretive work acts not only as a model of lucid analysis but also, increasingly, as a polemical resource for addressing situations where politesse falls short. As with all of his analyses, his current arguments for the pursuit of truth differ little at their core from arguments he has always made in the classroom. But their rhetorical constructs now strike alarms that no single action is likely to silence. His gibe about intellectual effectiveness at the theory symposium had been prompted by someone asking: If critical theory can't improve the human condition, why bother with it at all? What is the point of academic exercises if they remain merely academic? Responding to such apparently reasonable questions as if they had been posed by the tempter in *Paradise Regained:* "What dost thou in this world?" (4.372), Stanley Fish still descants on the Savior's "Think not but that I know these things, or think / I know them not; not therefore am I short / Of knowing what I ought" (4.285). But his actual words savor less and less of the ambiguity in the Savior's rebuff: he tailors his response to the immediate occasion. For instance, when the occasion is a demand that education budgets adhere to financial models designed for profit-making businesses, Fish's advice to cash-strapped academic institutions sounds like this:

Instead of saying, "Let me tell you what we do so that you'll love us," or "Let me explain how your values are our values too," say, "We do what we do, we've been doing it for a long time, it has its own history, and until you learn it or join it, your opinions are not worth listening to." Instead of defending classics or French literature or sociology, ask those who think they need defending what they know about them, and if the answer is "not much" (on the model of "don't know much about the Middle Ages"), suggest, ever so politely, that they might want to go back to school.[3]

While only readers of Milton will hear in these words an echo of "Think not but that I know these things," even academics unfamiliar with *Paradise Regained* will hear the admonition to be skeptical about why they are being asked "What dost thou in this world?" Trying to appease the underlying taunt ("If you're so smart, why aren't you rich?") that motivates such a question only risks putting the pursuit of truth up for auction. Similarly, when the occasion is a demand for "political balance" in the classroom, to counter what some call the academy's left-wing bias, Stanley Fish's "Think not but that I know these things" sounds like the following:

This is a mixture of nonsense and paranoia. . . . if conservatives really want to spend their lives teaching modern poetry and Byzantine art, they should stop whining and do the dissertations and write the books, and they'll get the jobs. . . . [Those arguing for political balance intend] taking higher education away from the educators . . . and handing it over to a small group of ideologues who will tell colleges and universities what to do and back up their commands by swinging the two big sticks of financial deprivation and inflamed public opinion.[4]

Invariably, the taunt "What dost thou in this world?" defines the world's doings in terms circumscribed by the interests of the taunter. The recognition that there may be, in fact, doings of interest that lie well beyond the taunter's circumscriptions has always distinguished academic priorities, set them apart, and made them, from the time of Socrates, difficult and hazardous to defend, but even more hazardous not to. "If the academic community does its usual thing and rolls over and plays dead," Fish warns, "in time it will not just be playing dead. It will be dead."

What is at stake in Fish's argument for the disinterested pursuit of truth is the survival not just of the academic community itself, branded "ivory tower" for its refusal to define limits to its interests, but survival of the very idea that interests cannot be both circumscribed and open to discovery at the same time. Conceptual freedom, the essence of humanist education, is a project logically and necessarily (but also fruitfully) at odds with the concretely realizable projects of the nonacademic world. The nonacademic project by definition must delimit human interests in order to make possible concrete realization of its objectives. The logic of the nonacademic project may be illustrated by a Fairfax, Virginia, Economic Development Council slogan: "Where the Quality of Life Is Matched by the Quality of Technology Jobs." So long as the two qualities in this formula can be made to "match," the nonacademic project will have achieved its objectives and thus be declared a success. (Anyone who doubts that life and technology jobs can be made to match underestimates the power of public relations advertising.) By contrast, the logic of the academic project requires looking into the value of the formula itself and each of its terms — quality, life, technology, job, matched — in addition to examining how each term relates to every other, and how the entire formula might affect or be affected by external conditions. The logic of the academic project and the logic of the nonacademic project will never be made to match. But the fruitfulness of the two projects being kept at odds lies in the academy's ability to explore and explain why they are at odds. So long as the academic project remains free to pursue truth rather than being forced to demonstrate results, it too can be declared a success while yet leaving the nonacademic project free to ignore or refer to its findings as it chooses. That is why, as he shapes academic policy around versions of "Think not but that I know these things," what Stanley Fish actually affirms is not an intellectual preference for staying aloof from politics — aloof, that is, from the political conditions that sustain all human activity, including the activity of humanistic inquiry. Rather, he affirms his own commitment, and that of the academy, to a definition of intellectual work for which the political consequences (as opposed to partisan consequences) could not be greater.

Partisan Plays

Not that distinctions between politics and partisanship are always easy to maintain. In debates framed by the devastating attacks of September 11, 2001, for example, political interests can lend academic discourse a certain currency that yields easily to partisan thinking. A provocative article by John Carey, published in the *Times Literary Supplement* a year after the attacks, begins moderately with "events in the real world inevitably change the way we read,"[5] but then it goes on to argue that Stanley Fish's reading of *Samson Agonistes* supports the ideology of terrorism. Carey's article stimulated not only academic debate about Samson, terrorism, and Stanley Fish, but debate also about the kinds of intellectual activity academics engage in whenever they make literary texts the site of political critique. We cannot avoid trying to make sense of inchoate experience by reading it through the organizing construct of art: human culture *is* cumulative interpretation. And as Fish demonstrates throughout his career, the interpretive frameworks we have are the ones we use: if our interpretive practices were formed around Milton, our political analyses will likely reflect Milton's influence. Since individual practices vary, moreover, myopic readings, self-indulgent or self-righteous readings, historically partial or culturally skewed readings may occur whether interpreters are politically motivated or not. But above all, humanists are motivated to read, teach, and think about art because they believe that the resulting expertise enables them to live more fully and to employ their talents to good effect in the world.

Yet since employing his talents to good effect in the world was what Samson had aimed at too, critical debate over the distinctions between politics and partisanship persists. Exactly why it persists, and is likely to persist as long as people continue to interpret Milton's dramatic tragedy, is an issue that receives penetrating analysis in the last four essays in this volume. The debate itself — and its relevance to academic work — was demonstrated in 2004 during a thought-provoking conference session on Samson. A single paper deftly juxtaposed the apocalyptic rhetoric of PNAC (Project for the New American Century) with the rhetoric of seventeenth century English millenarians, then segued logically through John Carey's valorization of a humanist Milton to critique Fish's unregenerate Samson, before moving on to identify Fish with the political Left because of his commitment to liberal humanism.[6] As soon as the paper session turned to questions from the audience, there burst from Stanley Fish yet another version of "Think not but that I know these things" in a fusillade of rebuttals: "We should have as *Miltonists no interest* in combating PNAC! To critics who argue it is wrong to make an idol of Milton, I argue there are *no consequences!* On the claims of my being in the liberal camp, *I do not stand on the left side of any issue!*" His final sentence was uttered with such vehemence that no one dared ask if this meant that Stanley Fish stood on the *right* side of any issue. Had they done so, he would have sent them home with orders to read *The Trouble with Principle*.

Nevertheless, even people adept at maintaining distinctions between politics and partisanship may slip political analysis into poetry readings (and vice versa) through the interpretive back door. The practice demonstrates that art cannot ultimately be separated from political life, although the academic approach to both art and politics remains, still fruitfully, at odds with the nonacademic approach. At a time when public debate on crucial political issues is often intellectually impoverished, or gets derailed by forces ignorant of, or actively hostile to, educational needs, academics struggling to meet those needs use their interpretive discourse as they should: to develop and exercise the skills required not only to read a work like *Areopagitica*, but also to read and write the larger book toward which it directs us. If interpreting "whatever thing we hear or see" is how human beings may be said to achieve personal autonomy, Stanley Fish's remarks on the autonomy of academic disciplines will illuminate, without specifying, the answer to the question "What dost thou in this world?":

> Autonomy is a social and political achievement [that] can only maintain itself by reconfiguring itself in the face of the challenges history puts in its way. . . . [I]t will seem paradoxical to some that instability could be the source of identity. . . . The paradox vanishes, however, when one realizes that the law (or literary criticism) does not remain what it is because its every detail survives the passing of time, but because in the wake of change society still looks to it for the performance of a particular task. That is what survives, a distinctiveness that rests not on an essential difference but on a difference in the sense of purpose (to secure justice or to interpret poems) informing those who think of themselves as lawyers or literary critics. Even when a practice is racked by debate, it is nevertheless itself so long as what is being debated is the best way to do the job the culture continues to assign to it.[7]

Identity survives in a distinctive sense of purpose. In the decade since these words were published, the culture has given increasing indications of a will to terminate the job assigned to higher education of developing interpretive autonomy — distinctive, purposeful, informed individual identity — among its citizens. What might be offered in place of this assignment can only be surmised from the record of enterprises devoted to achieving not autonomous identity but measurable results. When the power of information technology can be harnessed as George Orwell prophesied, to create the perception of material and cultural stability while putting neobrutalist policies into practice, interpreters capable of reading and writing the full story of what it means to be human have never been more needed.

The Contributors

However imperiled the academic pursuit of truth may at times seem (and historically it has never been entirely secure), as long as interpretive work continues, the disciplinary expertise upon which interpretation depends will maintain the vibrancy of the pursuit. Prominent in this interpretive work are the essayists of the present volume, whose contributions to *Milton in the Age of Fish: Essays on Authorship, Text, and Terrorism* bear witness to their own disciplinary mastery at the same time as they celebrate the extraordinary accomplishments of an illustrious colleague, admired mentor, and generous friend. The heterogeneity of their critical approaches points toward the eclectic nature of Stanley Fish's intellectual and professional attachments, but all focus on the poet with whom Fish is most constantly and tellingly associated, John Milton. Not surprisingly, given the current widespread interest in Milton as a political writer, nearly all of the essays take their analytical cue from what may be found in Milton's writings to define him in political terms, broadly or narrowly conceived. While none of the essays strays into the kind of partisan advocacy that might intrude on academic integrity, all demonstrate the disciplinary expertise that Fish himself (notwithstanding the trouble it might lead to) has elevated into a principle: "The sharper and the more limited the focus of your labors, the more likely is it that what you produce will be useful to the larger contexts you resolutely ignore. What society needs from academics are not grand schemes and grandiose visions, but precise formulations of intellectual problems and their possible solutions."[8] Or, in Milton's words, "To sequester out of the world into Atlantic and Utopian polities, which never can be drawn into use, will not mend our condition; but to ordain wisely."[9] Exactly how one might distinguish between the principles of John Milton and those of Stanley Fish is an intellectual problem for which there can be no precise formulation, but if a solution were possible, it would owe much to the wise ordaining of the present tributes, and to the interpretive activity inspired by Milton that characterizes academic politics at its best.

Instead of distinguishing between Fish and Milton, Marshall Grossman finds ways to sample and synthesize the two identities, exploring the "Importance of Being Fish" in a trivial play for serious people inspired by Joel Fineman's interpretation of Oscar Wilde. Grossman plots Stanley Fish's "onomastic destiny" from cues set by John Bunyan's piscatory symbol of Christian sin and salvation, Morris Zapp's comic escape from sexual misadventure, Fish's own remarks on our prospects for changing the world in "Theory's Hope" (his contribution to the *Critical Inquiry* symposium) and, intermittently, Slavoj Žižek's repulsion by certain group performances in bed and at board. Grossman portrays Fish getting hooked, via the symbology he inherits by accident with his name, into a Lacan-inspired "countertransference" (comically abetted by David Lodge) that leads him perpetually to read the self that he writes: "Fish, as writer and critic, stands in an estranged relationship to "fish" as shared signifier discovered in the text . . . while he reads the text, the text reads him." This reader-text transfer occurs because Grossman sees interpretation itself as a classic science fiction "trans-mat mishap," in which the amazing time-and-space machine that is literary experience mixes up particles of the being it is engineered to convey: "Fish leaves his mark on the text . . . and the text leaves its mark on Fish, defining for him a relationship of reader to text that both exemplifies his approach to seventeenth century literature and validates it with the putative approval of a seventeenth century writer." Grossman's witty psychoanalytic sketch of Fish's multifarious intellectual career makes a persuasive case for his argument that the theory he practices cannot be called interdisciplinary because psychoanalysis has in fact already been literary criticism since the moment of its inception. To prove it, Grossman delineates tropic transference in Freud's affective dream-work through Žižek's comic inversion of interpretive norms, to the predicative impertinence of metaphor, which in turn illuminates the rhetorical structure of repressed memory and, in consequence, the self-discovery that comes with reading a book. This sequential structure allows Grossman in his closing act to dramatize how it happens that, since the 1967 publication of *Surprised by Sin*, Fish has been able to recast Milton criticism from its traditional treatment of Milton's texts as models to be either rejected or imitated, into treatment of them as opportunities for critical interpretation of the self in history and of historical change. By this analysis, and regardless of whether an interdisciplinary label can be attached to it, Grossman demonstrates his agreement with Fish on political readings: interpretation that confers partisan significance on a literary text falls victim to the "Milton-one-of-us syndrome." The only cure for the malady, illustrated by the way *Samson Agonistes* collapses into its own uninterpretability while at the same time spinning off multiple interpreters, is to subscribe to a literary reading of both self and history which, in its unceasing pursuit of truth, "understands that the moment it desires and resists does not occur."

This is the kind of reading Barbara Lewalski discovers in Milton's construction of authorial citizenship, a hard-won achievement of self-fashioning that evolved over many years and that set Milton apart from conventional early modern authorial practice. His youthful self-consciousness about his poetic calling was historically new, Lewalski argues, and Milton's struggle to fit that vocational consciousness into a pattern answerable to religious and civic duty compelled him to hew a literary path independent of any form of patronage apart from that of his father. Tracking steps in Milton's campaign for authorial citizenship, Lewalski reveals aspects of his self-representation that are too often overlooked. For example, as the aspiring poet in *Mansus*, Milton is so tantalized by his own promise that he imagines his desired patron-friend as reversing their roles, with someone like the now aged Manso seeking out the poet, caring for him, and honoring him upon his death by erecting a monument much as Manso had honored Tasso. But at that moment, surprisingly, patronal honor disappears from the scene, and Milton projects his own Olympian apotheosis. This displacing of patronage by a higher recognition, argues Lewalski, shows Milton visualizing his way out of the career path indicated by patronage because, he comes to realize, it cannot sustain his sense of vocation. Similarly, in *Areopagitica*, Milton's argument for securing authorial copyrights fits into his developing picture of the self-authorized citizen, along with his portrayal of the writer's extraordinary public responsibility. This latter he represents symbolically as well, by having his own name printed boldly on the title page when neither the printer nor the bookseller could safely print their names. Milton's concept of authorial citizenship evolves from his early pastoral entertainments, where he assumes a public duty to foster moral reform, through

Areopagitica's concept of citizens as independently reasoning choosers, on through the arguments for civic virtue in the Latin *Defenses* and *Readie and Easie Way,* to his emphasis on choice in the final poems, where education is made central to *Paradise Lost,* and where the heroes of *Paradise Regained* and *Samson Agonistes* must each come to terms with their own callings. As Lewalski traces Milton's path to intellectual and creative independence, she shows him constructing the citizen-author as a public hero at the same time as he commits his autonomy to a vocation that, from his earliest writings, he had conceived as divine. Dependence on the higher patronage invoked in *Paradise Lost,* however, apparently did not liberate Milton's serviceable autonomy from the tactful diplomacy that would have been required by any other patron: Lewalski notes anecdotal evidence that he found Urania to be in need of a good editor.

The precision of linguistic events that structure Milton's self-authorship leads Annabel Patterson to examine the self-validation and vindication that he builds specifically on grammatical negatives, the lexical elements that empower his "positive negativity." Illustrated most dramatically in his life by his transformation of growing blindness, from the threat it posed to his literary vocation into heroic confirmation of it, Milton's positive powers of negation may also be discerned in the syntactic minutiae that reflect his early immersion in Latin sentence constructions. Patterson illustrates the grammatical consequences for his English poetry with instances such as the narrator's walking "unseen" and "not unseen" in *Il Penseroso* and *L'Allegro*. These negations throw into relief the "unreproved pleasures" whose grammatically implicit reproof contributes, lexically as well as philosophically, to the same exercise in denial as do syntactic counterparts in *Lycidas* and *Comus*. These cumulative negations articulate the Miltonic theme that Patterson phrases as "the inexpressibility of all that really

matters." So effectively does Patterson's argument sharpen
our awareness of lexical negation that by the time she for-
mulates this theme, early in the study, Milton's negatives
fairly leap from the page as we read. To explore further the meaning for Milton of his lexical negations, however, she turns to
the *Art of Logic,* where his chapter "On Privatives" reveals a
deeper logic than can be explained solely by his latinity. This
is the logic of privation, wherein may be found the elements
of Milton's philosophical transformation of blindness into a
posture of defense that is self-affirming: in effect, he faces
down the negative threat by controlling or denying its grammatical existence. The variations on this logic that play out
in the later poetry are demonstrated with great élan by Patterson,
whose final example — the heroic nonaffirmation of "Think
not but that I know these things" — reaffirms both Milton's
poetic heroism and the positive negativity of consequences that
may be expected from academic interpretation.

In a graceful exploration of visionary analogues to Milton's
divinely sanctioned self-authorship, Albert C. Labriola compares passages that define the ontological relationship of the
Father and Son in *Paradise Lost* with scenes from the apocryphal Martyrdom and Ascension of Isaiah, to demonstrate that
the perfection attributed by Milton to the Son lies more in his
voluntary humiliation than in his deity. Since God's announcement of the Son's begetting arouses the envy that leads to
heavenly rebellion in *Paradise Lost,* book 5, the precise nature
of this begetting has long been the focus of critical debate. In
Milton's poem, the envious Lucifer persuades his followers that
the begetting indicates a new policy of favoritism, as if one angel
among equals had been elevated. But in Isaiah's vision, the begetting is portrayed as the first stage of an elaborately graded
descent from godhead to full incarnation — from deity to angel
to man. Isaiah is guided by an angel through the seven heavens to witness this descent, which at each stage affords greater

perceptibility to the second person of the Christian Trinity. Although even before the descent begins, at the height of the seventh heaven, the Son can be distinguished from the Father (Isaiah is able to rank the divine persons — Father, Son, Holy Spirit), before the Son can assume mortal form he must take an intermediate step. In order to transform himself into the infant Jesus, he must first take on the form of an angel, in a sequence that requires moving two levels downward in the heavenly hierarchy before the transformation is sufficient to enable the angels to treat him as one among their kind. Yet no reversal of this transformation process is required, after the human form has been achieved, to accomplish the Son's resurrection. He regains his heavenly seat without retracing the steps of his descent: his deity is recognized and worshiped by the angels at every heavenly level despite his human form. This ascension in human form thus represents a hope for divine salvation that would not otherwise be apprehensible to mortals. By making visual the conferring of divine status on the mortal human form, the Isaiah analogues compare with Milton's vision of self-transformation as within the capacity of all human beings. This emphasis on visibility in the Isaiah account (the divine Son is ordered literally to "make your form like" lower beings) renders spiritual transformation as a distinctly human process. Labriola's study of analogues in the Isaiah vision thus not only supplements our understanding of the ontological relationship between the Father and Son in *Paradise Lost:* it also enriches our understanding of the analogue that Milton saw between divine salvation and the self-transformations made possible by the pursuit of truth.

Milton the millenarian draws Stella Revard to examine his use of another biblical image from the seventeenth century wars of truth, the book of Ezekiel's Chariot of Paternal Deity, comparing it with the use made by royalist Henry More, who is also a millenarian. More openly retains his millenarian views

even after the return of Charles II, absorbing them into celebration of the restored monarchy. As Charles's political approach
unfolds, however, More tempers his rhetoric: by 1668, though
still a millenarian and a royalist, he no longer sees the restored
king as a champion of religious reform. Meanwhile, Milton's
millenarianism, after the 1660 publication of *The Readie and
Easie Way*, in effect goes underground. In their religious, if not
their political, views More and Milton seem closely related:
both were committed to reform, and both espoused a toleration
that would expressly exclude Catholics, a stricture that More
elaborates on specifically political grounds. But what makes
comparing the two fascinating is their shared interest in
kabbalistic commentary on the vision of Ezekiel, Ma'aseh
Merkabah (Work of the Chariot). Revard shows how this work
appears to have informed both More's *Divine Dialogues* and
Milton's chariot of paternal deity in book 6 of *Paradise Lost*.
Comparison of these two works with their source reveals how
subtly the same text, itself already an interpretation of a text,
can be interpreted, even by like-minded individuals, to differing political ends. More the royalist uses the vision of triumphant righteousness to mount a covert critique of Charles's
failure to enact contemporary religious reform. Meanwhile,
Milton the dissenter uses the same interpretative resource to
prophesy ultimate divine vengeance, thus providing conceptual solace to those yearning for higher forces to right the
wrongs they now suffer. Simultaneously masking, revealing, and eluding the political intentions of its interpreters,
the Work of the Chariot — as Revard's stimulating inquiry
demonstrates — shows little sign that such work will ever be
completed.

In an illuminating historical study of the political agency
that Milton fought for in *The Readie and Easie Way* and
throughout his polemical career, Joan Bennett explores the subtle, telling discriminations that mark a widening conceptual
divide in seventeenth century England between monarchist

claims for personal autonomy and dissenter exercise of individual reasoning to achieve a just society. Challenging contemporary feminist readings of Milton's political significance that rely on nineteenth and twentieth century interpretive values, Bennett constructs a seventeenth century framework of feminist liberation theology to reveal feminist arguments for autonomy that are distinct not only from those of a later era, but also from each other. Bennett's comparative study of Mary Astell and Lucy Hutchinson, women who share with Milton the attributes of intellectual sophistication, religious faith, and political commitment, demonstrates that while the three share a sensitivity to interpretation as a means of working toward political autonomy, their interpretive approaches diverge as each makes arguments that in contemporary feminist terms might seem contrary to the interests of the cause. For example, Mary Astell uses Holy Scripture as an illustrative resource for polemical proofs to support arguments that, constructed along Cartesian lines in a sequence of logical steps, validate autonomy by their dependence on individual reasoning. Astell argues for women's equality, education, and public service in a style that itself justifies her claims for individual female autonomy. Yet in contemporary feminist terms, Astell undercuts her achievement by avowing her Tory support for absolute monarchy even in cases where the monarch is a tyrant, and by subordinating women to men in the social hierarchy. By contrast, Lucy Hutchinson treats Scripture not as an authoritative resource but as a storehouse of "dangerous memory" — patterns of oppression that, if humanity is to be saved, must be reformed through a hermeneutics of suspicion and proclamation that exposes received ideas to critique. Thus Hutchinson agrees with Milton, who argues in the divorce tracts for treating Scripture as a text to be interpreted toward a liberating higher truth, rather than enforced as a prescriptive rule. Since Hutchinson's model for reform demands that all members of the society assume equal responsibility, her liberation theology, like Astell's, leaves women in a social position of subordination to men. But because she emphasizes not individual autonomy but communal action, Hutchinson's case for individual agency as an instrument of change carries greater political force than does that of Astell, who leaves existing power structures in place and also exempt from critique. Meanwhile, in his own hermeneutics of suspicion, Milton, like Hutchinson, "gives his readers the most important tools" for feminist critique of power: "he requires us not only to understand who has power *over* whom, but also to examine the prior question: what is power *for?*" In Bennett's view, this central question leads both Milton and Hutchinson to portray divine power as "a kind of dance between the majesty of God the Father and the grace of God the Son" that is reflected in the terms Milton uses to articulate relations between Adam and Eve: "a kind of dance between 'glorious' 'Majestie' and 'sweet' 'Grace.'" Bennett's feminist liberation theology is thus simultaneously contemporary and historical, valuably confirming a hermeneutics that defines not only seventeenth century scriptural critique, but also any interpretive practice that aims toward advancing the pursuit of truth.

The departure point for the remaining four essays is the controversy over Milton and terrorism, sparked by John Carey in September 2002, that continues to the present. Joseph Wittreich brings organic richness to discussion of the slippage between critical analysis and polemic while interpreting *Samson Agonistes:* Milton criticism needs only to look to its contextual roots. Heading each segment of his ramifying argument with provocative remarks on Samson by Stanley Fish, Wittreich shows how critics and readers of *Samson Agonistes* have always used it as an interpretive lens for their times, just as the tragedy itself took shape in the manner of a "protest poem" that appropriated the biblical story in order to transform a moment in political history. This context-inversion, whereby art interprets history that in turn feeds upon art, transforms

Milton's final poems into the kinds of prophetic works that the British Romantics made of them: sources of "mythic paradigms of our history" in a hermeneutics that supplied the multiple roots of modern Milton criticism. One of these roots is the critical line of inquiry that begins with the Bible's influence over Milton and ends with Milton's influence over the Bible. Wittreich demonstrates this context-inversion at work by showing how readings of Milton's *Paradise Lost, Paradise Regained,* and *Samson Agonistes* have shaped a new biblical hermeneutic, especially by way of Samson, through critical analyses from authors ranging from Dr. Johnson to Malcolm X. This critical line evolves ultimately into a hermeneutics of the oppressed through the work of Ralph Ellison, Toni Morrison, and Philip Pullman, all of whom take from *Samson Agonistes* lessons about the ultimate futility and degradation of a politics of violence and revenge. Wittreich's ramifying contexts find Milton's resolution and hope for reaching beyond such politics in his commitment to a consciousness-expanding dialectic. By juxtaposing contrary ethical systems, as represented by the 1671 pairing of *Samson Agonistes* with *Paradise Regained,* interpreters may generate many questions and few answers, but the dialectic itself will nevertheless move the pursuit of truth forward.

Salutary historical checks of another kind are brought to the debate over Samson and terrorism by David Loewenstein, who places *Samson Agonistes* in the context of political upheaval in the seventeenth century rather than the twenty-first. The political turmoil to which Milton's tragedy spoke in its historical setting was aroused not by terrorism, but by antinomianism. Thus, "identification of Samson with a modern-day suicide bomber tells us more about out own fears and values than it does about Milton's poem." Exactly what it tells us about our fears and values, interpreters will continue to dispute, but Loewenstein points toward a different lesson from history that can be applied with greater reliability. This is the lesson that warns against indiscriminate use of politically volatile labels in critical debate. Like the seventeenth century label "heretic," against which Milton warns, the label "terrorist" will more likely curtail analysis than contribute to it, much as (one might add) unexamined assumptions about what motivates a "suicide bomber" serve no analytical purpose. But by citing evidence for Milton's support of state terrorism, exemplified by Cromwell's Irish campaign, Loewenstein reminds us that righteous claims by advocates of overwhelming force have the same hideous consequences (and may still fail in their political aims) regardless of who makes the claim, including Milton. For that reason, Loewenstein advocates another remedy for Grossman's Milton-one-of-us syndrome: we should face up to Milton's inconsistencies where they exist, instead of trying to pick and choose the evidence that supports our desired picture of him. Meanwhile, Loewenstein documents evidence from seventeenth century apocalyptic discourse to show how easily *Samson Agonistes* could have been read by Milton's contemporaries to answer to the terrifying religious terms that the revolutionary years had made familiarly political. Ultimately, however, Loewenstein sees the poem's complex treatment of religious terror as pointing not toward politics but toward anxieties that lie at the heart of Puritan providentialism.

Anxieties lie also at the heart of the reading that Michael Lieb gives to Stanley Fish's Milton. In a witty riposte to the charge that Fish supports terrorist ideology, Lieb offers himself — because of his own major work on Milton and violence — as Fish's ideological body double: "Lieb is an individual who delights in writing about violence," he advises John Carey, whereas Stanley Fish is demonstrably obsessed not with violence but vigilance, adherence to the inner light that leads to joining the angelic choir. Yet Fish's departure from this "Miltonic Paradigm" in his reading of Samson results in a conceptual divide so profound that it subverts Fish's own interpretive enterprise. In the resulting gap, Lieb takes up a defense of Fish, showing how Carey misreads him, and objecting to Carey's use of the word "terrorism" for describing Samson's activity. On historical as well as polemical grounds, Lieb argues, the term is inappropriate for Milton's Samson because it is too modern, and it is imprecise. As he probes the idea of terrorism for definitive meanings, however, Lieb finds that the most comprehensive definitions — ones that include the appalling theatricality of a bombardment that forces victims to "behold the spectacle of their own demise" — would as accurately apply to the campaign known as "Shock and Awe" as it does to terrorism. Thus, if Samson can be charged with one, Lieb suggests, he ought to be charged with the other. The more appropriate catchword for Samson, therefore, is not "terror" but "dread," the "living Dread" that is the divine vengeance into which Samson would transform his entire being. In the moment that Fish declares uninterpretable, the moment marked by Samson's standing in the temple of Dagon with "eyes fast fixt," Lieb finds Samson triumphant, having transformed himself into an embodiment of the living Dread in which he believes.

Only the churlish would deny Stanley Fish the pleasure of contributing to a volume that celebrates his own brilliant career. But in this instance his intervention is justified by the duty of responding to the now famous attack by John Carey, not to defend himself (others have done that for him), but to explain to Carey, and to anyone else who may be interested, exactly what it is that Stanley Fish really thinks about Samson and terrorism. Along the way, he also explains what he believes Carey and interested others truly ought to know about antinomianism, universally accepted moral standards, Enlightenment distinctions between the public and private sphere, judgment by outcomes versus the Miltonic principle of intention, the true path to obedience, the difference between majestic unaffected style and majestic affected style, the unknowability of faith, the anxiety of pious desire, the absence of external signs, the argument for liberalism, the priority of procedural means above substantive ends, and the distinction between doing literary criticism and doing any other activity in life whatsoever. Throughout, Fish explains himself with all the scintillating clarity and wit, impeccable logic, and sense of intellectual play for which he is famous, making every argument a fresh discovery, no matter how familiar the territory. And he concludes his performance with a flourish of such magnanimous precision that John Carey himself must be amused to suffer refutation at the hands of that crafty devil, Stanley Fish.

AUTHORSHIP
AND
AUTHORITY
• • •

1 • The Onomastic Destiny of Stanley Fish

Marshall Grossman

You see the ways the Fisher-man doth take
To catch the Fish; what Engins doth he make?

. . . .

Yet Fish there be, that neither Hook, nor Line,
Nor Snare nor Net, nor Engine can make thine;
They must be grop'd for, and be tickled too,
Or they will not be catcht, what e're you do.
— John Bunyan, "Apology for a Book," as quoted in
Stanley Fish, *Surprised by Sin*

Morris Zapp took his departure from Milan as soon as he decently could, if "decent" was a word that could be applied to the Morgana ménage, which he ventured to doubt. The troilism party had not been a success. As soon as it became evident that he was expected to fool around with Ernesto as well as Fulvia, Morris had made his excuses and left the mirrored bedchamber. He also took the precaution of locking the door of the guest bedroom behind him.
— David Lodge, *Small World*

> [T]he possibility of our changing [the world] — or of at least
> furnishing some of the formulations that might be adopted
> and adapted by those whose business it is to change it —
> depends on the nearsighted situatedness of those who remain
> within the borders of the academy. A "discourse . . . that
> speaks to the world outside the academy" will only emerge
> if we remain inside and produce the delimited analyses that
> just might get taken up by someone with a project a million
> miles from ours.
>
> — Stanley Fish, "Theory's Hope"

1. *What's in a Name?*

By beginning with these three epigraphs — given in chrono-
logical order — I set along a path which I hope will fulfill and
strategically exceed the task set for me by this occasion — to
say something celebratory about the remarkable intellectual
itinerary of Stanley Fish. This essay, in fact, began with an earlier and more manageable occasion: a 1993 MLA panel celebrating the twenty-fifth anniversary of the publication of
Surprised by Sin.[1] On that occasion I began by reading the first
two of my present epigraphs and confessing that my first reason for including the excerpts from Bunyan and Lodge was the
thought that, in the context of a panel discussion on the work
of Stanley Fish, they would be funny. Because the first thought
that I had about what I then spoke and now write — before,
in fact, I knew what it would be about — was that I would enjoy
quoting these lines, it is fair to say that the argument I am about
to make was, in historical fact, constructed as the support for
a joke. Despite this contingent fact, my argument is serious
and I mean to pursue it earnestly.

By way of dispelling the specter of triviality an argument in
support of a joke might rightly evoke, I propose to revisit —
from a literary historical point of view — the nontrivial related-
ness of names and things, as exemplified by the onomastic

destiny of Stanley Fish. In a brief essay on *The Importance of Being Earnest,* Joel Fineman asserts that Wilde's subtitle, "A Trivial Comedy for Serious People," indicates exactly the way in which the trivial may be taken seriously. "Farce," Fineman says, "is trivial because it imitates imitation (literature or literariness), which is nothing."[2] So, the first task set by my farcically selected epigraphs is to establish that the triviality of my citations, in fact, arises in relation to their status, in this context, as an imitation of imitation, which is at once literary and serious.

Fineman's way of taking Wilde's farce seriously was to recount the play's interrogation of the proprietary relations between proper and common nouns: "The opposition of meaningful words to meaningless proper nouns is therefore one instance of a more general system of opposition in *The Importance of Being Earnest* that manages consistently to juxtapose the serious against the trivial in such a way as to destabilize the integrity of meaningful binary antithesis." Now, if, in fact, the passages from Bunyan and Lodge are, in this context, funny, they are funny because (1) the quotations, without leading in any particular argumentative direction, attract attention to themselves as, respectively, punning and allegorical references to the author of *Surprised by Sin.* The allusive but apparent aimlessness and self-conscious reflexivity of such an opening may even lead some readers to suspect that they are about to read a parody of a paper by Stanley Fish; and (2) in a straightforwardly crude way, in this context, the epigraphs pose and (potentially) answer the question "what's in a name"? Thus, the juxtaposition of the trivial and the serious plays out as a juxtaposition of imitation and ontology. In the first epigraph, I quote Fish quoting Bunyan, as it were, in the act of being tickled by quoting Bunyan's insistence on tickling fish. The subtitle of *Surprised by Sin* is the *The Reader in "Paradise Lost."* So the passage from Bunyan is a fitting set-up for a book that will trace the cunning way that Milton goes about tickling and hooking one appropriately named reader. In the first instance, then, my playfully serious allusion to Fish is rather a quotation of Fish's seriously playful superposition of his surname on Bunyan's piscatory metaphor, thus implying — at the beginning of his book — that he, Fish, is indeed the "informed Reader" to be caught on Milton's hook, baited by sin.

Yet the fact that Fish and fish are homophones is surely trivial. The claim of Fish's book is not (*pace* Augustine) that Milton's angling was aimed directly at him, but rather that "the reader" in the book can be generalized to include also all those readers who happen not to be named Fish.[3] Yet one wonders whether this particular quotation would have found its way into the notes to *Surprised by Sin* without its supplemental implication of onomastic destiny. Bunyan's use of a piscatory metaphor to assert the salvific ambition of his writing supports Fish's contention that seventeenth century writers were, in fact, ambitious to engage their readers in such decisive ways. But there also remains a certain comic eroticism in various (more or less) spontaneously occurring constructions, as the word "fish" passes back and forth in our reception between its uses as a common and a proper noun. The humor in this comes largely from imagining not fish generally, or, as was Bunyan's probable intention, sinners under the metaphor of fish, but Stanley Fish, in particular, as the object of Bunyan's groping and tickling. Moreover, the eroticism I detect in the piscatory encounter is, after all, neither solely Fish's, mine, nor Bunyan's, but rather something already in the seventeenth century usage of "fishing" as a vehicle for erotic captivation. Bunyan and his contemporaries inevitably engage with an established Christian discourse of fishing that goes back through Augustine to Saint Peter.[4] There is, then, in my citation of Fish's citation, a certain troilism, a multiple interpenetration of contexts —

Bunyan's, Fish's, and mine — such that we find *The Reader in "Paradise Lost,"* to use Fish's subtitle, caught between and multiply reflected in the (acoustic) mirrors of fish, the common noun, and Fish, properly designating the author of *Surprised by Sin.* Insofar as the informed or fit reader represented in Fish's book as "the reader in *Paradise Lost"* is, in a note, represented as always and already typified by the author's name, one might wonder (*avant la lettre*) whether *Surprised by Sin* is to be, presciently, a "self-consuming artifact."

This troilism appears more concretely in my second epigraph. "Troilism" is defined by the *OED* as "Sexual activity in which three persons take part simultaneously." The word, a common noun in Lodge's usage, brings to mind the "bifold" authority that Shakespeare's Troilus finds in the dissonance of Cressida's behavior and appearance.[5] Etymologically the phonic reference to Troilus is adventitious; "troilism" derives — logically enough — from the French *trois*, and the earliest use recorded by the *OED* is dated 1941, but the association once made can neither be justified nor expunged.[6] My citation of David Lodge also assumes that readers will have made the commonplace assumption that there exists a certain mirroring relationship between Stanley Fish and the fictional Morris Zapp. Whether intended by Lodge or not, this assumption is so firmly established in public consciousness, that, in *Tenured Radicals*, Roger Kimball occasionally seems to support his protracted attack on Fish by quoting Zapp. "Zapp" as the proper name of a fictional character is, of course, more straightforwardly a motivated signifier than "Fish" or even "Troilus," both of which presumably precede the destinies that we attach to them only as a willful anachronism. In naming his character "Zapp," Lodge alludes to the staccato, perhaps impatient, intellectual style and confidence of the character and its putative model, while preserving the monosyllabism of each surname. (It is also interesting to note that Lodge — in what strikes me as a characteristically English move — recuperates the presumptive ethnicity implicit in "Fish," displacing it, however, to the given (though decidedly not Christian) name "Morris."

All of this is material for a dense meditation on the relation of a fictional character to its mimetic "original" in general and on Lodge's play with "Fish" and "Zapp" in particular. But what makes my citation of Lodge specifically farcical, in the serious sense attributed by Fineman to Wilde, is that the erotic situation to which it refers is offered, at least by me — and, I would argue, also by Lodge — not as an imitation of human action but as the signifier of an approach to literary criticism. It is thus reminiscent of the inversion of psychoanalytic explanation in Slavoj Žižek's claim to experience revulsion at certain sexual activities because they remind him of the way people share foods in Chinese restaurants.[7]

Like Lodge, Bunyan too presents sex as the lure of reading; his piscatory metaphor intensifies the Horatian injunction to instruct and delight by shifting from a perhaps more commonplace signifier of literary delight — for example, the sugar coating on the bitter pill of doctrine — to one of groping and tickling. This shift from a passive to an aggressive seduction of the reader precisely suits the argument of *Surprised by Sin*, in which the passage is quoted. If the reader, baited and manhandled (albeit erotically) by the text of *Paradise Lost*, is the *terminus a quo* of a certain literary, critical adventure, the citation from Lodge represents what is (or thus far has been) its *terminus ad quem*: Morris Zapp locks his door against sodomy. The locked door of Fulvia Morgana's guest room thus figures a bar between *The Reader in "Paradise Lost"* and its elided mirror image, which, with a certain clinical but subtitular precision, we might call, *"Paradise Lost" in the Reader*. I believe that this terminal choice has, in its exigence, certain ethical implications, particularly and pointedly for teachers of literature, in the area of pedagogy that is the provenance of my third epigraph.

2. *Is Verse Perverse?*

But first, to traverse the distance between the seductions of Bunyan-Fish and Fish-Zapp, which is also a distance traversed, in some way, by literary criticism in the past 35 years, I will recur again to Fineman's remarks on *The Importance of Being Earnest*, in which is embedded a specifically literary language, which in contrast to the "perennial philosophical dream of true language, of language that always means what it says . . . can never mean what it says because it never means anything except the fact that it is saying something it does not mean" (*The Subjectivity Effect*, 36). For Fineman, following Lacan, the irreducible discrepancy between a transparently referential or purely deictic "true language" and the literary language that gives the lie to the dream of such a metalanguage also defines the situation of "the self in writing":

> [I]f we are to speak of the relation of the self to the language in which it finds itself bespoken, then we must do so in terms of a critical discourse that registers the disjunction and the discrepancy between being and meaning, thing and word, and which therefore locates the self who is committed to language in its experience of the slippage between its immediate presence to itself and its mediated representation of itself in a symbolic system. Moreover, since Being, to be thought, must be thought as Meaning, even this self-presence of the self to itself will emerge only in retrospect as loss, with the self discovering itself in its own meaningful aftermath. (33)

It will, perhaps, be useful first to simplify and rephrase Fineman's very Lacanian observation in terms more directly appropriate to the present argument. The self at issue here is the subject of the symbolic — that is, the self we attain when we recognize and identify with a signifier — our name.

Following the custom of patrilineal denomination then prevalent, but which has in the interim weakened somewhat, Lacan calls this signifier *le nom-du-père*. Such an inherited patronym preexists the individual to whom it is attached, implicating the newborn child in a prehistory and accompanying range of assumptions and expectations of which it can know nothing. When the infant accedes to language and attaches itself to a family name, it therefore necessarily submits to an identification that is irreducibly extrinsic to it. In finding his or her name, the child finds himself or herself in the Other, encountering itself as a discursive signifier.[8] As a speaking subject the individual both speaks and bespeaks. When I use the pronoun *I*, the speaker and the spoken never coincide. (Witness the common experience of responding to a report of one's own words with the queasy conviction: "that doesn't sound like me," and common expressions like, "I was beside myself.")

This discursive mediation of the self to the self is made more peculiar by the fact that a subject so constituted can only recognize the unmediated self as that which was lost in the moment of its appearance. That is to say, one arrives at a discursive recognition of the self in language by positing — in discourse — this unmediated self who is speaking — but such a realization is itself a mediation and so this originary subject comes into being as belated and irrecoverable in the very moment when we are able to name it. Insofar as we are thus destined to live within the ongoing story of our lives, we can justly say that we read ourselves as we write.[9] This realization of the self as suspended between writing and reading holds true (and in the same way) for the authorial self we call Milton, the quasi-historicist "informed reader" posited in *Surprised by Sin*, the myopically situated author-reader designated by the proper noun "Fish," and the alternatively idealized reader defined within the discourse of any particularly occurring "interpretive community."[10] Now, Fish will, I suspect, want to know what if any consequences follow from a discourse that registers the constitutive failure of self-presence and the retrospective temporality it gives off, and it is in respect of this good question that I alluded above to the ethics of pedagogy, a field in which Fish has been significantly engaged as theorist and practitioner. I propose that the ethics of pedagogy be governed by an ethics of reading.

I suggested above that Morris Zapp's locking of the door against sodomy might represent a literary critical as well as a sexual orientation. Having alluded to psychoanalysis but conducted his discussion largely with the vocabulary of the analytic philosophy of names, Fineman unexpectedly ends his essay with a high Lacanian provocation: "This leaves us with the psychoanalytic conclusion that the fundamental desire of the reader of literature is the desire of the homosexual for the heterosexual, or rather, substituting the appropriate figurative embodiments of these abstractions, the desire of the man to be sodomized by the woman" (37). Fineman, no doubt, knew that a deep dead drop stands between this formulation and the discussion of Austin, Kripke, and Searle that precedes it.[11] It is, however, a shorter distance from the proposed "troilism" that sent Morris Zapp behind the locked door of Fulvia Morgana's guest room.

A more painstaking consideration of what is at stake in placing literature in the reader will bring us closer to understanding the tendentious inclusion of sublimated sodomy in Fineman's conclusion about the desire of literature and Lodge's comic placement of Zapp in the locked guest room of the Morgana ménage. A certain reading of sublimation — dating from Freud's *Three Essays on the Theory of Sexuality* — suggests that Fineman's sudden recourse to sexual terminology might imply an etiology in which an originally sexual aim is redirected into a literary one. However, mindful of Žižek's anecdote of the Chinese restaurant and Lacan's reworking of the development of the subject as function of "something that only a representation can represent [*Vorstellungsrepräsentanzen*]," I do not think that is the case.[12] Rather, the distinction between autological and heterological words with which Fineman began is prior to and includes the anatomical aims of desire. So Lodge's reference to sodomy need not be taken as an analysis resolving critical practice to redirected sexual desire, but rather to the ease with which the train of desire bumps along its semiotic tracks.

In the subtitle of *Self-Consuming Artifacts: The Experience of Seventeenth-Century Literature*, Fish would seem to have effected the reversal of the terms in *The Reader in "Paradise Lost"* that I am proposing, for this book is clearly about the operation of literature in the reader:

> A dialectical presentation succeeds at its own expense; for by conveying those who experience it to a point where they are beyond the aid that discursive or rational forms can offer, it becomes the vehicle of its own abandonment. Hence, the title of this study, *Self-Consuming Artifacts*, which is intended in two senses: the reader's self (or at least his inferior self) is consumed as he responds to the medicinal purging of the dialectician's art, and that art, like other medicines, is consumed in the workings of its own best effects.[13]

But we quickly discover that Fish conceives of this agency of literature in the reader as an assimilation of literature to the reader: "[W]hen we read — the work as an object tends to disappear — and . . . any method of analysis which ignores the affective reality of the reading experience cuts itself off from the source of literary power and meaning" (*Self-Consuming Artifacts*, 4). Although the writer and the reader of a "self-consuming artifact" may undergo a "painful process (like sloughing off a second skin)" (2), in the end it is the work that disappears and the reader who, though transformed, persists as an object of critical attention.

By inverting the subtitle of *Surprised by Sin,* I tried to suggest a somewhat different consequence in critical-historical practice: an account of what I am going to call "counter-transference," whereby, for example, Fish, in the corporeal presence rigidly designated by that proper noun, caught in the act of catching Bunyan, is — adventitiously and contingently, because his name happens to be Fish — groped and tickled and captivated, in one or another quadrant of the damp, metaphoric sea. Fish, as writer and critic, stands in an estranged relationship to "fish" as shared signifier discovered in the text. One is tempted to say that while he reads the text, the text reads him. Bunyan's "fish" is already allegorical, expropriating the marine critter to signify the sinner in a Christian symbolic. In this transfer from the biological to the theological, the sinner, under the figure of the fish, acquires some salient characteristics of the fish. The sinner must be tickled, lured, entrapped into reprobation. Yet these fishy characteristics are at the same time understood to be metaphoric. Bunyan pins a class of human beings under the name of the fish, and something fishlike attaches to the members of this class. This fishy bit is neither fully assimilated by nor ejected from the reader who recognizes that he or she has been addressed in Bunyan's figure of the fish — that is, the reader who recognizes the fish in the text as a figure of the reader. Something has been transferred from the sea to the page to the reader, and it is not easily returned.

Reading understood in this way may be thought of as a variation on a time-honored science fiction motif: the trans-mat mishap. The trans-mat mishap appears with remarkable consistency in countless examples. A marvelous machine is able to transport matter from one place to another by disassembling it to the atomic level and beaming the particles through space and reassembling them at a new location. The classic mishap is exemplified in the 1958 film, *The Fly.*[14] In this film, a fly happens to slip unnoticed into the transporting machine along with its inventor. The atomic elements of fly and man become crossed up in transit and two tragic figures emerge at the new location: a fly with the head of a man and a man with the head of a fly. I propose that when we read and identify ourselves in and through signifiers, which we recognize as our textual surrogates, we may find that similar exchange occurs. In the instance I have been so tediously explicating, a certain portion of fish is zapped into Bunyan's sinful reader where it encounters a certain portion of the reader Fish. Fish leaves his mark on the text — excising it to illustrate a theory of reading and thus foregrounding its signifying process — and the text leaves its mark on Fish, defining for him a relationship of reader to text that both exemplifies his approach to seventeenth century literature and validating it with the putative approval of a seventeenth century writer.

When Fineman provokingly characterizes the "desire of the reader" as "the desire of the man to be sodomized by the woman," he is concluding a discussion of *The Importance of Being Earnest*, a play in which sodomy is explicitly present — albeit on another, necessarily unseen, scene — as (dis)embodied in the imaginary character of Bunbury. But he had earlier found the thematics of the desire of an autological language crucially "invented" at the turn of the sixteenth century in Shakespeare's sonnets, in which the desire of the "homosexual for the heterosexual" becomes evident, he argues, in the contrast between the sonnets addressed to "the young man" and those addressed to "the dark lady" (*Shakespeare's Perjured Eye*, 17–23). Written in the aftermath of the Petrarchan ideal of a poem that would show its object and conduce also to the assimilation in virtue of lover and beloved, the sonnets addressed to the young man explore a self-consciously belated aspiration to an autologus, or presentational language, to which the answer is the frank heterologism of the sonnets to the dark lady: "Therefore I lie with her, and she with me, / And in our faults by lies flattered be."[15] For Fineman, "the subjectivity effect" arises from the disjunction of word and meaning and thing epitomized in the dark lady sonnets. I would argue, however, that the shift from the linguistic to the psychoanalytic vocabulary of sexual object choice — from autologous to homosexual and heterologous to heterosexual — cannot be taken as positing an etiology akin, say, to the developmental stages outlined in Freud's *Three Essays on the Theory of Sexuality*. The urge to do so — that is, the desire for a metalanguage that fixes desire in a temporally unfolded narration — is similar to that manifested by Žižek's table mate in the Chinese restaurant. It obscures the possibility that sexual desire is a function of linguistic *méconnaissance* — precisely the possibility that allows Lodge to bring Fulvia Morgana's ménage into the small world of literary criticism. In a biological sense we are secure in the knowledge that sexuality is prior to language. But in cultural terms can we be sure that the path of sexual desire is the signified and not the signifier of desire? This question brings us to the intersection — if there is such a thing — of literature and life.

3. Are We Milton Yet?

My third epigraph is taken from Fish's contribution to a polyphonic examination of the future of criticism, orchestrated by and presented in *Critical Inquiry*, on whose editorial board Fish sits. In it Fish responds (with even-tempered hostility) to the desire of practitioners of cultural studies and new historicism to effect social change through academic discourse in general, and, specifically to those who, in service to that desire, engage in an undifferentiated interdisciplinary eclecticism:

> I believe that it is by focusing narrowly that we have the best chance of getting it right and of speaking with power to the constituencies we do not directly address and, indeed, refrain from addressing. And I am sure that when we expand our focus and

broaden our aims we lose whatever rigor we might be capable of achieving. . . . [I]f you have your eye on a larger horizon — a horizon so large that it barely knows boundaries, never mind laws of entailment — almost anything you come across will seem relevant and capable of being plugged in unproblematically.[16]

I agree with Fish that what is distinctive and efficacious in literary critical work cannot entail extraliterary mediation. But one may still wonder whether Fish's discipline functions like the locked door that protects the integrity of Morris Zapp against the expectation that he fool around with Ernesto too. As a literary historian proposing to adapt a psychoanalytic model to (sympathetically) illuminate Fish's relentless defense of the integrity of discursive communities, which I begin now to see as also a surrogate for the integrity of the self, I intend no riposte to Fish's recognition that interdisciplinary research is only coherent when situated within a carefully restricted ambition. Rather, I am going to state explicitly what I hope has been already implicit in my argument — that psychoanalytic literary criticism is not interdisciplinary at all, because psychoanalysis — the talking cure — is (and always has been) a literary critical discipline.[17]

By beginning with Fish's playful identification with Bunyan's fish and Lodge's appropriation of a recognizable "fishiness" for his character Zapp, I hope to have made it clear that the Fish I am discussing is a fictional character — a written character with a more or less determinate relationship to the desiring subject bespoken in the publications under that name. The distinction I make between the discursive, fictionalized Fish and the flesh-and-blood person of that name is neither superficial nor trivial. I know nothing about the psyche of the actually existing Fish, and if I did, I would not be able to write about it even if I wanted to. What follows is speculation about the character Fish bespoken in a public discourse. As such, its efficacy, should it have any, will be strictly performative, which is to say it will work as a reading of that character's discursive presentation. In what streams does this Fish swim? For all his preoccupation with discursive boundaries, Fish has long occupied a liminal position as a public intellectual, a major academic administrator, and a self-identified "Miltonist." Like Oedipus, he makes his decisive choices at the place where three roads meet. But even as he occupies these different roles, Fish frequently situates himself as a Miltonist.[18] One might say, then, that the notion of Milton mediates the three faces of Fish. For the purposes of motivating my fictional Fish, I am going to give the structure of this mediation the psychoanalytic name "transference." Milton, the poet, was, of course, first and last a literary man, who also found occasion briefly to run a school, write a tract on education, spend the central portion of his career embroiled in the polemical exchanges of a political and cultural war, and administer a small, but important, government department. Transference, indeed.

Freud's theories of transference depend on the premise that emotions attendant on a repressed trauma, although they are never consciously experienced, remain mobile in the unconscious.[19] Lacking a narrative context to account for them, these unthought emotions persist in the unconscious as what Freud called "unbound affect"; we become aware of them only when they are transferred to something in consciousness that lends itself to representing the repressed material. Freud first notices this transference of affect in dreams, when "the remains of the day" are appropriated to represent something in the latent — that is, unconscious — dream thoughts.[20] The dreamwork opportunistically seizes residual memories and attaches to them the emotional affect of what cannot be remembered. This is a literary or rhetorical process.

This mobility of emotion is facilitated when disparate chains of signifiers are imbricated so that associated feelings may jump from an unconscious chain of signifiers to another, conscious one, the links of which are similarly configured. When analyzing Dora's first dream, in the earliest of his case histories, Freud imagined the distorting tropes of the dream-work as railroad switches across which affect turns from one set of tracks to another. "Now, in a line of associations ambiguous words (or, as we may call them, 'switch-words') act like points at a junction. If the points are switched across from the position in which they appear to lie in the dream, then we find ourselves upon another set of rails; and along this second track run the thoughts which we are in search of and which still lie concealed behind the dream."[21]

Lacan identifies the rhetorical mechanism underlying "the line of associations" as metonymy and that of the "points of junction," or "switch-words," as metaphor. The operative distinction here is between associations based on contiguity —one thing adjacent to another — and those based on resemblance — one thing like another.[22] Metonymies extend the tracks along which the semantic train rolls; metaphors establish the switches that allow it to cross from one track to another. For Freud, the intensity of feeling experienced in some neurotic phobias may be traced back to an originating trauma, but the assumption that interpretation consists in tracing the symptom back through the vicissitudes of its signification to reconstruct a narrative of trauma to which the emotion may be properly bound is not a necessary premise of the transference itself. We may return, for an example, to Žižek's antipathy for sharing dishes in Chinese restaurants. The table neighbor in Žižek's parable assumes that the shared food is merely the representative of a more deeply seated fear of sharing of sexual partners. Thus, the negative affect originates in a sexual experience, which is the cause or latent meaning of the manifest dislike of sharing food. Žižek suggests, however, that the transference may go in the other direction. Perhaps he resists sharing sexual partners because the affect attached to sharing dishes reminds him of the practice. The story is both funny and challenging because it underlines and disrupts a normative assumption in what Fish might call the interpretive community of psychoanalysis: that repression derives its energy from sexual rather than culinary indiscretions.[23] Moreover, it disrupts the narrative expectation of an earlier cause that shapes present behavior. Even shorn of its mythic contexts —repression and early trauma — transference of affect supports the finding that emotion is fungible along identifiably rhetorical pathways.

When through metaphor or metonymy a material sign is made the signifier of an unnamed other, the resulting compound sign is subject to two sets of associations that may be made on the basis of the signified and on the level of the signifier. For example, a rose may signify my love because both are beautiful, delicate, sweet-smelling, short-lived, and thorny. But the "rose," which signifies my love, may be drawn by its sound into an association with a "pose," "hose," or "toes." These strictly meaningless associations inevitably spill back into the signified. Is the nature of my unconscious desire suddenly revealed when the phonic associations produce "My love arose when I beheld the hose that sheathed her rosy toes"? The example is silly, but the question it poses is not trivial. Which comes first: the fetish or its representation? The fetish is itself a representation, but of what? Does the refusal to share dishes in a Chinese restaurant fetishize a fear of sexual profligacy, or is the avoidance of shared sexual partners a fetish appropriated to represent an antipathy to sharing food? If the revelation of desire is predicated on a collaboration of semantic determinations *and* representational contingencies, does the resulting dream (or poem) represent the latent desire or constitute it?[24] While the traumatic cause of unbound emotions remains unconscious, their associated affect is bound to a conscious narrative posterior to the affect itself. The appropriated sign — the fetish onto which affect is transferred — has, then, a character similar to that of the name "Ernest" in *The Importance of Being Earnest* or, for that matter, of gold in Marx's version of the fetish: it means everything precisely because it means nothing. The value of gold as monetary standard is extrinsic, as is the importance that accrues to Jack's being Ernest in earnest. Yet it is not purely formal.

Metaphor depends on a perception of impertinent predication. When the poet says, "My love is a rose," metaphor occurs only if the literal predication is rejected as impertinent. A neurotic — for whom "my love is a rose" — prevented by repression from recognizing the impertinence, might be presenting symptoms of *floraphilia*, which analysis could hope to resolve by eliciting from the unconscious the repressed tenor of the metaphor.[25] But, as will become clear in what follows, the tenor thus elicited need not be a *literal* fact of memory; a serviceable fantasy, itself a secondary metaphor, will do as well. The truth of desire is not the desired object but the formal (and temporal) structure that situates it with respect to the subject: the relation of the subject to his or her own desire.

For example, when Gertrude says, "Hamlet, thou hast thy father much offended," and he answers, "Mother, you have my father much offended," Hamlet resists the appellation of "father" to Claudius as impertinent, because Claudius is not literally his father; but he also rejects the metaphoric assimilation of Claudius to King Hamlet, which it implies.[26] Claudius is neither his father nor can he be understood to resemble his father. The issue is not whether Hamlet is arrested by a repressed childhood memory of his father — any more than it would be the discovery of the literal rose in the history of our hypothetical floraphiliac. Rather, it is the formal structures of trauma and transfer by which King Hamlet and King Claudius, the historical and the metaphorical rose, are absorbed. These structures inhere not in a putative memory of the past but in the present encoding of the text. We use our awareness of a text haunted by a set of implied but unspoken alternative locutions to make sense of what we read. Without imputing textual features to a temporally prior cause distinct from the text, we can see that the transference of emotion across words in a text correlates two contemporaneous and specifiable representations.

Unlike readers, psychoanalysts may aim to elicit the unthought associations that comprise an unconscious by working back through the distorted form in which they have reached consciousness. Bringing the repressed past into the discursive present is the putatively therapeutic work of "the talking cure." However, I have tried to demonstrate with the previous example that becoming aware of the configurations on which stray emotions map does not require constructing a narrative memory of some originary trauma. What psychoanalysts call "repetition automaton," for example, can also be understood as the circulation of emotion between two linked chains, in which the rhetorical scheme of an earlier chain unconsciously configures succeeding engagements according to a similar pattern. Freud called these preemptive configurations "complexes." The recovery of the repressed memory that formed the complex is a separate issue from the recognition of its rhetorical structure. Once the complex is established the structure is constant, the content variable — until it becomes available to conscious thought.

Transfer of affect is a general mechanism of the mobility of emotion, a way to explain, for example, why neurotics invest certain seemingly trivial objects, events, or performances, with apparently disproportionate importance. But the talking cure depends on a form of transference that is specific to it. This specifically analytic transference occurs when the analysand comes to identify the analyst with a significant figure in the repressed drama from which his or her putatively archaic emotions derive. This identification is not a matter of mistaking the analyst for the repressed figure but of placing the analyst structurally in the position of an other onto whom the analysand can project emotions originally evoked by the figure the analyst has come to represent. Freud at first thought this phenomenon, which he experienced as illusory love or hate directed toward him by his patients, represented the most difficult to overcome of the resistances.[27] Later, however, he came to see the transference as an essential element of the analytic process. Identification of the analyst with a key figure from the past enabled the analysand not simply to recall what had been repressed but to "work through" or experience the free-floating emotions attached to it. "Remembering" and "working through" in this way bind these emotions and allow them to be discharged into conscious memory, thus freeing the neurotic, for example, from repetition compulsion in which the emotion is bound by endlessly repeating the configuration of the unremembered scene in various opaque representations.[28] I come by this circuitous route to something that shares the general shape of Aristotle's melioristic view of tragedy, in which by identifying with the tragic hero the spectator is able to purge himself of pity and fear, to achieve, as Milton puts it in *Samson Agonistes*, "calm of mind, all passion spent."[29]

I propose, then, to broaden Aristotle's insight into the "therapeutic" value of tragic theater to include the possibility of a readerly transference. Such a model would describe an exchange of agency in two directions: the reader experimentally adopts and experiences the rhetorically structured subjectivity of the text to which he or she also brings — as on a parallel track — his or her historically situated rhetoric of the self. The reader experiencing and analyzing his or her transference from the text also countertransfers onto it his or her own unconscious affects and tropes. That is why we are able to discover what we feel by reading books.

Returning now to the question of Fish in *Paradise Lost* and *Paradise Lost* in Fish, we note that by virtue of its fascinated engagement with details such as names and sounds and random contingent associations, details whose singular virtue is that they cannot be historicized because they are impermeable to narrative motivation, such a criticism offers obstructions and alternatives to the profligate invention of Miltons and of Fishes. The critic who invents Milton, to use a phrase made current in John Rumrich's jeremiad against what he constructs as the conservative effect of *Surprised by Sin* on Milton studies, wishes to be penetrated by the text he or she penetrates, and so to invent himself or herself in the image of the author he or she invents.[30] But this self-invention can only succeed by failing. The nothing the critic is trying to contain by prescribing boundaries that determine the author as the cause of the text necessarily reappears (and disappears) elsewhere — in another, alternative history or at the horizon of excess. In psychoanalytic terms such a reading remains within the transference, repeating rather than working through the self-knowledge it might otherwise disclose. In terms more concretely pertinent to the current ascendancy of the historicist urge in Milton studies: something historical, some exigent happenstance — the sexual pun on Shakespeare's name; the iteration of the name Elizabeth in the designation of Spenser's mother, wife, and queen; Milton's problems with Mary Powell; the fishiness of Fish — is always available to resist naturalizing attempts to historicize. Like the unbound affect they are appropriated to represent, such details remain excessive, uncaused, yet decisive. The necessary contingency of the name thus demarks a bar between the literary and the world, and it is the persistent and constitutive failure of self-invention rather than the correction of the misprision of others that drives the *démarche* of critical history. It is with this sense of the reader — alternately deluded and frustrated — in search of himself as inscribed in the text he reads, that I now return to *Surprised by Sin* as it might figure within a brief but consequential retrospection of Milton studies since 1967.

In 1967, a bit belatedly, the context toward which Fish intervened was the tail end of a debate on the canon; that is, what we quaintly used to call the "Milton controversy." This early, premature, and ideologically confusing skirmish in the culture wars may seem parochial by current standards, but the passion of aggression that powered F. R. Leavis, T. S. Eliot, A. J. A. Waldock, and John Peter in their attempt to dislodge Milton from the canon (that is, to take *Paradise Lost* out of the standard curriculum) and the equally passionate efforts to keep him there assumed that it mattered in some significantly consequential way whether or not Milton's texts got into the youth (principally) of England.

The anti-Miltonists tended to represent Milton as an obstacle to modernism (and thereby to identify themselves with a high modernist exaltation of the autonomous and reflexive consciousness of self), who had been bad for poetry, and, with his polemical and doctrinal commitments, inimical to the aesthetic of the unmoored and alienated consciousness they understood modernism to promote.[31] Fish presented *Paradise Lost* as proactive. That Milton's poem is supposed to do something rather direct and aggressive in and to the reader is a significant literary, historical assertion because the process Fish describes differs from previously canonical constructions of the action of a text on the reader; for example, Hamlet's "to hold the mirror up to nature," causing virtue and scorn to recognize themselves and, in the shock of recognition, to speak what they always have been, what they ineluctably are; or, Spenser's classically epideictic "to fashion a gentleman" by putting examples before him. Spenser and Hamlet engage the reader in a way that is profoundly mimetic: Claudius *is* (always already) a murderer and to show him this murderer in the mirror is to make his murder speak. Red Cross *is* Saint George, even when he does not yet know it, and so too, generally speaking, are the gentlemen who will fashion themselves through their efforts to live according to Spenser's model. The concerns of the anti-Miltonists — that Milton subordinated poetry to doctrine, that his style was grandiloquent, his God unpleasantly authoritarian and defensive, and, most importantly, that he lacked a visual imagination — remained significantly implicated in the autological ambitions of epideictic mimesis and its assumption that the desire of the reader is emulous — that the self in writing and the self in reading meet at and become the object of their mutual contemplation. To be "surprised by sin" is a markedly different experience, posited, by Fish, as the result of a markedly different process. The reader is not engaged to model himself on an idealized Adam epideictically indicated. On the contrary, for much of the journey through the text, the reader has Adam at a distinct disadvantage, being, as he or she is, in a position to appraise Adam's education as a young man might patronize the impossible innocence of his father's childhood. Nor is Fish's reader of Milton to see himself or herself in Adam and, thus, to confront and bespeak, like Claudius or Gertrude, his or her sinful state. Rather, readers are to experience a collapse into their own putative origin, not only to experience the "education of Adam" but also to recognize in the reenactment of the narrative rise and fall of that experience — for the temporal moment — the finite boundary of human being. Fish posited for *Paradise Lost* a textual ambition to engage its reader in a process that finally rejects the visualization of mimetic selves because it recognizes in its own way that the "truth" of the self is always elsewhere. In psychoanalytic terminology, in Fish's *Paradise Lost* the self-in-writing (or -reading) finds itself caught between the mirrored images of the ego ideal and the ideal ego and disappears, putatively to be recovered at the end of the narrative, or the end of time. Thus, Fish, in his subsequent emphasis on reading as something that happens in time, was, I think, following Milton in recuperating the poem's subject by giving the place to which it withdraws the temporal designation "later."

It seems to me, therefore, that subsequent efforts to historicize *Paradise Lost* in and through the invention of one or another Milton — a Tory, nearly Anglican Milton, a progressive, working man's Milton, Milton the avatar of emerging capitalism and possessive individualism, even the moderately postmodern Milton I have hinted at in this essay — miss the historical point. To the degree that Fish's construction of the entanglement of the reader persuades us formally, it sets an agenda for literary history: it describes the change for which literary historians must account, and it challenges them to accommodate within that account a high degree of embarrassment about their need to rely on models of causality in situating a moment in which causality is metaleptically superseded. The door is thus at least ajar in Fish's description of the failure of the Chorus in *Samson Agonistes* to be properly dumfounded by its confrontation with Samson's and God's unintelligibility. Fish recognizes the perfervid anxiety behind the Chorus's desire to pass through Samson to what he signifies; faced with the spectacle of a story that does not signify, or rather, a story that signifies the uncertainty of its own meaning, the Chorus cannot stop inventing Samsons.[32]

I have always been much taken by the fact that Milton's 1671 volume reverses temporal expectation by "adding" Samson's story to Christ's. This may have been an aesthetic decision on Milton's part or it may have been a commercial move by the printer. However it came about, the resulting volume frames Samson's story with the antitypal repetition that precedes it. Unlike the Chorus, I am dumbfounded by this temporal suspension indicating that it is the future that makes sense of the past. The presence of the living Samson is a positive impediment to the symbolic function Samson. In a curious way, rather like the deaths of Dante's Beatrice and Petrarch's Laura, Samson's death is required to confer ethical agency on the story in which it occurs. Moreover, Samson's life as a signifier remains fungible postmortem. Manoa's notion of Samson's tomb as an inspirational shrine of the Hebrew youth is not fulfilled. The Philistine yoke is not thrown off. The tribe of Dan disappears from history until Samson is reborn as a supplement to the temptation of Jesus: "To which is added, *Samson Agonistes, a Tragedy.*"

To my mind, history can be properly literary only by being literary precisely in Fineman's terms; that is, by advertising itself as necessarily heterological, by recognizing that it constitutively cannot be the thing it seeks to describe. It cannot invent Milton and it ought not to be Miltonic. The critical impulse that seduces its reader to transfer his or her affections onto another Milton who is then posited as the cause of the text recalls to my mind a scene from Tod Browning's exceedingly strange film, *Freaks*.[33] The film, which features a group of circus "freaks," tells the story of a midget, Hans, who is infatuated with Cleopatra, a normal-sized trapeze artist. Learning that Hans is coming into money, Cleopatra marries him with the intention of doing him in and sharing his wealth with the circus's strongman. At the marriage celebration, the freaks signal their acceptance of the bride by chanting "Cleopatra, one of us," while passing a cup of liquor around the table. Unnerved by this welcoming ritual Cleopatra reveals her nefarious intentions and runs out into the woods, pursued by the freaks. In the film's final scene, her induction into the family of freaks is belatedly fulfilled; she is revealed to have been transformed into a creature that appears to be half woman, half chicken, and put on display in the sideshow. I appropriate this story, leaving it to the reader to cast Milton in the role of Cleopatra and the critic as Hans, or the other way around.

As an alternative to the "Milton-one-of-us syndrome," I propose a heterological and therefore literary history. This history only appears in the moment after the transference has been broken, and it bears analytical witness to the in-forming structuration that reading performs on it. It understands that the moment it desires and resists does not occur. The troilism to have been reflected in the mirrors of Fulvia Morgana's haute bourgeois boudoir does not occur because Morris, who is its point, is not there. He is, rather, behind the locked door of the guest room, awaiting transportation to another scene, another conference. The untimely (timely) appearance of Ernesto has frustrated Zapp's desire to be "sodomized" by the "nothing" of literature by superimposing an imminent threat of confrontation with the thing itself. But Ernesto is no more the real thing, no less a posterior effect of narrative, than Zapp or Milton or Fish; if the door were unlocked, nothing would happen. The unconsummated consummation would, however, remain, an afterimage in the mirror whose history is literature.

2 • Milton's Idea of Authorship

Barbara K. Lewalski

Milton spent much of his youth and his adult life engaging Foucault's question, "What is an author?" though his answers were hardly postmodern ones. I think it fair to say that no English writer before Milton fashioned himself quite so self-consciously as an author or considered quite so seriously and persistently what it means to be an author. He often signed his title pages "The Author John Milton" or "The Author J. M." He incorporated into his texts passages of autobiography that make something like a bildungsroman of his early life. He claimed poetry and also his polemic service to church and country as his vocation. In text after text he calls attention to himself as author confronting the problems of the work in hand. In *Paradise Lost,* he constructs his bardic role in four proems whose length and personal reference are without precedent in earlier epics. Miltonists have also been engaging the question of how to situate Milton as author in the early modern cultural landscape, where the practices of collaboration, imitation, appropriation, and exchange, the institutions of patronage and censorship, and the ownership and control of texts by printers and publishers produce a concept of authorship quite different from the Romantic image of the solitary writer expressing his or her own thoughts and deepest feelings.[1] We do well to resist ascribing to Milton a Romantic poetics, but we should nevertheless recognize that he develops an idea of authorship — especially for himself — that departs markedly from early modern norms.

I will survey Milton's complex engagements with the idea of authorship throughout his career, which Milton extrapolated, by stages, from his own experience as reader and writer and defined in terms that are distinctively his own. Stanley Fish offers us his culminating analysis of *How Milton Works*, characteristically focusing on Milton's stylistic strategies in work after work, strategies calculated, Fish argues, to produce specific effects in the reader.[2] My purpose here is to look instead to Milton's presentation of himself as a writer, both of poetry and prose, as he works toward a poetics and a rhetorical theory appropriate to worthy authors, and especially to such an author as John Milton.

At the core of that self-presentation is Milton's idea of authorship — both in poetry and prose — as a vocation, investing in that concept all the Puritan religious meaning of a "calling" made manifest by God-given talents and opportunities. Seventeenth century gentlemen (the class Milton could claim as a university graduate) did not see themselves making a career, much less a living, as a poet. Nevertheless, early to late Milton cast himself as a poet, not as a clergyman (though he had considered that role before being, as he put it, "Church-outed" by the Laudian prelates),[3] nor as a schoolmaster (though he ran a small academy), nor as a public servant (though he served as Latin secretary to the Commonwealth and to Cromwell). At Cambridge, in what is apparently his earliest statement of vocational intent, the English poem "At a Vacation Exercise," he proclaimed his desire to write on lofty subjects in English, especially epic and romance in the vein of Homer or Spenser.[4] During his nearly six years of "studious retirement" after university at his father's homes in Hammersmith and Horton he committed himself earnestly to learning and also to poetry, though, as *Sonnet VII*, "How Soon Hath Time," shows, he was painfully conscious that by comparison with his peers and by outside measures of success he had achieved little. At first he hesitated to present himself in the public arena: his epitaph for Shakespeare (1632) and his masque (1637) were published anonymously, and *Lycidas* (1638) bore only his initials — a pattern of deferral perhaps prompted by the early modern assumption that a gentleman should not stoop to print publication, but perhaps more by his desire to stake his claim on some great work rather than these occasional pieces. Probably in late 1637 or 1638, after all the study and soul searching, Milton proclaimed unhesitatingly in the Latin verse epistle to his father, *Ad Patrem*, that "it is my lot to have been born a poet" [Nunc tibi quid mirum, si me genuisse poëtam] (61).[5] This is bold and new. I can think of no previous English poet who made such a forthright claim to the role of poet as the very essence of his self-definition. That poem also thanks his father for providing him the kind of education he thought exactly suited a poet's needs: not only Latin and Greek at school but also private tuition in Hebrew, French, and Italian, and the opportunity and leisure after university to study all areas of knowledge. His sense of poetic vocation was reinforced by the gratifying praises his Latin poetry received during his Italian travels and especially in the Florentine academies, which he found to be an ideal environment to nurture poetic creativity and scholarship, combining poetic performance, social warmth, intellectual exchange, and literary criticism. In *Mansus* and the *Epitaphium Damonis*, written during and just after his Grand Tour, he alludes to plans for an Arthuriad, an English heroic poem addressed to the nation, having concluded, it seems, that this must be the major work God intended for him.

Some months later, when he entered the polemic fray with his antiprelatical tracts, he came to understand this service to church and state as another aspect of his vocation. In his autobiographical preface to book 2 of *The Reason of Church-Government* (1642), he described such writing as the most immediate demand laid upon him by God, akin to God's call requiring the Old Testament prophets Elijah, Jeremiah, and Isaiah against their wills to pronounce God's denunciations: "But when God commands to take the trumpet and blow a dolorous or a jarring blast, it lies not in mans will what he shall say, or what he shall conceal" (YP 1:802–03). Speaking as a scholar and an accomplished rhetorician, he complains that polemic does not allow for anything "elaborately compos'd," or for the "full circle" of learning to be completed, or for overlaying the text with "the curious touches of art" (807), but he willingly undertakes this "unlearned drudgery" since "God by his Secretary conscience" enjoins it (822). Even so, in this his first signed tract, he insists on introducing himself to his readers as a poet. In prose, he famously declares that, "led by the genial power of nature to another task, I have the use . . . but of my left hand," whereas the poet can soar "in the high region of his fancies with his garland and singing robes about him" (807–08). Confirmation of his poetic vocation came, he reports, from several sources: his teachers praised his style "prosing or versing, but chiefly the latter" as "likely to live"; the Italian academics and several "friends here at home" offered "written encomiums" and encouragement; but most important, "An inward prompting . . . grew daily upon me, that by labour and intent study (which I take to be my portion in this life) joyn'd with the strong propensity of nature, I might perhaps leave something so written to aftertimes, as they should not willingly let it die" (810). He still imagines that this will be a national epic in English that would advance "Gods glory by the honour and instruction of my country." Two years later, in *Areopagitica*, he is much more comfortable about claiming a vocation as scholar-teacher in prose: "When God shakes a Kingdome with strong and healthfull commotions to a generall reforming," Milton declares, he calls "men of rare abilities" (like himself) to discover new truths (YP 2:566). This explicitly stated concept of authorship — both in prose and poetry — as a God-given vocation with a national educative purpose was something new on the English literary scene.

That idea of authorship as vocation led Milton to resist or radically redefine one institution that commonly exercised considerable influence over what early modern authors wrote, literary patronage. Unlike Donne or Herbert or Ben Jonson or his college mate Edward King or most other gentlemen poets, Milton made no gestures to invite court patronage, while at Cambridge or later. After university he may have hoped, in accepting commissions for *Arcades* and *A Maske*, popularly known as *Comus*, to attract some better patronage, perhaps as tutor or secretary in a noble, soundly Protestant household like that of Bridgewater or the Countess of Derby. But in fact (as *Ad Patrem* indicates) he looked to his father as his only patron. He declined to have his name attached to the 1637 publication of *Comus*, set forth by its music composer Henry Lawes as a patronage gesture to Bridgewater. In *Mansus*, written in graceful acknowledgment of the attentions paid him in Italy by Manso, patron to Tasso and Marino, Milton fantasizes about finding some such worthy patron whose aid would enable him to write an English epic in Tasso's vein, thereby resolving the vexed question of career and livelihood: "O, if my lot might but bestow such a friend upon me, a friend who understands how to honor the devotees of Phoebus — if ever

I shall summon back our native kings into our songs, and Arthur, waging his wars beneath the earth, or if ever I shall proclaim the magnanimous heroes of the table."[6] But Milton's poem reverses genre expectations in that, instead of the expected emphasis on the duty of poets to honor their patrons, he insists on the duty and high privilege of patrons to befriend and assist poets. Echoing Virgil's line from the *Georgics*, "Fortunate senex" (49), Milton derives Manso's claim to immortality from his association with poets (including, by implication, himself), whose tributes honor him much more than he does them by hospitality, patronage, and memorials.[7] Recalling how Manso cared for Tasso during his last years, Milton imagines himself on his deathbed honored and cared for by a patron-friend who would erect a fitting monument for him and spread his fame. But, in a final reversal, that imagined patron does not proclaim the poet Milton's fame; instead, Milton pronounces his own praises in a projected apotheosis on Olympus. This eliding of the patron intimates that the patronage relationship will not do for an independent-minded and free-speaking Protestant poet, even as the apostrophe to Manso as an old man, however fortunate and vigorous, intimates that such patronage belongs to another era.

In his 1645 volume of *Poems* published by Humphrey Moseley, Milton addresses no patron or potential patron; instead, this as-yet-little-known poet is introduced to the world as scholar, humanist, man of the world, highly accomplished Latin poet, and English bard by personal tributes from a distinguished coterie of fellow scholars and artists: several Italian scholars and poets, Sir Henry Wotton of Eton, and the composer Henry Lawes. The first edition of *Paradise Lost* (1667), which is bare of all preliminary matter and which was published under one of the earliest publication contracts guaranteeing author's rights, is, Peter Lindenbaum argues, a landmark text in the evolution of a "republican mode of literary production."[8] The second edition (1674) contains commendatory poems by Marvell and Samuel Barrow, but again in the role of admiring readers and friends. In *Paradise Lost,* the only patron Milton acknowledges is his "Celestial Patroness" Urania (9.21).[9]

Milton's sense of authorship as vocation also stands behind his vigorous assertion in *Areopagitica* of an author's proper independence from state authority and control. This protest against prepublication licensing mandated by the 1643 parliamentary act came forth without printer's or bookseller's names — too dangerous for them — but with Milton's name boldly inscribed on the title page. The tract also explicitly approves that part of the law requiring identification of author and printer, both to ensure responsibility and as a means to secure authors' rights (YP 2:491). This work registers Milton's resentment and frustration, clearly founded on personal experience, at the affront prior censorship offered to the independence and autonomy he thought intrinsic to the author's role, and to himself as a virtuous and learned citizen-author:

> What advantage is it to be a man over it is to be a boy at school . . . if serious and elaborat writings, as if they were no more then the theam of a Grammar lad under his Pedagogue must not be utter'd without the cursory eyes of a temporizing and extemporizing licencer. . . . When a man writes to the world, he summons up all his reason and deliberation to assist him; he searches, meditats, is industrious, and likely consults and confers with his judicious friends; after all which done he takes himself to be inform'd in what he writes, as well as any that writ before him; if in this most consummat act of his fidelity and ripenesse, no years, no industry, no former proof of his abilities can bring him to that state of maturity as not to be still mistrusted and suspected, unlesse [he appear] . . . with . . . his censors hand on the back of his title to be his bayl and surety, that he is no idiot, or seducer, it cannot be but a dishonor and derogation to the author, to the book, to the privilege and dignity of Learning. (YP 2:531–32)

As a further insult, an author who wishes to make changes in press must "trudge again to his leav-giver," often many times, or else allow the book to come forth "wors then he had made it, which to a diligent writer is the greatest melancholy and vexation that can befall." How, he queries angrily, "can a man teach with autority, which is the life of teaching, how can he be a Doctor in his book as he ought to be, or else had better be silent, whenas all he teaches, all he delivers, is but under the tuition, under the correction of his patriarchal licencer to blot or alter" (532–33). For a brief period, Milton was given some licensing duties by the Commonwealth, but he seems to have fulfilled them according to his own lights. He mostly licensed issues of Marchamont Nedham's newsbook *Mercurius Politicus* after the date of publication and often in batches; and there is no record of his objection to any book. Indeed, in early 1652 Parliament called him to answer for allowing publication of the Socinian Racovian catechism, which was condemned, seized, and burned for its "blasphemous" denial of the divinity of Christ.[10]

Milton's view of authorship as vocation led him to emphasize, more than any predecessor or contemporary, the writer's public duty and responsibility to reform his society and its culture. His early entertainments, *Arcades* (1632) and *Comus* (1634), repudiate both court aesthetics and the wholesale prohibitions of extremist Puritans like William Prynne as they explore the power of the poet to effect cultural change. In *Arcades,* the figure of Genius embodies the curative and harmony-producing powers of music and poetry so that the virtues of Harefield are seen to be nurtured by good art as well as by its ruling Lady, the Countess of Derby. In *Comus*, Sabrina, as a figure from the world of poetry and myth, as a personage in Spenser's poem, and as a singer herself, figures among other meanings the power of worthy art to counter unruly sensuality and debased rhetoric. She is the good poet whose elegant songs and masque transformations free the Lady from the spells of the bad rhetorician Comus and confirm her in her own arts of song. And at the masque festivities at Ludlow Castle, the children's "victorious dance" (974) images the pleasure, beauty, and art that accord with the life of virtue, intimating that these can be best nurtured in the households of the country aristocracy. In his autobiographical preface to book 2 of *The Reason of Church-Government*, Milton supposes that a reformed poetry might supplant "the writings and interludes of libidinous and ignorant Poetasters" that corrupt English youth and gentry, and speculates whether drama or epic would prove "more doctrinal and exemplary to a Nation" (YP 1:818). He also proposes a national cultural program to reform "our publick sports, and festival pastimes" — the Sunday games, dancing, Maypoles and other festivities promoted by the King's *Book of Sports* — by substituting "wise and artfull recitations" of poetry in various public assemblies and theaters, "instructing and bettering the Nation at all opportunities, that the call of wisdom and vertu may be heard every where" (819). He claims for poetry a power akin to and perhaps surpassing that of the pulpit, "to imbreed and cherish in a great people the seeds of vertu and public civility" (821).

In *Areopagitica*, as Sharon Achinstein indicates, Milton addresses directly the issue of how to produce citizens for a reformed republic in the making.[11] He may be the first to do so. He proposes continuous unrestricted reading, writing, and disputation to exercise citizens in making the choices through which they will grow in knowledge and virtue, learn to value liberty, and act to secure it in the state. He describes many authors besides himself engaged in that project, "sitting by their studious lamps, musing, searching, revolving new notions and ideas wherewith to present, as with their homage and their fealty the approaching Reformation: others as fast reading, trying all things, assenting to the force of reason and convincement" (YP

2:553–54). He hereby validates and defends the emerging public sphere, the marketplace of ideas that was being created by the deluge of pamphlets and newsbooks.[12] Then, as it became increasingly evident that the English populace were not becoming the engaged republican citizens he hoped for, he made impassioned appeals to them in his two Latin *Defenses* to develop and practice the moral and civic virtues needed to preserve the Commonwealth. On the brink of the Restoration he still held on to a faint hope that his *Readie and Easie Way* might, with God's help, reverse "the general defection of a misguided and abus'd multitude," persuading "som perhaps whom God may raise of these stones to become children of reviving libertie" (YP 7:462–63). Also, in his *History of Britain*, written for the most part well before but published after the Restoration,[13] Milton sought to help his countrymen recognize their continuing danger from an innate characteristic evident in them from earliest times: though valorous in war, they sadly lack the civic virtues needed to sustain free governments and their own liberties — a failing they must counter by gaining "ripe understandings and many civil vertues . . . from forren writings & examples of best ages" (YP 5:1, 451).

After the Restoration, Milton's major poems create imaginative experiences intended to help readers gain moral and political knowledge, virtue, and inner freedom — the "paradise within" that is also the necessary precondition for gaining liberty in the public sphere. *Paradise Lost* makes education central. The Miltonic bard sets his poem in relation to other great epics and works in other genres, involving readers in a critique of the values associated with those other heroes and genres. And his representations of hell and heaven lead readers to rethink issues recently fought over during the revolution and Interregnum — monarchy, tyranny, idolatry, rebellion, liberty, and republicanism — inviting them to recognize as satanic any monarchy besides that of God and his vicegerent Son, who alone deserve that status. *Paradise Regained* and *Samson Agonistes* portray their respective heroes' hard intellectual struggles to come to a right understanding of themselves, of their different callings, and of a broad spectrum of moral and political issues that must precede their fulfillment of those callings. The temptation episode in the brief epic allows Milton to present Jesus' moral and intellectual trials as a higher epic heroism, as a model for right knowing and choosing, and as a creative and liberating force in history. Jesus' debates with Satan also offer a model of nonviolent yet active and forceful resistance to the Restoration church and state,[14] inviting readers to think rightly about kingship, prophecy, idolatry, millenarian zeal, the proper uses of civil power, the place of secular learning, and the abuses of pleasure, glory, and power. In *Samson Agonistes,* the blinded and defeated Samson, "Eyeless in Gaza at the Mill with slaves" (41) and engaged upon a painful process of self-scrutiny, has some reference to the situation of the defeated Puritans.[15] The drama offers a brilliant mimesis of the confusions attending moments of political crisis and choice, requiring readers — and especially the dissenters — to think through the hard questions raised by the revolution and its failure, so as to prepare themselves should God offer them (as Samson's final act offered the Danites) a new chance at liberty. Such questions include: How is a nation to know the liberators raised up by God to promote change? What signs are reliable indexes of God's favor to or rejection of leaders or nations? How can would-be liberators know themselves to be chosen or repudiated? Or know when they are led by God and when by their own desires? Does God ever inspire to action outside the law and outside his own law?[16]

Milton's idea of authorship as vocation also prompted him, from early on in his career, to make a uniquely close connection between a writer's life and his works. He does so playfully in *Elegy VI*, linking the festive lifestyle of his friend Diodati with his preference for writing "gay elegy," and locating himself with epic and hymnic poets — Homer, Tiresias, Linus, Orpheus — whose high subjects require an ascetic and chaste life. In *Apology for Smectymnuus* he insists in all seriousness that the high poet can only make his poem out of his own wide experience and the values and virtues he has cultivated within himself: "He who would not be frustrate of his hope to write well hereafter in laudable things, ought himselfe to bee a true Poem, that is, a composition, and patterne of the best and honourablest things; not presuming to sing high praises of heroick men, or famous Cities, unlesse he have in himselfe the experience and the practice of all that which is praise-worthy" (YP 1:890). He believed this profoundly and also the obverse: that any work of art necessarily reflects the nature of the author that produced it. That belief informs many of his judgments about good and bad writing, and sanctions his often fierce *ad hominem* attacks: as a good book contains the "lifeblood of a master spirit" (YP 2:493), so barbarous prose and verse are indicators of slavish ideas and (often) a depraved life. In the antiprelatical tracts, he makes stylistic vigor and satiric vehemence touchstones for moral force, devotion to truth, and prophetic zeal. The prelates' dullness and faults of style are evidence of their vacuity and lukewarmness in God's service. Bishop Joseph Hall's "blabbing Bookes," "toothlesse Satyrs," fashionable curt Senecan aphorisms, and "coy flurting stile" mark him as the false prophet personified, the antithesis of Milton as true prophet, whose rhetoric flows naturally from a mind "fully possest with a fervent desire to know good things, and with the dearest charity to infuse the knowledge of them into others" (YP 1:872–73, 948–99).

In *Eikonoklastes*, Milton describes *Eikon Basilike*, purportedly written by Charles I while in prison awaiting execution, as the direct reflection of that king's nature as a masquer devising fictions and using disguise.[17] Milton undertakes to unmask him as a hypocritical actor wearing a "Saints vizard." He castigates the king especially as a plagiarist of others' prayers, claiming some of David's psalms as his own (YP 3:553), and much worse, appropriating Pamela's prayer out of Sidney's *Arcadia*, "a prayer stol'n word for word from the mouth of a Heathen fiction praying to a heathen God; & that in no serious Book, but the vain amatorious Poem of Sr *Philip Sidneys Arcadia*; a Book in that kind full of worth and witt, but among religious thoughts, and duties not worthy to be nam'd . . . much less in time of trouble and affliction to be a Christian Prayer-Book" (YP 3:362–63). In the second edition of *Eikonoklastes*, Milton links the affront to God in offering him this prayer offered first to idols — "the polluted orts and refuse of Arcadia's and Romances" — with the wrong done to the author Sidney who has a right to his intellectual property:

> But leaving what might justly be offensive to God, it was a trespass also more then usual against human right, which commands that every Author should have the property of his own work reservd to him after death as well as living. Many Princes have bin rigorous in laying taxes on thir Subjects by the head, but of any King heertofore that made a levy upon thir witt, and seisd it as his own legitimat, I have not whom beside to instance. (364–65)

In both editions he denounces the king's book in terms that seem surprising coming from a poet: "I begun to think that the whole Book might perhaps be intended a peece of Poetrie. The words are good, the fiction smooth and cleanly; there wanted onely Rime, and that, they say is bestow'd upon it lately" (406). But this sentiment is glossed by Milton's earlier reference to the "easy literature of custom" (339) — facile court genres that are the product of feigning and mere elegance, not the bardic poetry Milton aspired to, which is the product of "industrie and judicious paines" and inspiration. Milton would have readers see the king's "idle" book and his own strenuous treatise as exemplars of two kinds of literature and two kinds of authors. The king's, patched up from unacknowledged borrowings, pretense, and foolish metaphors, promotes indolent, credulous reading and leads to idolatry. Milton's, like worthy poetry, promotes diligent effort, rigorous judgment, and difficult interpretation, leading to heightened moral and political discrimination.

In his Latin *Defenses,* Milton draws the closest connection between the lives and the writings of his opponents, Salmasius and (as he mistakenly supposed) Alexander More. In the *Defensio,* drawing on the widespread gossip that Salmasius was dominated by his wife, Milton links that slavery to an inferior with Salmasius's defense of a royal absolutism that enslaves others: "You have at home a barking bitch who . . . contradicts you shrilly; so naturally you want to force royal tyranny on others after being used to suffer so slavishly a woman's tyranny at home" (YP 4:1, 380). In the *Defensio Secunda,* he constructs a contest of character between himself — attractive, virile, chaste, honorable, a heroic defender of the state at the cost of his eyes, and a blameless servant of God — and the lecherous, treacherous, priapic Alexander More who jumps in and out of every serving girl's bed, and whose unruly and licentious personal life is thereby quite consonant with his base support of Salmasius, Charles I, and monarchy. Here (as to a lesser extent with King Charles), Milton sees a natural connection between a "slavish" personal life and a disposition to practice, or defend, or submit to, political tyranny. It is an acute psychological observation, though Milton's application here makes regrettable assumptions about gender hierarchy. As well, Milton thought that historians necessarily image in their art the quality of the societies they describe. In his *History of Britain,* Milton explains the absence of British historians before or contemporary with the Roman conquerors by the principle that cultures get the historians they deserve: "great Acts and great Eloquence have most commonly gon hand in hand" he declares, but when civil virtue and worthy action decline, "then Eloquence . . . corrupts also and fades; at least resignes her office of relating to illiterat and frivolous Historians" (YP5:1, 39–40).

His notion of life and writing as integrally fused led Milton to emphasize his own originality, both as prose writer and poet, in terms that depart radically from some early modern norms. For one thing, he resists the common early modern practice of collaboration. In the *Apology for Smectymnuus,* he indeed associates his voice with those of the five Presbyterian reformers who published under that pseudonym, claiming to write "not as mine own person, but as a member incorporate into that truth whereof I had declar'd openly to be a partaker" (YP 1:871). But he quickly removes himself from such incorporation by drawing in this same tract, as he also does in *The Reason of Church-Government* and the *Defensio Secunda,* an extended and revealing self-portrait that presents his own life experiences as ethical proof supporting the argument and rhetoric of that good man and author John Milton. Often, as in the divorce tracts and the *Readie and Easie Way,* he presents himself as a solitary voice opposing the multitudes, though on one occasion, in *Areopagitica,* he represents himself as a participant in a lively reforming scholarly community in which many men like himself are "disputing, reasoning, reading, inventing, discoursing, ev'n to a rarity, and admiration, things not before discourst or writt'n of" (YP 2:557). Yet even here he presents this activity as engagement rather than collaboration: individual scholars in their private studies are writing and sending forth texts which contest with other texts in the Wars of Truth, each scholar adding what pieces he can to Truth's dismembered body. Only once, in *Pro Se Defensio,* does he construct authorship as a collaborative activity, in the course of an effort to justify his embarrassing mistake in *Defensio Secunda* of ascribing authorship of the treatise *Regii Sanguinis Clamor (The Cry of the Royal Blood)* to Alexander More. He now claims that several known and unknown persons were involved, but that since he is sure that More had some hand in the preface and in overseeing the work's publication, he can properly hold More responsible for the whole, so that the question of primary authorship becomes irrelevant: "If I find that you wrote or contributed one page of this book, or even one versicle, if I find that you published it, or procured or persuaded anyone to publish it, or that you were in charge of its publication, or even lent yourself to the smallest part of the work, seeing that no one else comes forth, for me you alone will be the author of the work" (YP 4:2, 712–13).[18] Of necessity he was prepared to understand More's authorship in collaborative terms, though not his own. Yet his self-construction as an autonomous, independent author is complicated by the fact that as a blind man from 1652 on he had perforce to rely on many others — friends, pupils, amanuenses, printers — for research, checking quotations, transcribing dictation, proofreading, and presentation. Nor was he able after that date to exercise final control over his texts. But he did not refer to such assistance as collaboration.

Related to this, in his prose tracts he made explicit and insistent claims to intellectual independence of scholarly authorities. He often presents himself as a learned scholar who can when necessary invoke a wide range of authorities, but who is not constrained by and does not require support from them. Openly scorning the citation-laden margins of "marginal Prynne" and most other controversialists, Milton kept his own margins, as Douglas Trevor emphasizes, defiantly bare.[19] He also diverged far from contemporary norms of controversy in refusing to marshal patristic and contemporary theological authorities, denigrating the patristic texts especially as unreliable, obscure, contradictory, mistaken, absurd, heretical, corrupt, or spurious: a "petty-fog of witnesses" (YP 1:648). In the divorce tracts, and especially in the narrative he constructs about writing them, he underscores his sense of conflict between citing authorities and his own scholarly independence. In the (unsigned) first edition of his *Doctrine and Discipline of Divorce* (1643), his argument is based almost wholly on Scripture and on the painful experience of incompatible wedlock, with very few citations of authorities. In the second edition, Milton signed the preface and asserted pride of authorship, having decided, he stated, to show the clergy who denounced his first edition "a name that could easily contemn such an indiscreet kind of censure" (YP 2:434). In this edition and especially in *Tetrachordon*, he cites several rabbinical and Christian commentators on Genesis and Jewish divorce law, notably Hugo Grotius and the best English Hebraist, the "learned Selden," but chiefly, he insists, to satisfy "the weaker sort" who rely on authority. He also claims in *Tetrachordon* that he is "something first" in producing a full-scale treatment of divorce (YP 2:693), and he flatly denies being influenced by the authorities he cites: "God, I solemnly attest him, withheld from my knowledge the consenting judgement of these men so late, untill they could not bee my instructers, but only my unexpected witnesses to partial men" (716).

Milton's visceral distaste for seeming to peddle others' ideas like a pedant or a second-rate thinker is most evident in *The Judgement of Martin Bucer on Divorce*, a free translation of some parts of Bucer's *De Regno Christi*. Here Milton formally enlists the "the autority, the lerning, [and the] godlines" of Bucer (YP 2:439) to overcome opposition to his *Doctrine and Discipline*, but he uses much of his preface to construct an elaborate narrative about writing his divorce tracts first and then discovering confirming authorities: "I ow no light, or leading receav'd from any man in the discovery of this truth, what time I first undertook it in *the doctrine and discipline of divorce*, and had only the infallible grounds of Scripture to be my guide" (YP 2:433). He found Grotius only after he had finished the first edition of *Doctrine and Discipline*, a sequence of events indicating that God "intended to prove me, whether I durst alone take up a rightful cause against a world of disesteem, & found I durst" (434). He describes Grotius as an "able assistant," who broached "at much distance" somewhat parallel concepts of "the law of charity and the true end of wedlock" (434), and he claims to have used Fagius's "somewhat brief" comments chiefly to silence his critics (435). He heard about Bucer when the second edition of *Doctrine and Discipline* had been out for three months, and he was amazed to find "the same opinion, confirm'd with the same reasons which in that publisht book without the help or imitation of any precedent Writer, I had labour'd out, and laid together" (435–36). So, he insists on the status of a "collateral teacher" with those scholars (436), not as a disciple, casting them simply as character witnesses for him. In a postscript, he somewhat truculently defends the freedom he has taken in summarizing and epitomizing some parts of Bucer and freely condensing his prolix Latin, thereby boldly exercising an author's prerogative even as a translator: "[I] never could delight in long citations, much lesse in whole traductions; Whether it be natural disposition or education in me, or that my mother bore me a speaker of what God made mine own, and not a translator" (478). Milton would not have seen his practice in the *Arte of Logick* and *De Doctrina Christiana* as compromising this position, though both of them incorporate other texts. In the *Arte of Logick*, Milton indicates in his preface that his intention is to provide for students a one-volume compendium of Ramus and the most important Ramist commentary; and in his theological tract, he takes over what he agrees with from the common Protestant theological tradition as formulated by Wollebius and others, while arguing points of disagreement at very great length.[20]

In the divorce tracts, Milton also works out how, from this point forward, he will deal with Scripture as an authority. His interpretative touchstone is the essential spirit of the Gospel, charity, which must be "the interpreter and guide of our faith"

(YP 2:145). Stating flatly that "we cannot safely assent to any precept writt'n in the Bible, but as charity commends it to us" (183), he heaps scorn on those who rest "in the meere element of the Text" (145) with an "obstinate literality" and an "alphabeticall servility" (164). He also appeals regularly — in the divorce tracts, *Of Civil Power*, and *De Doctrina Christiana* — to the illumination of the Spirit to clarify what Gospel charity dictates, making Scripture authoritative only as it is understood by each Christian. This context is instructive for the passage in *Paradise Regained* in which Jesus seems to devalue books in terms that echo Milton's disparagement of scholarly authorities and insistence on his own originality, authorial parity with other writers, and divine illumination:

> However many books
> Wise men have said are wearisom; who reads
> Incessantly, and to his reading brings not
> A spirit and judgment equal or superior,
> (And what he brings, what needs he elsewhere seek)
> Uncertain and unsettl'd still remains,
> Deep verst in books and shallow in himself,
> Crude or intoxicate, collecting toys,
> And trifles for choice matters, worth a spunge;
> As Children gathering pibles on the shore.　　　(4:321–30)

As poet, Milton also proclaimed his originality in relation to the models and precedents that, like every Renaissance poet, he looked to and borrowed from constantly. He began at college with elegy, "which in imitation I found most easie; and most agreeable to natures part in me" (YP 1:889). But unlike Ben Jonson, who recommended learning the writer's craft by imitating a particular classical writer so closely as to "grow very Hee,"[21] Milton early to late approached his poetic models with great flexibility, making space for his own originality by drawing on many sources in any given poem, by flaunting his revisionism and, often, by claiming superiority to them all. *Lycidas*, as the *Variorum* commentary makes clear, echoes in nearly every line pastoral elegies by classical, neo-Latin, and vernacular Renaissance poets.[22] Yet no previous, or I think subsequent, funeral poem has the scope, dimension, poignancy, and power of *Lycidas*; it is, paradoxically, the most derivative and most original of elegies. When Milton lays out, in *The Reason of Church-Government* (1642), his plans to write English poetry in several genres, he characteristically looks to multiple models, classical and biblical: what "the greatest and choycest wits of *Athens, Rome,* or modern *Italy,* and those Hebrews of old" did for their countries. But he claims an advantage over all of them by reason of the true subject matter available to a Protestant Christian (YP 1:811–12). For the "diffuse" epic, he points to Homer, Virgil, and Tasso, and for the "brief" epic to the Book of Job. For tragic drama, he specifies Sophocles, Euripides, and the Apocalypse of Saint John, and for "divine pastoral drama," the Song of Solomon. For the high lyric, his models are the "magnifick Odes and Hymns" of Pindar and Callimachus, but especially the Psalms and other biblical songs, which, he claims, surpass all other lyrics "not in their divine argument alone, but in the very critical art of composition" (815–16). In the preface to *Samson Agonistes,* he cites as models Aeschylus, Sophocles, Euripides, the Apocalypse, and the *Christus Patiens* of Gregory Nazienzen. He begins that preface, his only extended commentary on a poem of his own, by quoting in Latin the first sentence of Aristotle's famous definition of Tragedy, but then proceeds to recast that definition in distinctly un-Aristotelian terms, tailored to his own drama: "Tragedy, as it was antiently compos'd, hath been ever held the gravest, moralest, and most profitable of all other Poems: therefore said by *Aristotle* to be of power by raising pity and fear, or terror, to purge the mind of those and such like passions, that is to temper and reduce them to just measure with a kind of delight, stirr'd up by reading or seeing those passions well imitated."[23] Milton's formulation revises Aristotle not only by emphasizing the moral profit of tragedy but also by changing the object of imitation: for Aristotle, it is "an action," the plot, or mythos; for Milton, it is the tragic passions, pity, or fear and terror, that are to be "well imitated" — a definition that locates the essence of tragedy in the scene of suffering — here, in Samson's agonies, pain-wracked struggles, and violent death.

Milton's radical revisionism is most in evidence, of course, in *Paradise Lost,* which makes an explicit and daring claim of originality as it proposes to "soar / Above th'*Aonian* Mount, while it pursues / Things unattempted yet in Prose or Rhyme" (1.15–16). But as critics have long recognized, the line directly echoes a line in Ariosto's *Orlando Furioso,* highlighting the paradox that Milton's originality is of a piece with his assimilation of literary tradition. The poem includes the full range of topics and conventions common to the Homeric and Virgilian epic tradition, and constantly alludes to many great models — Homer, Virgil, Ovid, Lucan, Lucretius, Ariosto, Tasso, Du Bartas, Camöens, Spenser, and more. But at a fundamental level, it repudiates the traditional epic subject — wars and empire — and the traditional epic hero who is the embodiment of courage and battle prowess. Milton's protagonists are a domestic pair, the scene of their action is a pastoral garden, and their primary challenge, laid down by God, is, "under long obedience tri'd," to make themselves, their marital relationship, and their garden — the nucleus of the human world — ever more perfect. Milton flaunts this revisionism in the proem to book 9 (1–47), claiming that his tragic argument — the Fall and the new heroism it calls forth, "the better fortitude / Of Patience and Heroic Martyrdom" — is "not less but more heroic" than "Warrs, hitherto the onely Argument / Heroic deem'd" (9.27–33). He hopes and expects to surpass all his models because his subject is both truer and more heroic than theirs, and also because he looks for illumination and collaboration to the divine source of both truth and creativity. Milton's bold claims of originality as an author are not separable from his claims as inspired bard.

Milton also sees himself as an author appropriating a remarkable, I venture to say unprecedented, number of cultural roles. In his poems and polemic tracts, he varies the mix of roles as genre and rhetorical purpose dictate: sacred priest, learned scholar, humanist critic, cosmopolitan man of letters, rhetorician, engaged patriot, satirist, reformist poet, epic hero, teacher, prophet, and bard. And, as appropriate, he calls upon the resources of learning, reason, passion, ardor, delight, invective, metaphor, and sublimity available to those several roles. In several early poems Milton portrays the poet as a dedicated priest "sacred to the gods" and a prophet whose lips are touched like Isaiah's with seraphic fire.[24] In the antiprelatical tracts, Milton develops a poetics of satire justifying fierce invective against the bishops as a "sanctifi'd bitternesse," and identifying himself with satirists and satiric poets who promoted ecclesiastical reform: Juvenal, Luther, Wyclif, Martin Marprelate, Dante, Petrarch, Ariosto, "Our Chaucer," "our admired Spenser," and "our old Poet *Gower.*"[25] He also identifies himself with Old Testament prophets who were "Transported with the zeale of truth to a well heated fervencie": Daniel destroying the image of Nebuchadnezzar or Elijah destroying Baal (YP 1:663, 699–700). In *Of Reformation* and *Animadversions,* he imagines himself at some near-future moment as a bard celebrating and helping to perfect the reformed society that will herald Christ's millennial kingdom: "Then amidst the *Hymns,* and *Halleluiahs* of *Saints* some one may perhaps bee heard offering at high *strains* to new and lofty *Measures* to sing and celebrate thy *divine Mercies, and marvelous Judgements* in this Land throughout all AGES" (YP 1:616). In *The Reason of Church-Government,* he presents himself rather as a prophet-teacher, called like Isaiah to denounce God's enemies but also called to advance Reformation by reasoned argument. In the divorce tracts, he compares himself with Josiah restoring the true meaning of sacred texts and as a counselor to Parliament in the mold of Cicero and other classical orators.[26]

In some works, Milton assumes a specific persona as he enacts a particular role. In *Areopagitica*, he famously presents himself as a citizen-advisor to the English Parliament, seeking to persuade them "what might be done better" to advance the public good and promote liberty (YP 2:486–88). To that end, he adopts the persona of the Greek orator Isocrates, "who from his private house wrote that discourse to the Parlament of Athens, that perswades them to change the forme of Democraty which was then establisht" (489) — though as Isocrates *redivivus* Milton writes out of a different ethics and politics. Isocrates proposed to reform Athenian morals by reinstating censorship over many activities of the citizens, while Milton insists that only reading of all kinds, forcing the continuous, free, and active choice between good and evil, will allow the good to advance in virtue and truth to vanquish error, thereby producing citizens with a developed Protestant conscience and a classical sense of civic duty. In *Eikonoklastes*, Milton identifies himself with the several Greek emperors who assumed that name to signify that they uprooted idolatry, breaking "all superstitious Images to peeces" (YP 3:343). Milton Ikonoklastes undertakes to destroy the idol many have made of the king within *Eikon Basilike*, and of that book itself, "almost adoring it" and setting it "next the Bible" (YP 3:339–40). In *The Readie and Easie Way*, Milton is an English Jeremiah who combines fierce invective and tragic vision with a bitter, prophetic lament for the imminent Restoration, as he cries out with that Prophet, *"O earth, earth, earth!* to tell the very soil it self, what her perverse inhabitants are deaf to" (YP 7:462).

In his role as bardic poet, Milton identifies himself, early to late, with the archetypal poet Orpheus. In *L'Allegro, Il Penseroso*, and *Ad Patrem*, Orpheus figures the prodigious power of the poet's song to move stones and trees and hell itself. In *Lycidas,* Orpheus's horrific death and dismemberment by the Maenads, who embody the savagery and mindless violence that can so easily overcome the fragile civilizing arts, figure the poet's peril in a world in which poetic talent, labor, and the noble desire for fame can be so early and so easily snuffed out — as Edward King's was and Milton's might be. After the Restoration, in the proem to book 7 of *Paradise Lost,* Milton reads in Orpheus's fate the danger to himself and his poem from contemporary Maenads, the Restoration worshippers of Bacchus:

> the Race
> Of that wilde Rout that tore the *Thracian* Bard
> In *Rhodope,* where Woods and Rocks had Eares
> To rapture, till the savage clamor dround
> Both Harp and Voice; nor could the Muse defend
> Her Son.   (33–38)

Often Milton casts himself as an author-hero whose writings themselves are a species of heroic action. In the second edition of *The Doctrine and Discipline of Divorce,* he portrays himself as a solitary and courageous romance knight who has uncovered lost truth against great odds. In *Eikonoklastes,* he is a warrior, the designated champion of the republic, who sallies forth to meet "the force of his [the King's] reason in any field whatsoever" (YP 3:340–41). In *Defensio* he is a scholar-combatant, ready to meet and overmatch Salmasius in sound latinity as well as in political philosophy and historical scholarship; his weapon is his massive Latin treatise, which stands in for his long-planned national epic. Its epic theme is the heroic action of his fellow citizens in defeating, judging, and executing their tyrant king. He presents *Defensio Secunda* as the second part of his prose epic, and his peroration makes explicit both that genre claim and his own heroic role as epic prose poet:

> I have borne witness, I might almost say I have erected a monument that will not soon pass away, to those deeds that were

> illustrious, that were glorious, that were almost beyond any
> praise. . . . Moreover, just as the epic poet . . . undertakes to
> extole, not the whole life of the hero . . . but usually one event
> of his life (the exploits of Achilles at Troy, let us say, . . . and
> passes over the rest, so let it suffice me too . . . to have celebrated
> at least one heroic achievement of my countrymen. (YP 4:1.685)

In *Pro Se Defensio*, Milton explicitly claims the role of epic
hero in writing those epic prose poems. When Salmasius "was
attacking us and our battle array . . . I met him [in *Defensio*]
in single combat, and plunged into his reviling throat this
pen, the weapon of his own choice." His polemic battle with
More (in *Defensio Secunda*) was a continuation of his compatriots' war: "for me alone it remains to fight the rest of this
war . . . against me they direct their venom and their darts"
(YP 4:2.698–99). At length, in the four proems of *Paradise
Lost*, he portrays himself as an epic bard who in that role is
also one of his poem's heroes: he dares to soar "Above th'Aonian
Mount," he ventures with Satan through hell and Chaos and
then struggles "to reascend / Though hard and rare," and he
courageously sings the second half of his poem, "In darkness,
and with dangers compast round" (*PL* 1.15, 3.13–21, 7.27).

Finally, Milton as author took on the role of prophet-bard,
developing a subtle and nuanced concept of the relation between authorship and inspiration. He formulated it first in the
autobiographical preface to book 2 of the *Reason of Church-
Government*, as he formally promised his fellow citizens to
become a national epic poet when the political crisis was past
and he had acquired the requisite qualifications:

> These [poetic] abilities, wheresoever they be found, are the
> inspired guift of God rarely bestow'd, but yet to some (though
> most abuse) in every Nation; . . . Neither do I think it shame
> to covnant with any knowing reader, that for some few yeers
> yet I may go on trust with him toward the payment of what I
> am now indebted, as being a work not to be rays'd by the heat
> of youth, or the vapours of wine . . . nor to be obtain'd by the
> invocation of Dame Memory and her siren daughters, but by

> devout prayer to that eternall Spirit who can enrich with all utter-
> ance and knowledge, and sends out his Seraphim with the hal-
> low'd fire of his Altar to touch and purify the lips of whom he
> pleases: to this must be added industrious and select reading,
> steddy observation, insight into all seemly and generous arts
> and affaires. (YP 1:816, 820–21)

This statement asserts that high poetry is not the product of
youth, or stimulants, or mere imitation — Dame Memory and
the Muses — but flows from inborn gifts and divine inspiration, conjoined with arduous study and wide experience of life.
As prophet-teacher in prose, Milton did not see himself as a
vessel for extempore enthusiastic testimony as did some
radical sectaries; and as bard he did not suppose himself a
vehicle for the Platonic divine afflatus. He indeed testifies in
Paradise Lost that his muse comes nightly "unimplor'd," and
"dictates to me slumbring, or inspires / Easie my unpremeditated Verse" (*PL* 9.22–24), but this does not mean that he saw
himself as secretary of the Spirit, taking down divine dictation.
To the contrary, in this same passage he reviews the complex
and reasoned literary judgments and decisions he has made
about various epic subjects, topics, and styles, "Since first this
Subject for Heroic Song / Pleas'd me long choosing, and beginning late" (25–26). Because his subject is sacred history, he supposes that its true meaning must be revealed to him (as to any
Christian) by divine illumination, and he also recognizes that
his visionary imagination and his "answerable style" are, in
some primary sense, inborn gifts. He acknowledges his
"Celestial Patroness" Urania as a figure for such inspiration
and for the divine aid he needs to overcome daunting obsta-
cles — "an age too late" (the Restoration era unfriendly to
sublime poetry), the cold English climate, and the burden of
advanced years, which might overwhelm him "if all be mine,
/ Not Hers who brings it nightly to my Ear" (*PL* 9.44–47).
With such impulses informing his poetic dreams, and with a
lifetime of poetic labor and practice to draw upon, Milton evi-

dently experienced his magnificent lines cascading forth as a divine gift. Nevertheless, he had to supply authorial labor and art not only before but also after this creative moment. His early biographer, Jonathan Richardson, heard that, when his amanuenses arrived in the morning, Milton would dictate perhaps 40 lines in a breath, and then "reduce them to half that Number."[27]

3 • Milton's Negativity

Annabel Patterson

This essay began with a hunch, based on a passing observation that Milton tends to put his positives — his most important positives at that — in negative form. My hunch was that he learned to do this from his deep familiarity with Latin. Many negatives later, I concluded that not only was the hunch possibly correct, but that far more can be learned from Milton's negativity, whether of syntax or vocabulary, than I had ever dreamed; and that it is not just a question of linguistic habit, but reflects the poet's deep psychological impulses and, dare I use the term, his world view. Paradoxically, this world view was eventually clarified by his not being able to see. I shall suggest that when his blindness closed in on him, Milton's understanding of how to put things crystallized for him into a pattern that, for some extraordinary reason which must have something to do with our own critical blindness, has hitherto gone unnoticed, or at least unremarked.

Let's begin with the young Milton, and with two familiar quotations: "Missing thee, I walk **unseen** / On the dry smooth-shaven Green" and: "Some time walking **not unseen** / By

Hedgerow Elms, on Hillocks green."[1] "Unseen" and "not unseen." Small words, easily lost in the rich texture of *Il Penseroso* and *L'Allegro*, poems whose texture consists of the pleasures of seeing as well as listening, both pleasures conveyed to readers through their own senses. Why would Milton choose these matched words to describe his own persona in different moods, morning and evening moods? Why not "Missing thee, I walk obscure, / By the silver fountains pure," or "Sometime walking in plain view, / Where congregates the rural crew?" *Il Penseroso*, it is true, thematizes invisibility by choice. The speaker walks "in close covert by some Brook, / Where no profaner eye may look," and asks Night to "hide [him] from Day's garish eye." Later he also invokes the "unseen Genius of the Wood." But why, in the lighter, seemingly simpler poem, would he see himself as "sometime walking *not unseen*," a weird double negative so gratuitous, especially in its discovered echo in *Il Penseroso*, that it jolts us into rethinking the "unreproved pleasures" of the poem, where the negative implies not freedom but the brooding presence of a figure of reproof.

Let us now look at the learned habits of writing in Latin. In *Ad Patrem*, the verse letter where Milton attempts to persuade his father that a literary career will be worth his costly education, he writes: "Quae mihi sunt nullae, nisi quas dedit aurea Clio" [I have nothing except what golden Clio has given] (line 14). *Nullae . . . nisi.* Not "I have only Clio's golden gifts." And he writes, "Nec tu vatis opus divinus despice carmen" [Nor should you despise the divine song of the poet] (line 17). *Nec . . . despice.* Why not, instead, "You should honor the heavenly work." And he writes, "Nec tu perge, precor, sacras contemnere Musas, / Nec vanas inopesque puta" [Do not persist, I beg of you, in condemning the sacred Muses, and do not think them vain and unuseful] (56–57). More of the same. *Nec . . . nec* and *inopes* instead of some other word that does not itself consist of a denial. And finally, should his appeal to his parent be successful, he looks forward to a different kind of life, one in which the values of *Il Penseroso* and *L'Allegro* somehow combine, at least as concerns his own place in the sight of others. "Iamque nec obscurus populo miscebo inerti" [I shall no longer mingle obscure] (103) (note that Hughes here catches Milton's habit and translates *obscurus* as "unknown" — with the unthinking rabble). Milton is promising his father that he *will* be famous some day, and that the scrivener's investment in a university education will pay off. Something is going on here, and it is not too early to suggest that *Ad Patrem* is the visible site of Milton's vocational anxiety, the place where the problem of self-esteem emerges in the formulas that spring (unasked?) to his writing hand.

Now to the 1640s, and the period of Milton's English prose. Here is Milton's account to the English public, that same *populus inertus*, of his literary intentions, from *The Reason of Church-Government*, published in January or February 1642:

> And the accomplishment of them lies **not but** in a power above mans to promise; but that **none hath with more studious ways** endeavour'd, and with more **unwearied** spirit that **none shall**, that I dare almost averre of my self. . . . **Neither do I think it shame** to covnant with any knowing reader, that for some few yeers yet I may go on trust with him toward the payment of what I am now indebted, as being a work **not to be rays'd** from the heat of youth or the vapours of wine, . . . **nor** to be obtain'd by the invocation of Dame Memory and her Siren daughters, but by devout prayer to that eternall Spirit . . . to this must be added industrious and select reading, steddy observation, insight into all seemly and generous arts and affairs, till which in some measure be compast, at mine own peril and cost **I refuse not** to sustain this expectation from as many **as are not loath to hazard so much credulity** upon the best pledges I can give them.
> (YP 1:820–21)

If we translate this passage, and I think we must, not least because it is extremely difficult to do, what Milton is saying is roughly this:

It is beyond human power to promise the accomplishment of my literary ambitions, but I almost dare swear that I have tried to do so by the most intense study (and I defy anybody to be more energetic than I have been). And I must confidently make a contract with any intelligent reader that what I have promised to produce will be available in a few more years, since it will not be the product of youthful enthusiasm or intoxication, nor arrived at by appealing to literary tradition, but rather the gift of the Holy Spirit; to which inspiration must be added industrious and select reading, steady observation [of the world], insight into all appropriate arts and affairs, and until this necessary preparation is completed, at my own peril and cost[,] I must continue to ask for patience and credibility from those who are willing to take the chance on me, on the basis of my best pledges.

But here is the twist. Does that anxious phrase, "at mine own peril and cost," refer, as I have allowed it to by inserting a comma, to the costs of his literary apprenticeship (costs that, we may notice, are now his and not his father's); or does it, without the comma, reach forward to govern his refusal to be hurried, his statement that asking for more time is reasonable, given the quality of his credit? That the entire passage is shaped by the commercial metaphor of debt, delayed payment, and personal credit connects it both back to *Ad Patrem* and forward to the market metaphors of *Areopagitica*. "Pledge" I might note, is a word that *could* be used in the sense of "to give assurance of friendship or fidelity to any by the act of drinking," precisely that which Milton rejects, but also, more dramatically, "to deliver, deposit, or assign as security for the repayment of a loan or the performance of some action." What is Milton delivering? His eloquence only, his word, his most peculiar negative positivism.

We have now established a *mentalité* for Milton in which syntactical negativity is the sign of vocational doubt completely entwined with remarkable confidence. But this is only one strain of Milton's early negativity. There is another, primarily elegiac strain, already visible in the early poems. There is Lycidas, who "must **not** float upon his wat'ry bier, / **Unwept**," a formula that alludes to the poet's responsibility for taking up a neglected topic, and will return in fully theorized form in the invocation to *Paradise Lost*, book 9. But there is also the purely pathetic and affective series of "no mores," from the "Willows and the Hazel Copses green," which shall "now no more be seen," to "Smite no more," "Weep no more," and again, "Weep no more." And then there is one of the earliest of Milton's great divine paradoxes, "the unexpressive nuptial song," which points to another theme, the inexpressibility of all that really matters. And then there is *Comus*, which, as I argued long ago, is tightly connected to *L'Allegro* and *Il Penseroso*, and which I can now see is a lexical, as well as a philosophical, exercise in denial.

The Lady is clearly an Il Penserosa. She has heard Comus's music as if it were the dance of "loose unletter'd Hinds," (174) and found herself in a world in which she does not know where to direct her "unacquainted feet" (180). Naturally, she is worried about keeping her "life and honour unassail'd" (220). She sings. Comus hears, and delivers an unctuous compliment. And her response is convoluted: "Nay gentle shepherd, ill is lost that praise / That is addrest to unattending Ears" (271–72). As for her brothers, their mouths are full of high-minded and high-class negatives. Among "unnumerous boughs" (349), they fear their sister "leans her unpillow'd head" (355). But, says the Elder Brother, *she* won't be anxious: "I do not think my sister . . . so unprincipl'd in virtue's book . . . (Not being in danger, as I trust she is not)" (366–70). The Second Brother is a little less sanguine. Beauty needs a guardian dragon "with unenchanted eye" (395) to defend it:

> You may as well spread out the unsunn'd heaps
> of Miser's treasure by an outlaw's den,
> And tell me it is safe, as bid me hope

> Danger will wink on Opportunity,
> And let a single helpless maiden pass
> Uninjured.   (398–403)

And his speech ends with the very odd phrase, "our unowned Sister" (407), which is no less disturbing for the legalistic gloss, "not being possessed as property."

Now I shall stop placing the negatives in context and simply list them as they fall, without line references: "unblench't majesty," "unlaid ghost," "unconquered Virgin," "unpolluted temple of the mind," "unchaste looks," "th'unwary sense of them that pass unweeting," "th'unarmed weakness of one Virgin," "unjust force," and, importantly, the "unknown" secretive herb Haemony, so unrecognized that the "dull swain / Treads on it daily with his clouted shoon." Half of these negatives have a negative point to make, the other half are actually positives. Comus does it too. He cites the "unexempt condition of humanity," Nature's "unwithdrawing hand," "spawn innumerable," all arguments for using Nature's bounty, else "Th'all giver would be unthank'd, would be unprais'd, / Nor half his riches known," to which the Lady replies, using his strategy against him, that Nature would be better pleased if her goods were used "in unsuperfluous even proportion." Is this just a lexical habit run rampant, or is Milton trying to suggest that, when you are lost in the woods or in a long, argumentative poem, it is not always easy to distinguish a good negative from a bad one? The negative formations of the Elder Brother seem a bit too conventionally moral, those of Comus a bit too obviously anticonventional. Yet those of Comus have an insidious appeal because they are more intelligent than simple carpe diem.

Pondering the phenomenon of seeing and unseeing, I realized that I should check to see if Milton had anything to say about negative positives, or double negatives, in his *Art of Logic*. He does not. Nor should I have expected him to do so, since the Ramistic logic on which he was expanding is concerned with the semantic substance of axioms, not their form. Thus, a negative is only a negation. I did, however, discover a strange chapter, "On Privatives," which begins like this:

> Privatives are negative contraries, one of which negates only in that subject to which the affirmative by its very nature belongs. And here what is affirmed is called *habitus,* by which someone possesses something, but the negative is called privation, by which someone is deprived of or lacks that something: examples are sight and blindness, or movement and rest. . . . In contradictories negation is infinite, negating is affirmative everywhere, that is, in any thing whatsoever; for example, whatever is not just is not-just. But in privatives the negation is finite, negating the affirmative or the *habitus* only in that subject to which the affirmative by its very nature belongs, or can belong. . . . Thus blindness is the negation of sight, not everywhere and in any thing whatsoever, but only in the thing to which sight by nature should belong. . . . Not everything, therefore, which does not see is properly called blind. (YP 8:267–68)

Later, he cites trees and stones as examples of things that cannot properly be called blind.

Now why would Milton choose this example, of all possible others, to illustrate the theory of privatives? The *Art of Logic* was published in 1672, when Milton had only two more years to live. Its editors in the Yale edition, Walter Ong and Charles Ermatinger, were "virtually sure that it was a much earlier composition," and after reviewing the various theories, conclude that the most likely time for its composition was during 1640–1647, or, even more closely, 1645–1647, when Milton was engaged in teaching Edward and John Phillips and a few other boys (YP 8:144–45). That is to say, it was conceived as a textbook in our sense of the word. The editors were using as an authority Francine Lusignan's 1974 dissertation on *The Art of Logic,* for which she used computer-assisted studies of his prose works, and they agree with her that, although *The Art of Logic* could have been revised later, "the technicalities, massive quotations, and cross references would seem to make *visual access* to the text imperative for extensive modifications" (YP 8:147; my italics). To me, it seems inconceivable that Milton would have chosen that particular example of a privative, blindness, without the personal stimulus of at least failing sight. And in his later writings, those that we know follow the more or less absolute loss of vision, the privation so experienced results in a new use for the negativity of expression, and particularly of self-expression. If in *Comus* the flurry of negative constructions seems somehow appropriate to a poem whose central message is "No," and if in *The Reason of Church-Government* the negative constructions are clearly related to Milton's embarrassment at not having produced more than minor literary works (the habit is catching), in *Pro Populo Anglicano Defensio Secunda*, which Milton produced after his blindness was total, we can see both the embedded influence of latinity and the searing effects of privation. The former, of course, is the consequence of our *reading* the *Second Defense* in both Latin and English, the second is made visible because Milton rises to self-defense, specifically on the issue of his blindness and what has caused it. Here, the theme of being seen — how he looks in the eyes of others — is refocused on the question of how his now blind eyes look in the eyes of others. Let us start with an English translation, which is partly my own, partly that of the Columbia edition:

> No one, so far as I know, who has only seen me, has ever thought that I am deformed in appearance: whether handsome or not, is a point I shall less insist on. My stature, I own, is not tall . . . but it is not true, that I am thus lean beyond example; on the contrary [when I was younger] . . . I was neither unskilled in handling my sword, nor unpractised in its daily use. . . . At this day, I have the same spirit, the same strength, [only] my eyes are not the same: yet to external appearance, they are undamaged, as clear and bright without a cloud, as the eyes of those whose sight is most perfect. In this respect only, and

against my will, am I a dissembler. In my countenance, in which [my adversary] has said, there is "nothing more blood-less," there still remains a color so very opposite to the blood-less and pale, that, though turned forty, there is scarcely anyone who would not think me younger by nearly ten years. Neither my body nor my skin is shrivelled.

Now the Latin:

> Deformis quidem **a nemine**, quod sciam, qui modo me vidit, sum unquam habitus [notice the appearance of that word, "habitus," from the logic of privation] formosus **necne,** minus laboro: statura fateo **non sum procera . . . sed neque exilis admodum . . . nec ferrum tractare, nec stringere** quotidiano usu exercitas **nescirem;** . . . Idem hodie animus, eadem vires, **oculi non idem**; ita tamen extrinsecus **illaesi,** ita **sine nube** clari ac lucidi, ut eorum qui acutissimum cernunt: in hac solum parte, memet **invito,** simulator sum: in vultu, quo **"nihil exsanguius** esse" dixit, is manet etiamnum color **exsangui** & pallenti plane contrarius, ut quadragenario major **vix sit cui non denis** prope annis, videar natura minor: **neque corpore contracto neque cute.** (CM 8:60)

Note first that in nine lines of Latin prose, there are 13 nega-tive constructions. Four of these are already built into the words themselves, **nescirem** (I did not know), **illaesi** (undam-aged), **invito** (involuntarily), **exsanguius** (more bloodless), the original insult that provokes the defense, and its rejection as **exsangui . . . contrarius.** Second, this passage has a striking literary antecedent; both the use of **formosus** and the negative construction derive from Virgil's second eclogue, where Corydon, hopelessly in love with the **formosum pastor**, reassures himself, having looked at his reflection in an unusually calm ocean, **"Nec sum adeo informis . . . si nunquam fallit imago,"** a line marvelously echoed by Marvell in *Damon the Mower:*

> Nor am I so deform'd to sight,
> If in my Sithe I looked right;
> In which I see my Picture done,
> As in a crescent Moon the Sun.[2]

But imagine the blind Milton, no longer able to see himself in any mirror, whether calm sea or shining scythe, calmly combining both **deformis** and **formosus** in a single, defiant self-portrait (or perhaps we should say ecphrasis), relying on the eyes of others for his mirror, the eyes of others being what in the past he has claimed to shun.

But then the *Second Defense* turns to what **really** hurts: that the *Regis Sanguinis Clamor* had been preceded with an epistle to Charles II, comparing Milton to Polyphemus, not merely **deformis** but justly blinded by Odysseus: **monstrum horrendum, informe . . . cui lumen ademptum.** Having defended his appearance, Milton writes:

> Would it were equally in my power to confute this unhuman adversary on the subject of my blindness? But, it is not. Then, let us bear it. To be blind is not miserable; not to be able to bear blindness, that is miserable. But why should I be unable to bear that which it behoves every one to be prepared to bear, should the accident happen to himself, without repining? Why should I be unable to bear what I know may happen to any mortal being, what I know has actually happened to some of the most eminent and best of men, on the records of memory.   (CM 8:63)

And he then proceeds to list not only Teresias and Phineus, the precedents that survive into *Paradise Lost*, but also Timoleon of Corinth, Appius Claudius, Caecilius Metellus, Dandolo, prince of Venice, Ziske, "the gallant duke of Bohemia," the humanist Zanchius, and patriarch Isaac himself. I am less interested, however, in the length and incoherence of this list in its first form (we tend to think only of the version in *Paradise Lost*, 3.33–36) than in the grammatical construction of the internal consolation: "Utinam de caecite pariter liceret **inhumanum** hunc refellere adversarium; **sed non licet**; feramus igitur: **non est miserum esse caecum; miserum est caecitatem non posse ferre**" (CM 8:63). Beautifully simple, in its chiastic form, the defense of the blindness surpasses the defense of the appearance primarily in its full understanding of what negativity actually is: To be blind is not tragic; it is tragic not to be able to bear blindness. Out of this hard-won paradox, masquerading as textbook formula, Milton would fashion both the despair and the reconciliation of *Samson Agonistes:*

> O dark, dark, dark, amid the blaze of noon,
> Irrecoverably dark, total Eclipse
> Without all hope of day. (80–82)
>
> · · · · · · · ·
>
> But he though blind of sight,
> Despis'd and thought extinguished quite,
> With inward eyes illuminated
> His fiery virtue rous'd
> From under ashes into sudden flame,
> And as an evening Dragon came. (1687–92)

In the *Second Defense,* Milton is not yet the evening dragon. He still has to work out in laborious, confessional prose his testimony to the effect that his blindness is not a punishment for his defense of the regicides, but rather a sign of exceptional privilege: "I am not conscious of any offense . . . recently committed or long ago, the atrocity of which could have called down this calamity upon me above others. . . . I am still persuaded that I have written nothing, which was not right and true and pleasing to God" (CM 8:67). And here too the heart of the matter is conveyed in a negative syntax: "**nullius . . . nullius . . . nihil non rectum ed vera.**"

So we seem to have reached a point where Milton's negativity has found its true subject. It has gone beyond the modesty topos of being unseen, which is really, in the youthful poems, a boast, or the hortatory remarks to his father on not underestimating the value of a literary career, which we could put down to vocational insecurity, or the series of self-denying ordinances that mark the vocabulary, as well as the ethos, of *Comus.* Negativity has become the language of self-defense, which is the most purely negative form of self-promotion. As

Milton scrutinizes all the recesses of his heart, and all his previous writings, none of them seems to him to have conceivably justified the wrath of an angry god. And the *Second Defense* continues for several pages to develop the thesis of a heroic blindness brought about by his rigid adherence to duty.

> "I neither repine at, nor repent me of my fate": **Me sortis meae neque pigere neque poenitere**; "I neither believe, nor have found that God is angry": **Deam iratum neque sentire, neque habere.** "The divine law, the divine favour, has made us not merely secure (**incolumes**), but, as it were, sacred from the injuries of men; nor would seem to have brought this darkness upon us so much by inducing a dimness of the eyes, as by the overshadowing of heavenly wings": **nec tam oculorum hebetudine, quam coelestium alarum umbra**.   (CM 8:72–73)

But why did Milton have to go through a negative syntax, an admission, as it were, of the adversary's position in order to arrive at self-reassurance? In order to replace the ugly word **caecitas** with the glorious phrases **oculorum hebetudine** (which we might not unreasonably translate, remembering *Il Penseroso*, as "a dim religious light") and **coelestium alarum umbra,** the shadow of angels' wings, he had, we might say, to look the worst in the face, to place it before our eyes, and his inward eyes, sentence after sentence, in order to deny its force, along with its grammatical and logical existence.

But we are still not finished. There is one more major encounter with negation at the end of the *Second Defense*, after Milton has defended the leaders of the revolution, especially, of course, Oliver Cromwell. In this section of the tract, although the use of praise by negatives denied is not completely abandoned, it becomes merely a trace effect, completely overshadowed by the roll call of real heroes, and the use of superlatives, which in Latin rise off the page like an alleluiah: "**dignissimum, rectissimis, excellentissimo, fortissimorum,**" and, piled into a single phrase, "**modestissimos, & integerrimos, & fortissimos**" (CM 8:228). When promoting others, Milton did not hedge his grammatical bets.

But now we have to acknowledge how he brought the *Defense* to a close, not with the defense of others, but again with a defense of himself. Here is the final paragraph, in this case almost entirely in my own translation:

> As for myself, . . . I have performed, certainly **not unwillingly,** I hope **not in vain**, the service which I thought would be most of use to the commonwealth. . . . If our last actions **should not sufficiently answer** the first, they themselves [the citizens] will see it. I have celebrated actions glorious, lofty, almost beyond praise, with testimony, I had almost said a monument, which will **not speedily perish**; and if I **have done nothing else**, I have discharged my trust. As the epic poet . . . undertakes to embellish not the whole life of the hero whom he proposes to sing, but one particular action of his life . . . so likewise it should be enough either for my duty or for my excuse that I have celebrated at least one heroic action of my countrymen. If, after such brave things you are basely delinquent . . . posterity will speak and bring in the verdict: The foundation was strongly laid, the beginning and more than the beginning was famous; but it [posterity] will want to ask, **not without a certain mental disturbance**, who raised the entire work, who fastened the pediment? To such beginnings, such virtues, **if perseverance was not added,** it will lament. It will see that the harvest of glory was abundant, but that **men did not match (defuisse)** the materials: but there **was not lacking (non defuisse)** one who could advise rightly, encourage, spur on, adorn both what was done and who did it, and could celebrate them with worthy praises for all ages to come.

What stands out in your mind as you read this? The certainty, or the doubt? The job has been done not unwillingly and not in vain, **haud gravatim . . . haud frustra,** "*If* our last actions should not sufficiently answer. . . . If I have done nothing else." Milton is by now more or less confident that he has discharged the trust of which he spoke in *The Reason of Church-Government*, although that was a covenant to leave behind a very different kind of monument. And why does he add that curious phrase, "it should be enough either for my duty or for my **excuse**"? The Columbia edition translates, "duty and excuse," but the Latin says firmly, "**vel ad officium, vel ad excu-sationem**." Surely this prose leaves us "not without a certain mental disturbance" (**non sine commotione quadam animi**); certainly not with "calm of mind, all passion spent."

Of course, Milton did not have to rely on his defenses of the English republic for his monument to posterity. In *Paradise Lost*, he added another ingredient to the complex structure of neg-ative thought and expression, one that had been implicit in his language all along but that now became, and I choose the word deliberately, inevitable. For his sublime topic, Milton redis-covered a sublime use of the word that says, Yes and again Yes, because it appears at first to say No. He rediscovered words like **immutable, immortal, infinite**, words that form one phrase, one great iambic pentameter, in the angelic song in book 3 (373). In fact, Milton stole this line from Joshua Sylvester's transla-tion of Guillaume de Salluste Du Bartas, where it appears in the opening definition of God alone in the universe before Creation:

> God all in all, and all in God it was:
> Immutable, immortall, infinite,
> Incomprehensible, all spirit, all light,
> All Majestie, all-selfe-Omnipotent,
> Invisible, impassive, excellent.   (*First Day*, 44–48)[3]

He could use similar tactics to give us his unique vision of an Edenic happiness into which, philosophically and theologically speaking, negativity had not yet penetrated:

> Our two first Parents, yet the only two
> Of mankind, in the happy Garden placed,
> Reaping immortal fruits of joy and love,
> **Uninterrupted** joy, **unrivall'd** love,
> In blissful solitude.   (3.65–69)

But it turns out that the fallen angels also understand, in a negative way, how to make a negative into a positive. They are, Satan says, "irreconcilable to our grand Foe" (1.122), their "mind and spirit remain / **Invincible** (1.140–41), their strength "undiminished" (1.154); you can not count them, "so numberless were those bad Angels seen" (1.344), in "thick array of depth immeasurable" (1.549); and they are learning to live with absolute negativity as permanence. In "inextinguishable fire" (2.88), they must remain "**unrespited, unpitied, unreprieved**" (2.185). This last phrase may contain a memory of the lament of the ghost in *Hamlet*, that he has been carried off without the opportunity to repent his sins, "unhouseled, disappointed, unaneled" (1.5.77); but Milton did not really need a literary model to explore the semantic, affective, and philosophical force of the particle "-un," when doubled, tripled, or quadrupled. Against the would-be undoing force of the fallen angels' despair, the poem posits the idea of steadfastness, as in the definition of the angel Abdiel's position during the rebellion, "Among innumerable false, **unmoved, / Unshaken, unseduced, unterrified**" (5:897–98), another of those great three-negative pentameters, and one that foreshadows, of course, the courage of Jesus in *Paradise Regained*.

Negative constructions are also required to define Milton's eccentric position on redemption, as expressed by the Son in defiance both of double predestination and Arminianism, of too little and too much human initiative:

> Father, thy word is passed, man shall find grace;
> And shall grace not find means, that finds her way,
> To speediest of thy winged messengers,
> To visit all thy creatures, and to all
> Comes **unprevented, unimplor'd, unsought?**   (3.227–31)

If this tiny negative particle, "un-," is crucial to Milton's theology, so it is, of course, to his poetics, here in *Paradise Lost* explained for the first time as doing what has not been done. *Lycidas* had challenged him to make sure that Edward King was not "unwept," but now Milton produces a cluster of words that speak to his larger ambition. In the invocation to book 1, he claims that *this* poem will reach for "Things **unattempted** yet in prose or rhyme," a more resonant statement than Ariosto's "cosa non detta in prosa mai, ne in rime," which, of course, it replies to and upstages. In the invocation to book 7, he warns that "Half yet remains **unsung**," a word that gathers propositional as well as structural force in the invocation to book 9, where he deplores the captivity of previous epics to military values, "the better fortitude / Of Patience and Heroic Martyrdom / **Unsung**." And let us not forget, in this cluster, the famously disingenuous statement that his verse is "**unpremeditated**" (9:24), and that he himself, like Abdiel, is in the defeat of the Restoration "**unchang'd** / To hoarse or mute, / Though fall'n on evil days" (7.24–25).

Given the vocational importance of "unsung" in Milton's vocabulary (and it will return significantly at the opening of *Paradise Regained*), it is rather startling to find that Astarte, one of the most important of the pagan deities listed in book 1, is described as "not unsung" in Sion (1.442) — that is to say, her worship has spread from Syria into Israel. And by similar token we should notice that Satan enters paradise "all unobserved, unseen" (4.130), a formula Milton had adopted to describe his "own" relation to the world in *Il Penseroso* and *L'Allegro*. Does this leakage of a special, privileged, positive negativity into the territory of the demonic mean that the negative formulation is not so significant as we thought it was, merely, after all, a lexical, latinate habit? Or should we thereby recognize Satan as a demonic blend of *L'Allegro*, *Il Penseroso*, and the poet himself? *L'Allegro* ends by calling its catalog of the pleasures of the eye "these delights." Something has happened to the aesthetic sense (blindness, perhaps), when landing in paradise "the Fiend / Saw **undelighted** all delight" (4:285–86), a phrase that is not merely a negative, not merely an oxymoron, but also Milton's coinage.

Milton is not just using his philological reflexes at such moments, but demanding that we pay attention to what is truly a negative, truly a positive, though the mere grammatical form of words and sentences may at first glance obscure that extraordinarily difficult distinction, never more difficult than in a poem where the adversary has declared "Evil be thou my good," and tempted so many of Milton's readers into some version of skepticism or Manichaeanism. The distinction becomes more difficult to make when the negative and positive electrodes are built into the word itself, and into an already complex word, as is characteristic of *Paradise Lost*, rather than being the result of a relatively simple "not" formula, as in the anxious autobiographical passages in the prose.

How far can Milton stretch this exercise, and our minds? After the Fall, very far. Consider the perverse formations of Sin and Death in book 10. One is to build a bridge "Smooth, easy, **inoffensive** down to Hell" (10.305), in which, Hughes assures us, the word "inoffensive" carries its Latin force "free of stumbling-blocks." But is that all it carries? Surely, after "smooth" and "easy," we are tempted to read "inoffensive" as a particularly clever negative-positive-negative, since the bridge is, in reality, deeply offensive and dangerous to human beings, yet the word "inoffensive" already has, in Milton's day, assumed a soothing or reassuring character, as in Eve's preparations for dinner with Raphael, nonalcoholic and easy to swallow — smoothies, in fact:

> For drink the Grape
> She presses, **inoffensive** must, and meaths
> From many a berry, and from sweet kernels prest
> She tempers dulcet creams.   (5.344–47)

The other project of Sin and Death is to "destroy, and **unimmortal** make / All kinds" (10.611–12), which is equally perverse, and Milton's coinage to boot, as though language had to stretch to encompass the eschatological narrative perhaps too simply and conventionally stated in the very second line of the poem, where we are invited to hear how "mortal taste / Brought

Death into the World." Another Miltonic coinage generated by these dark powers is "**unhidebound**," a description of Death on his way out of hell and anticipating a feast of humans (10.601). John Leonard suggests that Milton used a negative where "hidebound" alone was what he wanted, indicating that the lexical habit is getting of hand. But, in fact, "hidebound" does not only mean hungry, ravenous. It can also mean "having the skin tight and incapable of extension," therefore *unable* to eat, unable to expand.[4]

One could go on like this for quite a while, and a proper person would count the instances, and perhaps grade them in terms of cognitive challenge. Perhaps others will do so now that the phenomenon has been drawn to their attention. Instead, I want to move toward closure by remarking that, of the two poems we see as rounding off Milton's career by creating yet another unresolved issue — the question of whether violent, destructive action or passive resistance is the most heroic — Milton's negativity resolves itself into two different patterns. On the one hand, there seems to be in *Samson Agonistes* both a decrease in the number of negative constructions and a tendency for the complex word that takes negative form to carry a negative meaning. First, there is the negativity of blindness, "irrecoverably dark," (81) and "inseparably dark" (154). Then, there is his regret for his "former servitude" to Dalila, "**ignoble / Unmanly, ignominious, infamous**" (416–17). Then, Manoa advises Samson no longer to serve the Philistines with his miraculous strength: "Better at home lie bedrid, not only idle, / Inglorious, unemploy'd" (579–80). Samson complains of "maladies innumerable" (608) and "wounds immedicable," (620). Dalila begs Samson not to be strong primarily in "uncompassionate anger" (181), and Samson replies that her behavior to him has raised in him "inexpiable hate" (839). Dalila also compares or contrasts her behavior with the "inhospitable guile" (989) of Jael in her assassination of Sisera. These melancholy constructions are more powerful, I suggest, especially as they accumulate, than the opening, conventionally heroic adjectives that describe Samson as he once was, "Irresistible Samson" (126), "When insupportably his foot advanc't" (136), or the "**invincible** might" (1271) that the Chorus hopes God will once again put into the hands of his deliverer, all adjectives that remind us of the defiant fallen angels, and ask precisely the questions about Milton's view of violence that recent events have brought back into the foreground of Milton criticism.

On the other hand, in *Paradise Regained*, Milton seems to go out of his way to recover the youthful, innocent and Stoic force of the simpler negative marked by "un-." For in this poem we are assured that humility — not thrusting one's self forward — is essential to modern heroism, or to modern ideas of heroism. Thus, the opening lines of the poem express a series of paradoxes:

> Thou Spirit who led'st this glorious Eremite
> Into the Desert, his Victorious Field
> Against the Spiritual Foe, and brought'st him thence
> By proof **th'undoubted** Son of God, inspire,
> As thou are wont, my prompted Song, else mute,
>
> . . . .
>
> to tell of deeds
> Above Heroic, though in secret done,
> And **unrecorded** left through many an Age,
> Worthy t'have **not** remain'd so long **unsung**. (8–17)

With "not . . . unsung" we revisit that curious formula of *L'Allegro*, "not unseen," as well as the fact that the protagonist of this poem is, like that of *Il Penseroso*, "obscure, / **unmarkt, unknown**" (24–25) when he comes to his coming-out occasion, the baptism by Saint John. His great victory occurs in the desert, in secret, with no spectators, and is achieved only by saying no. And at the end of the poem, of course, "Hee **unobserv'd** / Home to his Mother's house private return'd." I say "of course" because the demureness of Jesus' victory over temptation and his ethos of delay and renunciation have been understood by everyone who reads the poem. What has also been unmarked and unknown is the way the vocabulary of this ethos maps onto and is quietly empowered by the long stream of Milton's negative constructions heretofore, constructions that began, apparently, when he contemplated the problems of his own tardiness and invisibility in the field he hoped would make him famous.

Thus, in the person of Jesus and a perfectly rigorous, restrained biblical narrative (though not the one readers would have expected when they purchased a poem entitled *Paradise Regained*), Milton was able to solve the psychological and ethical problems of reputation and fame. Narrator and hero have merged. Together they explain what "passive fortitude" must really mean, which *Paradise Lost,* still in urgent communication with classical epic, was unable to do.

There is now a *structural* relationship between being "unsung" and "unknown" and the particular kind of heroism Jesus manages, which comes from being "**unshaken**" 'and "**unappall'd**" and having an "**untroubl'd** mind" after Satan's more active, physical threats in book 4, and *not* like the incessant reader, "uncertain and unsettl'd" in his mind. He is "**invincible**" (2.408) only in his temperance, thus canceling out the militarist use of that word both in *Paradise Regained* and its wishful thinking echo in *Samson Agonistes.* Accordingly, the diminished Satan in this poem is not allowed to garner the power of the great extremist negatives marshaled in Satan's speeches in *Paradise Lost,* book 1. The only ones he is still allowed are the smaller, elegiac ones, "**unfortunate**" (1.358) and "**unpitied**" (1.414), or the brilliant Miltonic coinage, "**unconniving,**" used by nobody else subsequently, a word Satan had to invent to obscure the question of whether his freedom to exit hell now and then was really by divine permission or his own enterprise:

Yet to that hideous place **not** so confined
By rigor **unconniving** but that oft
Leaving my dolorous Prison I enjoy
Large liberty.   (1.362–65)

This is glossed by Hughes as "unwinking," ever watchful, a
gloss that obscures the theological issue of how much of
Satan's activity on earth God is responsible for. In fact, the word
"connive" more often carried already, in Milton's day, its modern meaning or meanings, of which the most usual is "to shut
one's eyes to an action that one ought to oppose, but which
one covertly sympathizes with; to wink *at*, be secretly privy
or accessory to." And surely Milton was here echoing, with a
peculiarly ironic inflection, the particularly nasty speech of God
in *Paradise Lost*, 10.616–32:

See with what heat these Dogs of Hell advance
To waste and havoc yonder World, which I
So fair and good created, and had still
Kept in that state, had not the folly of Man
Let in these wasteful Furies, who impute
Folly to mee, so doth the Prince of Hell
And his Adherents, that with so much ease
I suffer them to enter and possess
A place so heav'nly, and **conniving** seem
To gratify my scornful Enemies,
That laugh, as if transported with some fit
Of Passion, I to them had quitted all,
At random yielded up to their misrule;
And know not that I call'd and drew them thither
My Hell-hounds, to lick up the draff and filth
Which man's polluting Sin with taint hath shed
On what was pure.

In fact, Satan explicitly renounces the *good* Stoic negatives that
characterize the Son. "The wisest, **unexperienc't**," he warns,
"will be ever / Timorous and loth, with novice modesty . . . /
Irresolute, unhardy, unadvent'rous" (3.240–43). This is a version of the voice in Milton's ear that he imagined in the *Reason*

of Church-Government berating him for his inactivity on behalf of church reform: "Timorous and ingratefull, slothfull, and ever to be set light by. . . . Dare not now to say, or doe anything better then thy former sloth and infancy" (YP 1.804–05). But novice modesty in *Paradise Regained* is to be a lasting *habitus*. "Prediction else," the Son responds to the temptation of the kingdoms, "Will **unpredict**" (4.395), a seeming paradox that requires our careful attention. And when he is offered the temptation of the kingdom of the mind, the world of *Il Penseroso*'s "lonely Tow'r," he who has earlier said, "To me is **not unknown** what hath been done / Worthy of Memorial" (2.444–45), now creates the unanswerable chiasmus. Instead of the adjustment offered in that early chiasmus about the loss of sight, "non est miserum esse caecum; miserum est caecitatem non posse ferre," the Son replies to the temptation of too much reading: "Think not but that I know these things; or think / I know them not."

TEXT
AND
CONTEXT
● ● ●

4 • The Son as an Angel in *Paradise Lost*

Albert C. Labriola

1. *Introduction*

One of the most vexing issues in Milton studies involves the begetting of the Son in *Paradise Lost,* an episode that has generated disparate commentary. While commentators tend to focus on the begetting of the Son as either literal or metaphorical, most of them opting for the latter, I contend that they have not broadened their outlook adequately in order to encompass other begettings of the Son. The Son of *Paradise Lost* is thrice begotten literally, not metaphorically: first as divine, second as angelic, and third as human. The first begetting occurs before the action of *Paradise Lost* begins. The second, which happens as part of the action of *Paradise Lost,* is the earliest event in the epic, which is recounted in book 5. And the third begetting, the Son's voluntary humiliation in becoming incarnate, is prophesied during the celestial dialogue in book 3 and included in Adam's dream-vision in book 12.

In the first begetting, the Father endowed the Son with divine nature akin to, but not the same as, his own. The Son when begotten a second time, as an angel in the earliest episode in Milton's epic (5.600 and following), resembles in nature and form the following: Michael, Raphael, Uriel, Gabriel, Abdiel, and Lucifer (that is, Satan before his downfall). Because the form and nature of the Son are like theirs, other angelic beings can and do discern the lineaments of his countenance more clearly than when he was wholly divine. Moreover, during the celestial dialogue in book 3 of *Paradise Lost,* the epic narrator discerns the Son as an angel at the right hand of the Father. Also, as Adam and Eve encounter the Son immediately after each of them is separately created, and when the Son judges them after their transgressions, he is an angel. Finally, begotten a third time, an event foreseen but never enacted in *Paradise Lost,* the Son will assume the form and nature of humankind throughout his temporal ministry of approximately three decades.

Since the earliest event in *Paradise Lost* dramatizes the begetting of the Son as an angel, that is the originary moment of the epic, whose significance cannot be overestimated because the Son appears in Milton's epic only and always in the form and nature and with the features of an angel.[1] Indeed, his resemblance to the angelic cohorts has great significance since it becomes the means by which his ontological relationship with the Father is clarified. Though at first glance my proposition of the angelic Son or christological angel in *Paradise Lost* may seem highly unusual, there are numerous analogues and discussions of the Son as an angel. I will cite only three: the apocryphal Martyrdom and Ascension of Isaiah; *De Doctrina Christiana,* the theological treatise traditionally attributed to Milton; and the so-called Junius manuscript with its biblical poems, most notably *Genesis* and *Christ and Satan,* which Milton may have known through his likely friendship with Francis Junius, the Dutch scholar.[2] In what follows, I will focus only on the first of the three analogues, the Martyrdom and Ascension of Isaiah, an extracanonical book composed and redacted from the second century BCE to the fourth century CE. It recounts Isaiah's vision during his ascent through the seven heavens, with an angel as his guide and narrator. More than any other work, the Martyrdom and Ascension of Isaiah is the most cogent analogue of all three appearances of the Son — divine, angelic, and human — relevant to Milton's epic. As such, this work brings new light to an understanding of the Son in *Paradise Lost* and his ontological relationship with the Father.

2. *The Martyrdom and Ascension of Isaiah*

Unlike *Paradise Lost,* whose earliest episode is the begetting of the Son as an angel, the Martyrdom and Ascension of Isaiah presents the Son in his wholly divine nature and form. Though with the Father in the highest or seventh heaven, the Son is subordinate to him. Their ontological relationship becomes evident when the Son's appearance is contrasted with that of the Father. Isaiah notes that from all of the heavens, the praises of the angels "were directed to that Glorious One" — namely, the Father.[3] But his "glory [Isaiah] could not see," nor could "the angel who (was) with [Isaiah]," nor could "any of the angels," whether they were in the lower six heavens or even in the seventh heaven, where the godhead dwells (172). Ascending to the seventh heaven, Isaiah learns from the angel guiding him that he will "see the light where the Lord is and his beloved" (169), respectively the Father and the Son. Throughout the ascent and during the account that he receives after having entered the seventh heaven, Isaiah learns of the relationship of the divine persons by denominations such as the following: "the One who is not named . . . and his Chosen One," "the primal Father and his Beloved, Christ, and the Holy Spirit," "the Father of the one who is greater," "the Most High and his Beloved," and "the Father of the Lord" (165–69). These denominations suggest that the Father is the begetter of the Son; and of the divine persons only the Father always was. And always residing in the realm of the *invisibilia*, he is manifested, but paradoxically concealed, by the brightest light. Such paradox and mystery befit his status, for the Father is ineffable and inexpressible, and he transcends apprehension, except by the Son, who mediates between him and all other beings.

As Isaiah ascends from the first to the seventh heaven, he encounters a different choir of angels at each level. Though all angels praise the godhead, Isaiah notes that at each level or in each choir, the praise varies for the godhead enthroned in the seventh heaven. But he neither names the various choirs of angels nor specifies the differences in their angelic praises of the godhead. At each of the first five levels or choirs, Isaiah observes a throne in the midst of the angels; and the angel seated on the throne "had more glory than all (the rest)" (166). At the second level, in fact, Isaiah prostrated himself to "worship" (167) the enthroned angel, but his angelic guide prevented him from doing so.

Upon arriving in the seventh heaven, Isaiah views the Lord Christ: "his glory was great and wonderful," and "all the righteous . . . and the angels came to him." They "worshipped him, and they all praised him with one voice, and [Isaiah] was singing praises with them, and [his] praise was like theirs" (171). While the Father is invisible because of the brightness surrounding him, the angels can and do approach the Son, whom they "worshiped" and to whom they "sang praises" (171). In the seventh heaven, Isaiah too apprehends the Son: "I saw one standing (there) whose glory surpassed that of all, and his glory was great and wonderful" (171). Isaiah's description of the Second Person lacks details, but it nevertheless implies that he has an upright posture. Though the Son's glory surpasses that of all others, Isaiah stresses that it does not exceed the Father's. For the Son and the Holy Spirit both "worshiped" the Father (172–73).

In the seventh heaven, Isaiah acknowledges not only the divine manifestations of the Father and the Son but also "the angel of the Holy Spirit" (172). By his unfolding account, Isaiah is ranking the divine persons: the inapprehensible Father is the highest, the apprehensible and angelic Son is second, and the Holy Spirit also in the semblance of an angel is third. This hierarchy of progressive sublimation or, from a different vantage point, of successive subordination, dramatizes the ontological interrelationship of the divine persons. Equally important to our understanding of this ontological interrelationship are the two transformations that Isaiah views in the Son, who becomes, first, an angel and, next, a human being. Upon arriving in the seventh heaven, Isaiah learns from his guiding angel that "the Beloved" — the Son — "will . . . descend into the world . . . [,] (he) who is to be called Christ after he has descended and become like you in form, and they will think that he is flesh and a man." In "his descent," moreover, the Son "will be concealed even from the heavens so that it will not be known who he is" (173–74). The significance of the phrase "his descent" cannot be overestimated because it describes the devolution of the Son from wholly deific status to an incarnate condition. In this devolution, the intermediate or transitional stage is angelic. Isaiah observes that the Son *was transformed and became like an angel* (171; emphasis mine). Despite the Son's appearance as an angel, the guiding angel instructs Isaiah to "worship this one" (171), an affirmation that distinguishes the christological angel from other angels. The former, because he is deific, elicits worship, which is reserved for the godhead; the other angels elicit praise.

In the Martyrdom and Ascension of Isaiah, the Father makes a comprehensive announcement soon after the Son is begotten as an angel, an announcement directed to the Son but overheard by Isaiah: "Go out and descend through all the heavens. . . . And you shall make your likeness like that of all who (are) in the five heavens, and *you shall take care to make your form like that of the angels of the firmament*" (173; emphasis mine). Viewing the "Lord" who "went out from the seventh heaven into the sixth heaven," Isaiah heeds the voice of his guiding angel: "Understand, Isaiah, and look, that you may see the transformation and descent of the Lord" (173–74). But in the sixth heaven, the Lord retains his angelic appearance from the seventh heaven, thereby eliciting praise and glorification from the angels in that lower level or choir. Beginning at the fifth heaven, the Son assumes the form and nature of the angels in the respective choir or level through which he is descending (174).

After the Son as an angel descended from the first or lowermost choir of angels "into the firmament" (174), the account shifts abruptly. Isaiah witnesses events in the lives of Mary and Joseph, learning of her mysterious impregnation. He learns, as well, of the next literal begetting of the Son — in the form and nature of humankind. As an infant, Jesus was not recognized as divine. As an adult, while he performed "great signs and miracles," his "adversary envied him and roused the children of Israel, who did not know who he was, against him" (175), after which Jesus was crucified. When Jesus after his Resurrection eventually ascended through the seven heavens, he did so without being progressively transformed into the form and nature of the angelic beings through whose choirs and levels he was passing. Unlike his descent, during which he assumed the respective form and nature of the angels in the five lowermost choirs or levels through which he was passing, the Son ascended as a human being in his postresurrectional state of glorification and exaltation. Nevertheless, at every level of his ascent, he was recognized, praised, and worshiped as the Lord. Finally, Isaiah saw that the Son "sat down at the right hand of that Great Glory, whose glory . . . I could not behold. And also I saw that the angel of the Holy Spirit sat on the left" (176). Here, the divine persons manifest themselves to Isaiah in three ways: the Father, deific; the Son, glorified and exalted though human in form; and the Holy Spirit, angelic. In fact, in the Martyrdom and Ascension of Isaiah, the Holy Spirit, from the outset, appears as an angel, never as wholly divine, perhaps to suggest his tertiary status among the divine persons.

3. *The Begetting and Exaltation of the Son as the Angel of the Lord in* Paradise Lost

The portrayal of the Son in the Martyrdom and Ascension of Isaiah, the antecedent Jewish theology of the angel of the Lord that underlies that apocryphal book, and the endeavor by early Jewish Christians and Ante-Nicene Fathers to construe the Second Person as subordinate to the Father supply the contexts that illuminate Milton's characterization of the Father and the Son in *Paradise Lost*. In the Martyrdom and Ascension of Isaiah, the Son's transformation into an angel represents an intermediate stage between his wholly divine and incarnate manifestations. Such is true also in *Paradise Lost*. The Father's decree to the angels announces this literal begetting of the Son as an angel:

> This day I have begot whom I declare
> My only Son, and on this holy hill
> Him have anointed, whom ye now behold
> At my right hand; your Head I him appoint;
> And by my Self have sworn to him shall bow
> All knees in heav'n, and shall confess him Lord:
> Under his great vicegerent reign abide
> United as one individual soul.[4]   (5.603–10)

In this decree, the Father's reference to the Son, "whom ye now behold," indicates that the previous manifestation of the Son as wholly deific prevented the angels from beholding him. Like the Father, he may have been darkened with excessive light. The angelic cohorts, however, can and do now clearly apprehend the Son as an angel, because the godhead has chosen to reveal itself more fully to lesser beings by adopting their very nature and form. Accompanying this transformation of the Son is the Father's decree that the Second Person, though manifested as an angel, is anointed. By this decree the Father designates this newly begotten manifestation of the Son as the anointed one, or Christ, and as the "Head" (5.606) of the angels, what *Paradise Lost* continually refers to as the kingship of the Son. At the same time, the Father reaffirms the divinity of the christological angel, or *theangelos*, whom the angels will continue to acknowledge as their "Lord" (5.608) and whom they will continue to worship on bended knee though they apprehend the Son in a nature and form akin to their own.

Abdiel also emphasizes the divinity of the Son, whom he acknowledges as the creator of the angels, the one who "circumscribed their being" (5.826). Though brief, this account of the Son as the creator anticipates the use of the word "circumscribe" in book 7, when the Son uses golden compasses "to circumscribe / This universe, and all created things" (226–27). In his unfolding argument, Abdiel will develop the view that the Son who created or circumscribed the angels is circumscribed or delimited, in turn, by his recently begotten angelic nature and form, the effect of which is the following: "all angelic nature joined in one, / Equal to him begotten Son" (5.834–35). That is to say, the Son by his transformation shares the angelic nature as it devolves from the seraphim of the highest rank through the lower choirs or ranks. Indeed, the Martyrdom and Ascension of Isaiah drives home this very point — that the Son is transformed from a greater to a lesser and lesser angel in his descent. The parodic enactment of this humiliation of the Son is Satan's devolution from a greater to lesser angel when he "casts to change his proper shape" (3.634) to that of a "stripling Cherub" (3.636) in order to deceive Uriel. And if the continuum of the Son's humiliation is charted to include his incarnate manifestation, the parodic counterpart is the lament — "O foul descent!" (9.163) — by Satan who, when enclosed within a serpent, is "mixt with bestial slime" (9.165) to "incarnate and imbrute" (9.166) himself.

Elaborating on the view that the Son is begotten literally as an angel, Abdiel explains the Father's intent: "How provident he is, how far from thought / To make us less, bent rather to exalt / Our happy state under one head more near / United" (5.828–31). In using the word "bent," Abdiel conveys (at least) dual significance: that the Father is "inclined" to exalt the angelic nature and form by choosing them for the manifestation of the godhead, and that the godhead suffers voluntary humiliation (or is "bent" by stooping or bowing), but the angelic nature and form undergo corresponding exaltation. Continuing, Abdiel argues that the angels are not by the Son's

> reign obscured,
> But more illustrious made, *since he the head*
> *One of our number thus reduced becomes,*
> His laws our laws, all honor to him done
> Returns our own.   (5.841–45; emphasis mine)

If the angels are being exalted and the godhead humiliated, Abdiel further underscores this view by using the crucial word "reduced" and positioning it to describe simultaneously both the Second Person and the angels under his headship. That is, the godhead in the Son is "reduced" or lowered from wholly deific status when he "becomes" an angel, but the angels when "reduced" under the Son are being (re)led by him, who now is "circumscribed" by their own nature and form. As an angel, the Son, in the language of Abdiel, is subject to the "laws" of his lower nature. For instance, he lacks omnipresence and omniscience. In due course, when the Son becomes a man, he will be subject to the laws of humanity — most notably, the delimitations of time and space — and thereby suffer mutability and mortality.

Consistent with the Martyrdom and Ascension of Isaiah, *Paradise Lost* depicts the adverse reaction of some angels to the Son's appearance in their nature and form. Not praising the Son because his form was like theirs, these angels in the apocryphal book anticipate Satan and his cohorts in Milton's epic. Furthermore, in the Martyrdom and Ascension of Isaiah, the envy that the "adversary" on earth (as the apocryphal book calls Satan) incites against the Son as a man becomes integrated into the fallen angels' adverse reaction to the Son as an angel in *Paradise Lost*. Since the Son is "anointed" (5.605) by the Father, who also does "appoint" (5.606) him as "Head" (5.606) of the angels, Satan reacts by professing that this most recent angel "now hath to himself engrossed / All power, and us eclipsed under the name / Of King anointed" (5.775–77). Satan's real anxiety, to be sure, derives from his view that the christological angel has supplanted his leadership of the angels. After all, the epic narrator describes Satan in the following way:

> he of the first,
> If not the first Archangel, great in power,
> In favor and pre-eminence, yet fraught
> With envy against the Son of God, that day
> Honored by his great Father, and proclaimed
> Messiah King, anointed, could not bear
> Through pride that sight, and thought himself impaired.[5]
>
> (5.659–65)

Elsewhere, while seducing Beelzebub to be his principal confederate, Satan speaks of himself as "the chief" of "all those myriads of which we lead" (5.684). During his speech that lures one-third of the angels "into the limits of the north" (5.755), Beelzebub refers to Satan as "the most High commanding" (5.699). From Satan's perspective, the Father should have proclaimed him, not the most newly begotten angel, as king. Accordingly, Satan denies that the godhead (1) has honored the lesser nature of the angels by inhabiting it, (2) has undergone voluntary humiliation by experiencing the limitations of that lesser nature, and (3) has manifested itself more fully by interacting in their nature and form with the very beings that it created. Abdiel, on the other hand, by affirming what Satan has denied, emphasizes that the angels are not by the Son's "reign obscured, / But more illustrious made" (5.841–42).

4. *Resemblances between Begettings of the Son as an Angel and as a Man*

The Martyrdom and Ascension of Isaiah presents the christological angel as an intermediate state through which the deific Son passes in order to become human, a view that accords with the concept of gradation that we traditionally associate with the Great Chain of Being. To enter the world, the deity would descend through the heavens, departing from the seventh one where he divinely dwells. Inhabiting those realms while descending through them, he would adopt the form and nature of their respective beings, which are lower than deific but loftier than human. Thereafter, the deity, upon entering the world below the firmament, would inhabit the human condition and appear in human nature and form. The apocryphal book narrates these two descensions as consecutive occurrences in a continuous process of humiliation. For Milton, the begetting of the Son as an angel begins the process whereby the deity reveals itself more fully to its created beings — first to the angels, then to humankind. The first begetting occasions the rebellion of Satan, who perceives the proclamation of the Son's kingship as a usurpation of his own role, which he construes as that of principal leader or governor of the angels. The second begetting, prophesied in the epic, will occur because of the anticipated transgressions and eventual fall of humankind and the deity's endeavor to offer redemption. *Paradise Lost,* moreover, integrates these two separate and distinct descensions into a prolonged characterization of the Son, emphasizing his voluntary humiliation. To expound this point, I will comparatively cite the similar, indeed nearly identical, discourse of the Father's decrees in Milton's epic — first, as the Son is begotten as an angel in book 5; then, during the celestial dialogue in book 3 as the Father anticipates the Son begotten as a man.

First, in both decrees in *Paradise Lost,* the Father refers to the Son as "anointed" (5.605, 3.317), a denomination that pertains to the christological angel and to Jesus. Second, the Father designates both the christological angel and the incarnate Son as the "Head" of the angels (5.606, 3.319). Third, in both decrees, he commands the angels to "bow" their "knees" (5.607–08, 3.321) because the Son is still the Lord, whether he appears as an angel or as a man. Fourth, in both instances the Father describes the Son's "reign" (5.609, 3.318) as lasting. Fifth, in book 5, all of the angels "abide" (609) under the headship of the angelic Son, and in book 3 all angels that "bide / In heaven, or earth, or under earth in hell" (321–22) fall under the Son's authority. Sixth, in both pronouncements the Father cites particular choirs of angels — Thrones, Princedoms, Powers (5.601, 3.320) — that come under the kingship of the Son. And the Father terms another choir Dominations (5.601) in the one decree, and in the other he analogously uses Dominions (3.320).

Most important is the seventh similarity in the Father's two discourses. When the Father commends Abdiel for providing "the testimony of truth" (6.33) about the begetting of the Son, he condemns Satan and the fallen angels, "who reason for their law refuse, / Right reason for their law, and for their King / Messiah, who by right of merit reigns" (6.41–43). Likewise, after the Son volunteers in the celestial dialogue to undergo a second humiliation by becoming human, the Father proclaims that the Second Person "hast been found / By merit more than birthright Son of God, / Found worthiest to be so by being good, / Far more than great or high" (3.308–11). The use of the word "merit" in both decrees highlights the Son's twofold humiliation as an angel and as a human being, lesser states that he assumes rather than coveting the divinity into which the Father begat him. In accordance with Paul's letter to the Philippians

(2:6–11) and with the prologue of John's Gospel (1:14), the Son in *Paradise Lost* does not cling to his divinity but willingly relinquishes it in acts of humiliation and love. Indeed, in the letter cited above, Paul recounts that the Son, "though he was in the form of God did not regard equality with God as something to be grasped." Rather, "he emptied himself, taking the form of a slave, coming in human likeness," humbling himself and "becoming obedient to death, even death on a cross." And "because of this, God greatly exalted him." When integrating these passages from Paul into the celestial dialogue, Milton highlights the Father's emphasis on acts of humiliation. Because of such acts, the Son's "merit" (3.290), more than his divine birthright, distinguishes him as "worthiest" and as "being Good" (3.310), a homophonous wordplay on "God." Therefore, the Son acts both goodly and godly while he accrues merits to be "Imputed" (3.291) to humankind and as he conforms his will to God the Father's plan of redemption.

5. Conclusion

From what I have recounted, *Paradise Lost* presents a prolonged characterization of the Son, in the course of which he is differentiated ontologically from the Father. Such differences explain, for instance, why the Son during the celestial dialogue in book 3 lacks the divine attribute of omniscience. While some commentators contend that the Son's lack of omniscience indicates Milton's subordinationist, if not Arian, view, I am emphasizing another perspective: that the Son as an angel participates in the celestial dialogue with lesser knowledge than the godhead. This point becomes clear when the Father asks of the angels, "Which of ye will be mortal to redeem / Man's mortal crime?" (3.214–15). This question, if earnest, is posed for all of the angels to hear and for one or more of them to volunteer; but only the Son as an angel replies. In doing so, he thereby manifests the perfectibility of the angelic nature by exercising its fullest capability of self-sacrificing love. More important for our purposes is the fact that the Son as an angel in *Paradise Lost* establishes an important analogue of the Second Person's appearance as a man, precisely what Milton recounts in *Paradise Regained*. With more limited knowledge than he possessed as an angel, the Son reflects, in turn, the perfectibility of the human nature that he inhabits. Indeed, the Father announces to the angels in *Paradise Regained* that "This perfect man" (1.166), Jesus or the Son on earth, embodies "consummate virtue" (1.165). Finally, the Father in *Paradise Regained* affirms that Jesus "by merit call'd my Son" will "earn Salvation for the Sons of men" (1.166–67). This affirmation validates the greater importance of the voluntary humiliation of the Son, rather than of his divine birthright, as the more perfect way and means of expressing his goodliness and godliness. Therefore, the Son in *Paradise Lost* is the angel of the Lord, and in his reprise in *Paradise Regained* he is both Son of God and Son of humankind. In his former appearance he is the *theangelos*, in the latter, *theanthropos*.

5 • **Milton and Henry More**
The Chariot of Paternal Deity in *Paradise Lost*, Book 6

Stella P. Revard

While some twentieth century critics have condemned Milton's war in heaven as tiresome and pointless, most agree that the battle suddenly comes alive when the Son of God enters the scene, ascends the Chariot of Paternal Deity, and driving against Satan and his assembled army expels them from heaven.[1] Yet exactly what the chariot signifies and how the episode should be interpreted is, even now, a matter of wide speculation. Some of Milton's earliest critics simply viewed the Son's chariot as a Homeric battle chariot, the divine counterpart of Satan's sun-bright chariot, seen earlier in the battle.[2] The eighteenth century commentator Robert Thyer also compared the scene of the Son's going forth to the episode in Hesiod's *Theogony* when Jupiter ventures out against the Titans.[3] Later critics, such as G. Wilson Knight, took a contemporaneous view of the episode and regarded "Messiah's God-empowered chariot" as the ultimate war machine — "a super-tank or a super-bomber."[4] Stanley Fish takes an interesting view of Knight's commentary, viewing Knight's book as an attempt to make Milton's epic germane to the crisis that the British people were facing during the second world war (66–82). Milton's poetry provided comfort and inspiration to a nation beleaguered by evil forces. In this context the vision of the chariot insured the triumph of good. The onrushing chariot of God in book 6 is a "gigantic, more than human airplane" (see Knight, 159; Fish, 67). Still other critics viewed the chariot as a spiritual vehicle that reveals to Satan the meaning of the Son's deity.

That Milton drew details for his description of the Chariot of Paternal Deity from the prophet's vision in Ezekiel 1:4–28 has long been known.[5] The earliest editors of Milton, including Hume, Richardson, and Newton, cite Ezekiel and several other passages from Psalms, Daniel, Revelation, and Isaiah as Milton's principal sources for *Paradise Lost*, 6.749–59. Ezekiel, of course, as editors sometimes note, does not refer to a chariot per se: his vision describes four *chayyoth* — living creatures or cherubim — who support a throne with the likeness of a man seated on it. Although the early editors call attention to the passage in Ezekiel, none cite the Merkabah as Milton's source nor speculate how Milton might have known the extensive Jewish commentary on Ezekiel in the Kabbalah. Neither do twentieth century critics such as Denis Saurat and Harris Fletcher, while calling attention to Milton's Hebraic studies and his investigations of the Kabbalah, comment upon his possible use of the Merkabah.[6] Until Michael Lieb began his interpretive studies of Merkabah with *Poetics of the Holy* in 1981, the seminal article on the Milton's use of the Merkabah in the war in heaven was by J. H. Adamson, an article first published in 1958 and reprinted in *Bright Essence* in 1971.[7]

While Adamson speculates on how Milton might have known the Jewish mystical tradition, he advances Henry More, Milton's contemporary, as a key figure. He admits that Sir Walter

Raleigh's *History of the World* and the work of Alexander Gill the Elder may have also had a part to play, but he believes that it was More who brought the Kabbalah to Milton's attention and influenced his portrayal of the chariot in book 6 of *Paradise Lost*. Building on Adamson's work in an important article published in *Milton Studies* in 1999, Michael Lieb has not only reexamined the question of More's kabbalistic studies and his possible influence on Milton, but has also provided a definitive study of the development of kabbalistic studies in the Renaissance from writers such as Pico della Mirandola and Johannes Reuchlin.[8] My own interest is less on how More and Milton came to their knowledge of the Kabbalah, but rather on how these two men of different political persuasions, though like intellectual backgrounds, used the Kabbalah to interpret Ezekiel's vision both as a political as well as the theological statement for the post-Restoration world of the 1660s.

A leading member of the circle of so-called Cambridge Platonists, More (1614–1687) was six years younger than Milton. Having been admitted to Christ's College, Cambridge, in 1631, just as Milton was leaving the college, he proceeded to the B.A. and M.A, and was then elected fellow, remaining at Cambridge all his life.[9] Although Milton and More almost certainly knew one another directly or indirectly, there is no evidence that they were intimate friends. They were, however, acquainted with many of the same people, both at Cambridge and in London, and Milton undoubtedly would have known the various treatises More published in the 1650s and 1660s. More was a member of the circle around Anne Conway and knew many of the intellectuals in London in the 1650s, including Samuel Hartlib, Robert Boyle, and John Beale.[10] Although More remained loyal to Charles I and warmly welcomed the return of monarchy in 1660, he retained his position at Cambridge throughout the Commonwealth era and seemed in many ways to have been unaffected by the political changes that determined the course of Milton's life.[11] Modest and scholarly, More declined preferment both before and after the Interregnum. Politically, the parliamentarian Milton and the royalist More seemed to have little in common, but intellectually they shared a good many philosophical, theological, and scientific concerns of their time. More was interested in Cartesian philosophy and in the scientific and medical investigations of men like Harvey and Boyle, who, like him, belonged to the Conway circle.[12]

More's first excursion into kabbalistic learning resulted in the treatise, *Conjectura Cabbalistica*, published in 1653, which used the first part of the Kabbalah, or Ma'aseh Bereshith (the Work of Creation), as its focus.[13] More's *Conjectura Cabbalistica* would likely have interested Milton for its exposition of the first chapters of Genesis, but it would not have provided Milton with insight into Ma'aseh Merkabah (the Work of the Chariot).[14] Moreover, More does not refer to the Merkabah in his other treatises of the 1650s and the early 1660s, the very time when Milton's own kabbalistic studies would likely have been coming to fruition and when he was completing book 6 of *Paradise Lost*. It was probably not before the early 1660s that More expanded his investigations of the Kabbalah to include the second part or the Merkabah, of which he makes extensive use in books 4 and 5 of *Divine Dialogues* (1668). He later greatly expands his work on the Merkabah, writing both a Latin commentary on Ezekiel, *Visionis Ezekieliticae seu Mercavae Expositio*, and his *Catechismus Cabbalisticus*, first published in 1677 in Christian Knorr von Rosenroth's *Kabbala Denudata* and reprinted in More's Latin *Opera Omnia* in 1679.[15]

Adamson speculates that More's interest in the Kabbalah followed from the common ground it possessed with Platonism and Neoplatonism and the writings of Philo Judaeus. Both in *Divine Dialogues* (1668) and in his Latin treatises on Ezekiel (1677), More is concerned with reconciling the Jewish mystical writing and the so-called Christian Kabbalah of Pico and Reuchlin with Pythagoras, Plato, and Neoplatonism. Central to all these writings is the concept of the Logos, the figure that commentators on Ezekiel identify as the one who sits upon the amber throne of the chariot.[16] Adamson argues that both More and Milton take their view of the Logos or the Son of God from this kabbalistic tradition, More explicating it in *Divine Dialogues*, Milton employing it as the basis for his description of the Chariot of Paternal Deity in book 6 of *Paradise Lost*. Adamson explains that the vision of the chariot in kabbalistic thought came to have "two distinct though related meanings." Primarily, the chariot was the "mystical vehicle which carried the ecstatic worshipper into the realm of essence" and made possible the "personal union with the Divine." The chariot, however, was also "an elaborate symbol for the Logos steering the universe," signifying "a universal harmony of all being with the Divine will."[17] This second function, Adamson argues, was crucial both to Milton and More. As evidence of More's view, Adamson cites a note to book 3, chapter 10 of *The Immortality of the Soul*, a treatise More first published in 1659. The note, however, does not date from this early period, but was added later by More when his kabbalistic studies were more advanced.

> But the greatest Power over all hath Jesus Christ, or the Soul of the *Messias*, united with the eternal *Logos*, as is manifest from the Vision of *Ezekiel* or the *Mercavah*; which is nothing else but a Representation of this so mighty Polity and Government of Christ, reaching from the highest Aethereal Regions, or from what the *Cabbalists* call the *Ariluthick* World to this *Asiathick* and *Terrestial* World, in which our selves are. (Adamson, 111)[18]

Although it appears unlikely that More inspired Milton's kabbalistic studies, it is quite clear that both men were applying themselves seriously to investigations of the Merkabah at the very time when *Divine Dialogues*, More's dialogues on God, providence, the kingdom of God, and *Paradise Lost* were being completed. Although *Paradise Lost* was published in 1667 and the *Divine Dialogues* in 1668, there is a remarkable consonance between the views of Ezekiel's chariot in both. In *Divine Dialogues* More describes the man on the chariot's throne in Ezekiel's vision as the "Heavenly Humanity of the Son of God," united in the Soul of Messias or the eternal Logos, who creates or recreates the universe through his steering of the chariot (2:296–97). Adamson argues that the description of the Chariot of Paternal Deity in *Paradise Lost* is also adapted from the Merkabah. As in the *Divine Dialogues*, the Son functions as Logos — he restores heavenly order, ending the war and effecting a return in heaven to the primal union it enjoyed before Satan fractured heavenly harmony. Adamson admits that, unlike More, Milton did not attempt to work out the technically precise meaning of the chariot that is contained in More's *Divine Dialogues* and his later treatises on Ezekiel. However, Adamson maintains that More's interpretation of the divine chariot as the vehicle of the Logos was ideally suited to convey Milton's concept of the war in heaven as the basic conflict of harmony against disorder, of Logos against chaos. Moreover, Adamson argues that it was More who brought to Milton's attention this aspect of original Jewish thought that he so effectively exploits in book 6.

All this is well and good. If we went no further, we could confidently conclude that More and Milton shared an interest in Kabbalah that found its way into their writing in the 1660s. While it is possible, though not likely, that Milton knew More's *Divine Dialogues* before its publication in 1668, the work having been completed by 1666, it is more likely that the two pursued their kabbalistic studies independent of one another.[19] Yet, whatever our verdict on More's influence on Milton's kabbalistic studies, there is more to be said about the relationship of More and Milton — both theologically and politically — and about their uses for kabbalistic learning in *Paradise Lost* and *Divine Dialogues*. Although Adamson links More to Milton as an interpreter of Kabbalah, he says nothing

about the connection between More's and Milton's other theological studies. Although politically conservative, More shared
theological views with many of the most radical sects of the
1640s and 1650s, even while carefully dissociating himself from
the Fifth Monarchists and the Quakers.[20] He was an ardent millenarian who endorsed the millenarian views of the celebrated
Joseph Mede, master of Christ's College, Cambridge.[21] More's
crowning theological works were commentaries on Revelation
and Daniel, published in the 1680s, *Apocalypsis Apocalypseos*
and *An Exposition of the Divine Visions of the Prophet Daniel*,
treatises that, in fact, carry on Mede's work on Revelation and
Daniel. It is well known that Mede's view of Revelation had
a marked impact on contemporary millenarians throughout the
civil war era. Mede's *Clavis Apocalytica* (1627) was one of the
texts that in 1643 Parliament had translated into English as
The Key of the Revelation, a translation that was banned after
1660. Mede also had an impact on Milton, both in the 1640s
or later when he composed his theological treatise, *De Doctrina
Christiana*. The analysis of the millennium that appears in chapter 33 of *De Doctrina* is clearly based on Mede, for Milton pos-
tulates, as Mede had, that the thousand-year personal reign of
Christ on earth is not passed, but is to come, that it will occur
at the Second Coming but before the actual judgment, when
Christ in person with his saints will set up his thousand-year
kingdom on earth.[22]

For many Milton critics the Restoration is the watershed
for interpreting Milton's more radical religious and political
views. The passage that I have just alluded to in *De Doctrina*
is often dismissed by critics, some on the grounds that *De
Doctrina* may not be his work, others on the imprecise dating
of the treatise itself. It is perfectly clear, however, in Milton's
prose works from *Of Reformation* through *The Readie and Easie
Way* that Milton continued until the eve of the Restoration
to espouse views of the millennium similar to those of Mede

and More and to those of the most radical sects of Puritanism. Because he was later constrained by censorship, it is less easy to ascertain whether Milton retained his millenarian views after Charles II's return. In comparison, the royalist More continued to express freely millenarian views, both before and after the Restoration, and in fact until the end of his life.[23]

The principal text for the millennium is Revelation 20:1–7. However, the first chapter of Ezekiel was also viewed, especially during the civil war period, as a description of the millennial coming of Christ. Puritan sermonists often cited the vision of the chariot as a prophetic prognosis of Christ's victory over the tyrannies of the earth. For them, the chariot was not just, as in kabbalistic writings, a vision of the Logos's recreative powers, but a vision of Christ's Second Coming. Several civil war sermonists allude to Christ's appearance in Ezekiel's chariot to celebrate the victories of parliamentary forces. For example, in a sermon preached in 1647 to celebrate a parliamentary victory, John Carter uses the description of Ezekiel's chariot to argue that the current events in England were moving toward the millennium. He states that "the man sitting above upon the throne, is *Lord Jesus Christ*" and the creatures that convey the chariot are directed by him: "The living creatures, or Cherubins they are Angels, good Angels, which are immediately under the Command of Christ."[24] Similarly, in a thanksgiving sermon for another of Parliament's victories (1649), Peter Sterry interprets Ezekiel's chariot as a military conveyance, as a symbolic revelation of Christ, and as a prediction of the coming millennium. "The Likeness of a *Man*," who appears on the throne of Ezekiel's chariot, says Sterry, "is the *Glorified Person* of our Saviour." He interprets Parliament's military victory as Christ's punishment of his enemies: "*Iesus Christ* is now comming forth with his Garment dyed Red in the Blood of his Enemies." Citing the numbers of Daniel, which were often used to date the commencement of the millennium, he predicts the immediate arrival of Christ to succor the faithful: "*Iesus Christ* shall begin to appeare for his People" (11–12).[25] In the decade before the publication of *Paradise Lost* and *Divine Dialogues,* Puritan preachers frequently evoked Ezekiel's chariot as a vision of Christ, as a battle engine, and as the vehicle that would convey the returned Christ to earth to give succor to Christians and prepare the world for the establishment of Christ's monarchy on earth. Whether these preachers had recourse to kabbalistic commentaries to support their views of Ezekiel or whether they merely used Scripture to support their millenarian interpretations is not clear. However, the very existence of such references to Ezekiel's chariot during this era must have had an impact on Milton and More, both of whom later employ Ezekiel's vision to support their millenarianism.

In 1660 at the restoration of Charles II, both Milton and More express millenarian sentiments, although from completely opposite political poles. In *The Readie and Easie Way,* Milton urges England not to re-admit monarchy, but to remain true to the expectation of Christ's return to earth — "even to the coming of our true and rightfull and only to be expected King, only worthie as he is our only Saviour, the Messiah, the Christ, the only heir of his eternal father, the only by him anointed and ordaind since the work of our redemption finishd, Universal Lord of all mankinde" (YP 7:444–45). In contrast, More in *An Explanation of The grand Mystery of Godliness,* also published in 1660, is rhapsodic about Charles II's return, speculating that the reestablishment of monarchy in England might presage — indeed, might even precipitate — the establishment of Christ's kingdom on earth.[26] Throughout the 1660s, More continues to refer in his various theological treatises and in *Divine Dialogues* (1668) to the coming millennium, though he no longer connects the restored monarchy of Charles II to its imminent realization.[27]

As Richard Ward in his *Life of More* maintains, More remained loyal to the monarchy all his life, frequently expressing the opinion that Christians owed allegiance to their legal sovereigns.[28] However, there is reason to believe that More did not find in Charles II the strong support for Reformed Protestantism that he had hoped for. Probably, More's millenarian views would have brought unease to the monarchy, which connected such views with Cromwell's defeated Puritans. On the other hand, More undoubtedly would have viewed Charles's accommodations of Roman Catholicism with similar unease. With several of his closest associates at Cambridge University, More himself had come under scrutiny for his so-called latitudinarian views. More was a firm believer in toleration, even though, like Milton in *Of True Religion* (1673), he did not extend toleration to countenancing Catholicism. He felt that persecution was bad in itself and moreover diverted men from the proper concern for true religion. He regretted the persecution of Protestant sects and wished to bring all reformed Christian sects into closer communion with one another. Expressing such views in the "Preface to the Reader" of *An Explanation of The grand Mystery of Godliness* (1660), More found himself under attack by Joseph Beaumont, the author of *Psyche*, and by Ralph Widdrington, who accused him of being a heretic and denounced his so-called latitudinarianism as subversive to the Church of England.[29] More was deeply upset and wrote *An Apology* (1664) to defend the orthodoxy of his views, but the label of latitudinarian stuck to him.[30] Moreover, he was not inclined to change his views about toleration, which he affirmed through the voice of his principal interlocutor in *Divine Dialogues*.[31]

A cause that also informs both Milton's and More's millenarianism involves their opposition to the growing influence of Catholicism both abroad and in English life. It prompts Milton's publication of *Of True Religion* in 1673, and it is also the focus of More's *An Exposition of the Seven Epistles to the Seven*

Churches. In the "Epistle Dedicatory" to *An Exposition*, More remarks on the vast difference between "the Truth and Purity of the Protestant Religion" and "Popery," which many in the present age *"can* not or *will* not, discern" (sig. A4^{r-v}). As he repeatedly makes clear in his other treatises and in *Divine Dialogues*, the Roman Catholic Church is the Babylon of Revelation and the pope the Antichrist. Such statements inevitably have political overtones in an England where the heir to the throne, Charles's brother James, was a Catholic.[32]

When he published the *Divine Dialogues* in 1668, More asserted that the *Dialogues* did not have any political intent. However, he discreetly chose a pseudonym under which to publish the work: Franciscus Palaeopolitanus — the old politician. Both More and his publisher took pains to declare in the preface to *The Last Two Dialogues* that the *Dialogues* did not concern current political affairs, although they admitted the impossibility of separating the kingdom of God without from the kingdom of God within (1.a7^r). More and his publisher also affirmed that all good Protestants possessed a "sincere and unspotted Loyalty . . . to their Lawful Sovereigns" (2.a4^v).[33] *Divine Dialogues* is unlike any other work that More composed in his lifetime, his usual treatise being an explication of some religious or philosophical matter. Although *Divine Dialogues* concerns the nature of God and his kingdom, More approaches the subject broadly as a discussion between seven interlocutors and models it on Plato's *Republic* and the numerous Renaissance works also in dialogue form, such as Castiglione's *Courtier*.[34] His principal interlocutor is Philotheus (the lover of God), said to be modeled on Ralph Cudworth, More's close associate at Cambridge. More's other interlocutors, however, often develop philosophic or political arguments at length, particularly Philopolis (the lover of state), a character probably representing Anne Conway's elder brother, Heneage Finch, a barrister and later chancellor to Charles II. More himself was either represented by Euistor (the man of criticism, philology, and history) or by Bathynous (the deeply thoughtful man).[35] *The Last Two Dialogues* caused some concern at Charles II's licensing office and were thoroughly scrutinized by Samuel Parker, the principal censor, who, as More confided in a letter to Anne Conway, asked for some changes and modifications.[36]

More presents a lengthy exegesis of Ezekiel's chariot in book 5 of the *Dialogues*, connecting it not only with the vision of the four beasts in Revelation — the lion, the ox, the man, and the eagle — but also with the prophecies of Daniel that millenarians believed were the blueprint for the millennium.[37] But in order to understand More's interpretation of Ezekiel's cherub car, as Philotheus calls it, we must go back to book 4 and the discussion of the kingdom of God. The discussion begins with Philopolis asking Philotheus for a definition of the kingdom of God, both internal and external, which Philotheus accordingly provides. Since, as Philopolis maintains the kingdom of God is among men (*Divine Dialogues*, 2:26), then the question becomes how is it manifest and what the phrase, "Thy kingdom come," means in political terms. Philotheus argues that God's kingdom has physical, moral, and political dimensions, for the kingdom on earth will ultimately be the millennial kingdom Daniel foretells in 2:44 (2:51–56). But this kingdom cannot come until little Horn (the two-horned beast of Revelation) is defeated, nor can the kingdom of the saints emerge until the beast is not (2:56–57). At this point Philopolis takes over from Philotheus as principal interlocutor and the discussion becomes political rather than theological. For, although Philopolis reviews the history of the papacy, he does so from a political viewpoint. Rather than exploring the idolatries and theological errors of the Catholic Church, he denounces the pope as a dangerous political enemy, whose violence and tyranny continue to oppress men and states. In the process of the discussion, More also exonerates Luther and Calvin and Reformed Christianity from the charge that they were rebels against the rightful sovereignty of princes or of the Church itself.[38] It is an interesting tactic to put these criticisms of Catholicism into the mouth of the politically astute man rather than the theologically interested one. By so doing, More is indirectly cautioning the monarchy on the dangers of Catholicism, including a reminder that Catholics were responsible for such acts as the massacre at Paris and the plots against Queen Elizabeth (2:159, 166–67). Philotheus concludes, "the *Apocalypse* has its eye upon Religious accounts as well as Politicall" (2:211).

Philotheus's account in book 5 of the first chapter of Ezekiel comes as an appendage to his explication earlier in the book of the outpouring of the vials in Revelation. This explication is prompted, in turn, by Philopolis's earlier question, *"What Success the Kingdome of God is likely to have to the end of all things"* (*Divine Dialogues*, 2:219). Although More's treatment of Ezekiel's vision is flavored by his kabbalistic studies, his intent in *Divine Dialogues* is not to explicate Ezekiel kabbalistically, as he later does in his Latin treatise *Visionis Ezekielitiae seu Mercavae Expositio,* but to coordinate the vision of Ezekiel with that of Saint John in Revelation.[39] Philotheus has just finished his presentation of the New Jerusalem when Philopolis queries whether there are any other visions or prophecies that explicate "this excellent state of the Church" (2:280). Philotheus refers him to Ezekiel's vision of the cherubic chariot of God, explaining that the chariot was the throne of God in heaven, seen by Ezekiel, and also by Moses and Aaron on the Mount (2:282). He elaborates further that the aim of the Son of God — the driver of the chariot — was to enlarge the kingdom of God even to the earthly regions, ultimately bringing it to earth as the New Jerusalem. This, Philotheus states, is the meaning of *"Thy Kingdome come"* (2:281). Therefore, he maintains that what Ezekiel sets forth in his vision is "the Pattern of the Angelicall Polity over which God immediately rules," presaging the "great design of all," namely that "in the fulness of time the Church upon Earth may be his

Chariot as fully and commandingly as the Angelicall Orders in Heaven" (2:282).[40] In order to demonstrate this, Philotheus compares the elements of Ezekiel's vision with their counterparts in Revelation. The color of amber out of the midst of the chariot is likened to the transparent gold of the city of the New Jerusalem, both being of a pure angelical nature (2:283). The spirit that moves the self-guided chariot is, Philotheus explains, the "irresistible progress of Divine Providence administered by his Angelicall forces" (2:284). The wheels of the chariot are full of eyes, denoting the "Circuits and Periods of times and Ages . . . carried by a Special Providence of God, who oversees all things" and signifying also the "assistance of the Angelicall Orders in Humane affairs" (2:284). The wheels, therefore, are the "Circumvolutions of Providence, and Periods of *Kingdoms* and *People* and *Nations*" (2:287–88).[41] As Philotheus continually points out, "the meaning of *Ezekiel's Mercavah* is not *Physicall,* but *Moral, Spiritual,* or *Divino-politicall*" (2:289). He also attempts to link Jewish and Christian mysticism with Pythagoreanism, explaining thus that the number four, which denotes the number of cherubim that make up the chariot, corresponds to the Pythagorean Tetractys. The cherubim also correspond with the four beasts of Revelation — lion, ox, man, and eagle (Rev. 4:6–8). Each has four faces signifying the four parts that make up their polity — the lion denotes the military part, the man the administration of justice, the ox the laboring part, and the eagle the sacerdotal and philosophic part, that is, the speculative and the devotional (2:290–91).[42] The rider of the chariot is the "Heavenly Humanity of the Son of God," whose very title is written in the amber light of the chariot. He is the same as *"the God* of *Israel,* and the surrounding *Rainbow* emblematizes him the God of the whole Universe" (2:296–97). The chariot itself is "the Type of the state of Perfection in the Church," of which God drew a shadow for the Israelites in the vision he gave to Ezekiel. This

"Heavenly *Idea* of that state of the Church," set forth in Ezekiel's vision, "will be actually on Earth when the *new Jerusalem descends from Heaven, and the Tabernacle of God is amongst men*" (2:299). At that time, Philotheus goes on to explain, the Elders and the four Beasts will acknowledge "from whom and for whom they reign, even for the manifesting of the glory and honour and power of God in the Kingdome of his Saints" (2:308). This then will be "the universal Reign of *Christ*, called the blessed *Millennium*" (2:451).[43]

Throughout this long and detailed analysis, More's thrust is clear. The chariot is not just a symbol of divine glory, but of the fulfillment of Christ's kingdom of earth. As he explains more fully in his later treatise, *Visionis Ezekieliticae seu Mercavae Expositio*, the vision of the man on the throne is the soul of Messias or the Logos, who will become the earthly Jesus and in the fullness of time the returned Messiah, who will control his kingdom as he controls the chariot. More closely connects his interpretation of the chariot not only with Revelation but also with the prophecies of the kingdom of Messiah in Daniel, to which millenarians turned when they wished to assign the date and time of the coming millennium. Thus, there are unavoidable political implications to Philotheus's exegesis.

More's *Divine Dialogues* were popular in their time, but they cannot, of course, be considered a direct source for *Paradise Lost*.[44] Nonetheless, More's exegesis of Ezekiel's chariot, in drawing from the Christian Kabbalah, shares perforce a great deal with Milton's description of Messiah's Chariot of Paternal Deity in *Paradise Lost*. Moreover, it is not only their reliance on kabbalistic material that is striking, but also their views that the chariot functions to move the kingdom of God toward the millennium. Like More, Milton draws his description of the throne of the chariot both from Revelation 4:2–6 and Ezekiel 1:26.[45] Like More, he emphasizes the interconnectedness of the chariot's parts — its self-propelled spirit, its steady movement onward, its circumspect eyes and forward-moving wheels, and the radiant amber light that proceeds from Messiah's sapphire throne. Ezekiel's four-faced living animals become in Milton, as in More, cherubic beings, whose four-foldedness is also emphasized.

> forth rush'd with whirl-wind sound
> The Chariot of Paternal Deity,
> Flashing thick flames, Wheel within Wheel, undrawn,
> Itself instinct with Spirit, but convoy'd
> By four Cherubic shapes, four Faces each
> Had wondrous, as with Stars thir bodies all
> And Wings were set with Eyes, with Eyes the Wheels
> Of Beryl, and careering Fires between;
> Over thir heads a crystal Firmament,
> Whereon a Sapphire Throne, inlaid with pure
> Amber, and colors of the show'ry Arch.   (6.749–59)

However, when he describes the Son seated on the throne of the chariot, Milton departs from both Ezekiel and Revelation and includes other material, both biblical and classical, to expand the portrait. As though to emphasize the Son's priestly role, he describes him endowed with the Urim, which were on the breastplate of Aaron: "in Celestial panoply all arm'd / Of radiant *Urim*, work divinely wrought" (6.760–61). With his bow and quiver hung beside him, moreover, he less resembles the priest wearing the breastplate of judgment than Homer's angry Apollo descending from Olympus in book 1 of the *Iliad* to punish the impious Achaeans. Yet, the "ten thousand thousand Saints" (6.667) who accompany him seem a foreshadowing of the saints in Revelation, chapter 20, who are to rule with him in the millennium. At the climax of the chariot's progress, Milton returns us to Scripture, conflating Psalm 18:10 with Ezekiel's description of the sapphire throne: "Hee on the wings of Cherub rode sublime / On the Crystalline Sky, in Sapphire Thron'd" (6.771–72).

As with More, Milton's description of chariot is directed toward a specific purpose. Milton's Son goes forth to claim his kingdom, and the manner in which the chariot is described makes it clear that it is his millennial kingdom he is establishing. As in More's *Dialogues,* the chariot does not merely symbolize the angelical kingdom of heaven that Messiah rescues from satanic misrule but also prophetically the kingdom on earth that he is to assume with the saints. Of course, like More, Milton was wary of Charles II's licensers and deliberately refrained in book 6, as in the rest of *Paradise Lost,* from referring specifically to the millennium. He chooses to express his views kabbalistically by adopting as the signifier for Messiah's millennial kingdom the chariot that had been interpreted by millenarians as the symbol of that reign. On one level, he alludes in *Paradise Lost* to nothing further than the victory of Messiah over Satan at the end of the heavenly war. However, for millenarians, that very heavenly war, described in Revelation, chapter 12, was not a past one but a future one. Similarly, the cherubic chariot of Ezekiel might express nothing more than the creative spirit of God. However, it had been used by the civil war sermonists and by millenarians such as More to symbolize the advent of Christ's millennial reign, and to me it appears clear that Milton affirms with the progress of the chariot a belief that the Son will assume at last his kingship on earth.

Then the logical question for us to ask is whether the vision of Ezekiel's chariot, as used by More and Milton, carries a political as well as a theological message to those living in Restoration England in 1667 and 1668. Although More expresses loyalty to the reigning sovereign, he is none too happy with Charles's attitude toward Reformed Protestantism. Charles had not turned out to be the champion of the Church that More had hoped for in 1660. In his commentary on *An Exposition of the Seven Epistles to the Seven Churches* in Revelation, he identifies the Church of England with the Church of Sardis in Revelation, castigating it for its "looseness and slipperinesse in those points of Apostolick Doctrine which the Reformers had recovered" ("Epistle Dedicatory," sig. A5ᵛ). He cautions Lord Robartes, the dedicatee, on the potential mischief that will occur if the Church of England does not hold firm to the sacredness of the Protestant religion and guard against the Church of Rome and look on its opinions as "rejectaneous" (sig. A6ʳ). In the "Preface to the Reader," he refers back to the views that he expressed concerning the kingdom of God in his recently published *Dialogues* (sig. aʳ). He adds, "it is left to the Protestants to compute the approach of the final Ruine of Antichrist and the blessed *Millennium* according to their own progresse in the Mysterie of real Regeneration and indispensable Duties of Christianity" ("Preface," sig. cʳ). He likens the state of Christians at the present moment to that of Jews wandering in the wilderness before coming to the promised land, and sternly warns against any peevish and false return to Egypt, that is Rome ("Preface," sig. c3ʳ).

Whereas More makes no direct attack on the policies of Charles II, his position on Roman Catholicism would have allied More to the parties that were seeking to curb Charles's dealing with Catholic France and Catholic Rome and who were all too aware that Charles's heir was his Catholic brother James, the Duke of York. Moreover, More's radical millenarianism put him in company with strange bedfellows. One of them would have been John Milton, a fellow alumnus of Christ College and a man for whom millenarianism and dissent went hand in hand. At the beginning of book 7 of *Paradise Lost* Milton could covertly denounce a Stuart Bacchus and his revelers immediately after he had covertly described at the end of book 6 the defeat of a kingly Satan or Antichrist. Moreover, in book 12 he could have Michael advise Christians living in the last days to persevere in Spirit and Truth until "the day / Appear of respiration to the just, / And vengeance to the wicked, at return / Of him so lately promis'd" (12:539–42). The Son's decisive victory over Satan in book 6 driving the chariot symbolic of approaching millennium delivers a similar message to those politically and spiritually oppressed by the Stuart regime. It is perhaps ironic that the erstwhile parliamentarian Milton and the loyal royalist More shared views on the millennium, which they expressed (despite Charles's censors) by adopting the Kabbalah's symbolic language and making use of the radical Christian reinterpretation of Ezekiel's vision. By reading More's *Divine Dialogues* in conjunction with *Paradise Lost,* book 6, we can come to a better understanding of Milton's intent in employing the cherubic chariot as the engine to defeat a corrupt kingship.

6 • Mary Astell, Lucy Hutchinson, John Milton, and Feminist Liberation Theology

Joan S. Bennett

About twenty-five years ago, the authors of *The Madwoman in the Attic* pronounced that John Milton's works embodied an "undeniable misogyny." The implication in 1979 was that literary scholars wishing to read and teach as feminists would need to combat the influence of Milton on students who might be seduced by his poetry's beauty into absorbing its patriarchal assumptions.[1] During the 1980s, the scholarship of Diane McColley and others discredited the claim of misogyny, but many teachers who consider themselves feminists still feel that Milton is a problem.[2]

The most common approach at present seems to be influenced by the poet's categorization as a member of the emergent bourgeois social class.[3] Students are advised to bracket treatments of women and gender in Milton's poetry as outdated since people in the seventeenth century believed women should be confined to a private, domestic sphere of influence and submit within that sphere to male authority. Meanwhile, historians caution that in the seventeenth century, because the household estate functioned as a unit of the state, "the distinctions between public and private, political and nonpolitical, were less clear" than in the nineteenth and twentieth centuries.[4] Literature students nevertheless tend to imagine that the terms "hierarchy" and "subordination" have always represented ordering principles like those of the capitalist corporate and academic structures against which twentieth century feminists struggled, and that Milton must have created his Eve as a model for the bourgeois housewife.[5] It is assumed that, as a man of his times, Milton could not have imagined the vision for women's intellectual accomplishment and entry into positions of public influence that would emerge with nineteenth and twentieth century feminism.

I will suggest that such assumptions, although more responsible than the claim of simple misogyny, are historically inadequate. To focus more clearly on the modes of human agency available to women in the seventeenth century, we will look briefly into the experience of two writers, Mary Astell, born at the beginning of the Restoration period, and Lucy Hutchinson from Milton's own generation, both appropriate representatives of the times of which Milton was a part.[6] That most feminist theories have been unable satisfactorily to account for the writing of these women leads me to suggest using a lens that, to my knowledge, has not yet been used in studies of early modern writers who, like Milton, Mary Astell, and Lucy Hutchinson, were deeply religious, intellectually sophisticated, and politically committed. Feminist liberation theology is a glass through which we can gain a clearer view of the powerful resource available in Milton's poetry for twenty-first century feminist readers. At stake are ways of thinking about the terms "reason," "power," and "liberty," and ways of reading texts that contain a "dangerous memory."

I

> "[N]ot *Milton* himself wou'd cry up Liberty to poor *Female Slaves*."
>
> — Mary Astell, *Some Reflections upon Marriage*

English and American feminists in search of ancestors have been tempted to give the title "first feminist" to Mary Astell (1666–1731), a pioneering advocate for the education of women, reform of marriage, and involvement of women in public roles.[7] Like some twentieth century feminists, Astell combed the Scriptures for evidence of divinely sanctioned female ability, power, and authority, finding, for instance, that Deborah "overthrows the pretence of Natural Inferiority" because "it was God who Inspir'd and Approv'd that great Woman, raising her up to Judge and to Deliver His People Israel," and "tho' she had a Husband, she her self Judg'd Israel and consequently was his Sovereign" (*Reflections*, 24). Likewise, the Shunamite widow who sustained the prophet Elijah at Zarephah was clearly an authority figure, whereas her husband "is hardly taken notice of, and this no otherwise than as performing the Office of a Bailiff" (25). Reporting many similarly persuasive cases, Astell demonstrates that "the Bible is for, and not against us" (28).

Astell's biblical references function as evidence within her most frequently chosen genre, the political pamphlet, which allows her to exercise her skill in logical argumentation. Her faith in reasoning relates closely both to her religious faith and to her faith in women. Since a "Rational Mind is too noble a Being to be Made for the Sake and Service of any Creature," she maintains, women were made for the service of God only and not of men. As a struggling single woman dependent on patrons, Astell well understood that marriage was economically inevitable for many women and was, in any case, the divinely instituted method for propagating the human race. Nevertheless, she earnestly advocated the single state for as many women as could manage it. Even if a husband should come to own a woman's property and body in marriage, however, she taught that "the Mind is free, nothing but Reason can oblige it, 'tis out of the Reach of the most absolute Tyrant" (13).

As was the case for many of her late seventeenth century contemporaries, Astell's faith in rational argument and the potential power of "the Mind" was inspired by her understanding of the writings of René Descartes, whose philosophical method involving personal memoir and reflection seemed to allow for the ability of each rational creature to arrive at truth simply by proceeding with careful logic through to a clear perception. For this mental activity, access to tutors, schools, and universities was not necessary; one need only reason one's way carefully to God's truth. When this "radical consciousness of self" with its focus on individual human agency is seen to have been "important to the growth of feminism," Astell is regarded as both "an early prophetess of the Enlightenment" and "a forebear of nineteenth- and twentieth-century feminism."[8]

However, Astell has also presented a puzzle for historians of feminism who have been surprised to find her protofeminism embedded in an extremely conservative religio-political world view. Astell was a high church Tory, arguing tenaciously for the divine right to absolute power of the English monarch and of the bishops of the Church of England. Her advocacy of women's education and possible state service was an integral part of her conservative political beliefs. She wrote vigorously against the right of Dissenters to pass what she considered their heresy on to their children, perpetuating political "party," the inevitable and unacceptable result of religious toleration.[9] *Some Reflections upon Marriage* is more fundamentally about the political order than it is about domestic relationships. This tract, as Patricia Springborg points out, is part of a sustained attack by Astell on the social contract theory of her primary polemical targets, John Locke and other influential Whigs, for whom "Milton himself" — pronounced by Astell "a better poet than either divine or politician" — served as a surrogate. As Springborg explains, Astell's "challenge to Locke to extend to women against domestic tyrants the liberty he claimed for subjects against the Crown was [meant] . . . to expose to ridicule the tenets of contractarian liberalism and certainly not to endorse the space they appeared to open up" for women.[10] Since both Astell and the Whigs held that wives should be subordinate to husbands with whom they had made an actual marriage contract, she argued by analogy that it was unacceptable to believe that, because of a fictional or metaphorical social contract, political subjects could hold authority over a monarch.

Her position on how to deal with unjust superiors is the same for the domestic and civic realms. Acknowledging that "one Person is not in reality better than another, but as he is more Wise and Good," she holds nevertheless, "this world being a place of Tryal, just Retributions being reserv'd for hereafter," that "Respect and Obedience, many times, become due for Order's sake to those who don't otherwise deserve them" (*Reflections*, 58). With husbands, as with magistrates, although "the Head many times stands in need of the Inferior's Brains to manage it" (62), the power of such a head over wife or people must be tolerated and obeyed unless either the head willingly accepts advice or Providence removes his power.

Thus, although Astell seems to have advanced a feminist cause by proclaiming women's equal abilities, advocating education for women and their service in the public sphere, and denying the distinction between public and private that the new Whig view of history was in the process of imposing, at the same time, the very reasoning she used in support of these positions advocated submission by both women and men to the absolute power of a divine-right monarchy, whether the monarch be just or unjust, and by the same token, submission by a wife to a husband's rule even though, as she urged all as yet unmarried young women to consider, there are "100,000 Tyrants" ruling over the women subjected to them in marriage (*Reflections,* 17).

In attempting to explain the fact that Astell and other late seventeenth century advocates for women's advancement were Tory absolutists, Catherine Gallagher observes in these women's world view the development of an idea that she calls "singularity," which is an "absolutist impulse to obliterate intermediate levels of social power [such as households] between the individual subject and the monarch." Astell's faith in the ability of each person's unaided reason empowered her to view individuals, particularly women, as independent units, each singly connected as directly to the divine as to the human monarch. Gallagher finds Astell's contribution to feminism thus located in the "modes of female subjectivity that absolutist thought first enabled."[11]

In spite of her modes of female subjectivity and her attempts to better the lot of women, however, Astell believed that, except in the rare instances where Providence intervenes to grant female power, only a "Prospect of Heaven" can console the wise woman, who in her meditation "will discern a time when her Sex shall be no bar to the best Employments, the highest Honour" (*Reflections,* 75) and that, meanwhile, for almost all women — especially those chained in marriage — "the superior Force of Men, keeps Women from Acting in the World, or doing any thing considerable" (23).

In contrast to Astell's perception that men as a class keep women as a class from "doing any thing considerable" in the world, we may now consider the experience of Lucy Hutchinson, a contemporary of John Milton's who acted very much in the world, affecting the course of English history — albeit in a direction that Astell deplored — and whose writing has long

influenced posterity's reading of the history of her time. Her
extensive literary works, in addition to her history, include
Order and Disorder, an original biblical epic composed at
about the same time that *Paradise Lost* was published; a personal theology, *On the Principles of the Christian Religion*;
the first complete English translation of Lucretius's natural philosophy; and some very moving lyric poetry. I would like to
consider some of the reasons why such a woman has never been
proposed as an early feminist, and what this silence says about
feminism as well as about her. We will certainly locate some
of these reasons in the fact that this brilliant, politically active
historian and poet was married, raised eight children, and
embraced a religio-political theory that saw marriage and the
household as the divinely given locus and source of social and
political agency, including revolutionary agency.[12]

II

> "[S]he that would not delight in such an honourable and
> advantageable subjection, must have wanted a reasonable
> soul."
>
> — *The Life of Mrs. Lucy Hutchinson*

Lucy Hutchinson's biography of the revolutionary Colonel
John Hutchinson, her husband, has provided historians for
two centuries with detailed information about and analysis of
the English civil war in the north of England.[13] As the work of
a republican Dissenter justifying the actions and beliefs of a
Puritan regicide who died unrepentant in a Restoration prison,
the *Life*, although it probably circulated as a manuscript publication after its completion in the 1660s, would not, David
Norbrook points out, have escaped the notice of the royal censor had any publisher been willing to try to put it into print.[14]
Titled *Memoirs* by Julius Hutchinson, the descendant who
decided to have it printed in 1806, this account was thereafter

primarily associated with its male subject, John Hutchinson, even though the narrative's perspective, and its strong authorial voice, are clearly those of its female author.

N. H. Keeble, who published a new edition of the *Memoirs* in 1990, did recognize Lucy Hutchinson's own voice in it, observing that Colonel John Hutchinson of the *Memoirs* is the literary creation of Lucy Hutchinson. Hutchinson appears to Keeble to be a puzzling "mirror-image" of Mary Astell. "Whereas Mary Astell's prophetic feminist thought was married to a staunchly conservative Tory politics and episcopalian religion," he observes, "Lucy Hutchinson's radical religion and politics could tolerate only wifely domesticity in women." He turns to feminist theory for an explanation of what he sees to be Hutchinson's case. Recognizing the power of her voice as well as the extensive space she gives to her own story and opinions in the *Memoirs*, Keeble concludes that she invented a narrative persona, rendering "Mrs. Hutchinson" as a figure talked about rather than as the speaking voice, thereby exemplifying a "duplicity," predicted by the theory of writers like Sandra Gilbert and Susan Gubar as "the inevitable strategy of women writing in androcentric cultures."[15]

Although it is true that Hutchinson was writing in an androcentric culture, this interpretation illustrates a limitation placed by current feminist theory on our ability to encounter her work, a limitation reflected also in the reading of the autobiographical fragment that Julius Hutchinson had included at the beginning of the *Memoirs*. Because the fragment breaks off at the point of her marriage, Sidonie Smith felt that it was "as if her own life story ended after marriage when marriage subsumed her identity in her husband's." It took a reader immersed in the literary experience of the English republican movement to feel certain that this interpretation was mistaken and to demonstrate that the original autobiography was actually "a rich and ambitious narrative" that was "very self-consciously a story of the enormously complex historical causes that enabled it to be written." David Norbrook explains that the royalist women writers' commitment to individualism — Gallagher's "singularity" — contrasts markedly with the commitments of seventeenth century English republican historiography, in which "monarchism was condemned as an ideology that placed too much emphasis on individual whims and desires" while "republicans insisted on the individual's subordination to the common good."[16] Lucy Hutchinson viewed agency itself from the perspective that the republican John Milton articulated on the eve of his own political imprisonment in 1659, when he urged his endangered readers "to place every one his privat welfare and happiness in the public peace, libertie, and safetie."[17]

The *Memoirs* contain many narratives that illustrate the way in which Lucy and John Hutchinson coordinated their efforts for the creation of a just society within an order that, while it gave the husband a governing role, required that he govern by right reason and that the wife guide her actions by her own right reason as well, rendering male and female both very powerful. "Right reason" was a more complex phenomenon than the individualistic reasoning process that Astell admired in the Cartesian method; Christian humanist right reason required exercise in community and action in society.[18] Such action, or praxis, in turn required reflection that led to new understanding. The Hutchinsons worked together on theory, as when they jointly came to the realization that they did not believe infant baptism to be willed by God. Lucy, prompted by approaching childbirth, had been reading on the subject, found herself concerned, consulted John, who read the same pieces after which they prayerfully and intently reread the Scriptures until they became confirmed in a belief in adult baptism and resolved to uphold one another in a commitment, in spite of expectations of their community, not to have the coming child baptized (210–11). This was simultaneously a family decision and a community action undertaken with religio-political intentions and consequences.

They worked together politically, John asking Lucy to persuade Henry Ireton not to allow John to be called to serve on the Council of State at the conclusion of the war. The fact that she turned out to be unsuccessful both she and her husband took as a sign not of her lack of skill but, on the contrary, a sign that, given John's strong desire to return to private life, Lucy's very strong ability to persuade, and Ireton's constancy in seeking all true talent for the public service, God clearly wanted John to serve (237). They worked together in military maneuvers, as when Lucy, arriving by chance in the city of Nottingham at the beginning of a battle, managed to dissuade an infuriated army regiment from attacking a militia of youths incited against them by Presbyterian townspeople until their commander, General Monck, could be reached. Simultaneously, she sent a runner to her husband, who was in the same location as the general, so that when a renegade officer went alone to the general and obtained an order to sack the city, John was able to persuade the general to issue a countermand (276).

We may note in these instances and many more that Lucy saw herself as indeed subordinate to John but, equally importantly, that she did not experience this subordination as a barrier to her personal liberty, self-expression, or ability to affect public outcomes. On the contrary, she found her selfhood fulfilled, her initiative and collaboration — her agency — expected, valued, and as effective as actions taken by men.

Reflecting, in her biblical epic, on the creation of male and female, Hutchinson shows why she could not have accepted Astell's assumption that a person locked in an oppressive marriage could still be free in her mind, her "reason." For Hutchinson as a Christian humanist, reasoning could not be separated from relationships in praxis in society. When in her epic she amplified the Creator's saying "it was not good that man should be alone," she offered similes to convey its meaning to anyone who might be tempted by "singularity." "Man" (male or female), if without an "associate" who "doth both soul and sense participate," will experience life like an instrument with "strings screwed up too high" or a bow that is bent and not released. Such persons will either break themselves off from the social body or else "crack the instrument." Humans "for each other's mutual help were made," and human nature is "for society designed" (*Order and Disorder*, 3.335).

The heart of this mutual help is a shared practical wisdom, whether in the family or larger society, among "sweet friends" for whom "equal delight it is to learn and teach." Providence created a world of plenitude, not scarcity, a world in which

> Wisdom imparted, like th'increasing bread
> Wherewith the Lord so many thousands fed,
> By distribution adds to its own store,
> And still the more it gives it hath the more.   (3.375–78)

Shared wisdom, when acted and reflected upon, is the exercise of right reason, which is modeled on divine love. Reason in this large, complex sense is shown by Hutchinson to be God's purpose for human society, a view shared by Milton's angel Raphael, who encourages Adam and Eve to "retain / Unalterably firm his love entire/ Whose progeny who are" (*Paradise Lost*, 5.469–503). Like Raphael, Hutchinson teaches that

> Love raiseth us, itself to heaven doth rise
> By virtue's varied mutual exercise.
>   (*Order and Disorder* 3:381–82)

In her autobiography, Hutchinson describes herself as having flourished within the kind of hierarchy that we find in Milton's prelapsarian Eden. "Never man had a greater passion for a woman, nor a more honourable esteem of a wife" than her husband for her. "Yet," importantly for her own freedom as well as his, "he was not uxorious, nor remitted not that just rule which it was her honour to obey, but managed the reins of government with such prudence[19] and affection that she who would not delight in such an honourable and advantage-able subjection, must have wanted a reasonable soul." Her hus-band's love for her, "the highest love he or any man could have," Hutchinson reflected, "was yet bounded by a superior: he loved her in the Lord as his fellow-creature, not his idol." Her husband's governance liberated Lucy Hutchinson's humanity precisely *because* "he loved God above her," fulfilling his commitment to the God who mandated at Creation that human love and liberty be grounded in justice (26). His power over her was valid because it generated a power in her for the free exercise of her own ability to enact justice.[20]

In *Order and Disorder*, when Lucy Hutchinson narrated the visit of the angels to Abraham and Sarah, the biblical story on which Milton based the angel Raphael's visit to Eden, her interest, like Milton's, was not in gender roles but in right use of social privilege in the family-state complex. In the time of the matriarchs and patriarchs, she observed pointedly, "Great women were not delicate and nice, / Bred up in idleness" (12.227–28).[21] As Milton's Adam was a king whose royalty needed no retinue, so in the time of Abraham, "kings fed flocks and councilors served the plough." Sarah's preparing food and Abraham's waiting on visiting travelers showed not that Sarah was inferior to Abraham but that the nobility of both was manifested by their service (12.227–42).

Just as Hutchinson embedded the *Memoirs'* account of her own and her husband's lives in the larger story of the attempted republic ("it being necessary to carry on the main story for the better understanding of the motion of those lesser wheels that moved within the great orb" [104]), so, too, she incorporated the significance of all those experiences into her biblical epic. Like Milton, she grounded her reading of her own age in the revelations of Genesis. In contrast to Astell, who used the sacred stories as polemical proofs, Hutchinson found in the narratives a complex and dangerous memory waiting to be transformed, in the retelling, into a historical will for change and renewed hope for humanity.[22]

Whether Milton and Hutchinson met or were aware of each other is not known.[23] Although they lived in different parts of England, each author was connected to the Earl of Anglesey, who kept valuable but dangerous manuscripts safe for both of them as movers in what Norbrook calls the "shadow public sphere" of Dissenters in the Restoration period.[24] In the introduction to his edition of *Order and Disorder*, Norbrook wonders what Milton would have thought of a woman poet who took it on herself to write an epic on the same subject as *Paradise Lost*.[25] Without being able to answer that question directly, we may notice Milton wrote his *Sonnets IX* and *X* commending the right reason and the poetry of women. Unlike the young John Hutchinson, who, upon first seeing an excellent sonnet written by the woman he would eventually marry, "could scarcely believe it was a woman's" (*Memoirs*, 47), John Milton expected no less from gifted and dedicated women such as the Lady Margaret Ley, whose wisdom and literary gifts earned from him the epithet "Honor'd *Margaret*" (*Sonnet X*). To his pupil Richard Jones, Milton held up the example of Richard's mother, Lady Ranelagh, Milton's close friend of many years, to guide young Richard in the right use of his further studies at Oxford.[26] Our primary concern here, however, is not so much what Milton would have thought of Lucy Hutchinson as how twenty-first century readers with feminist interests and commitments may most fruitfully experience the poetry of both.

III

"The question now is whether the original explosive power of these symbols and myths . . . the 'dangerous memory' . . . can be recovered and reactivated."
— Míguez Bonino, *Toward a Christian Political Ethics*

For readers seeking access to the deep power of Milton's art, an individualistic feminism descended from the Enlightenment is an inadequate guide and can be an unnecessary hindrance. The highly "singular" Margaret Cavendish, Duchess of Newcastle, a royalist contemporary and neighbor of Hutchinson who drew upon her own Cartesian subjectivity to experiment with several genres and who has also been called a "protofeminist," felt that poets should not tamper with the Bible's "plain narrative."[27] Her conservative preference came from the same awareness that led many of her Dissenting contemporaries to reimagine and retell the narratives. Retelling biblical stories was for Dissenters like John Milton and Lucy Hutchinson, as it is for liberationists today, a way of activating the stories' power for present use. Their expectation that biblical texts would liberate anew required a radical confidence that "revelation is not closed." They share Milton's view that "the light which we have gain'd, was giv'n us, not to be ever staring on, but by it to discover onward things more remote from our knowledge" (*Areopagitica*, 1018).[28] Ultimately, it required seeing a way forward from reflection on the stories to social action and a way back from actions taken to a deeper understanding of the meaning of those actions through reflection on the stories.

Feminist liberation theology exercises a hermeneutics that can open texts like Milton's, as it opens the Bible, to the needs of a feminism that wants women to exercise agency not merely as individual thinkers or members of the class "woman" but as builders of a society that frees the full potential contribution of each member — female and male — to the whole. Let us, then, take a brief look at some hermeneutic principles of feminist liberation theology, guided by the theologian Elisabeth Schüssler Fiorenza.[29] The method assumes as its beginning point that women's struggle for liberation has always gone on just as other dimensions of oppression have been struggled against before now, and it examines both the oppressive and

the liberating dynamics of religious texts to assess their function in the current struggle.

Practicing a "feminist critical theology of liberation" adds
a qualification to the scriptural hermeneutics of liberation
theology. Both practices find in Scripture, especially in Genesis,
Exodus, and the Gospel portrayals of Jesus' "preferential option
for the poor," a driving force for their own work. However, the
feminist version believes it vital to understand that the very
Scripture that liberates also contains for women and other
marginalized people important materials of their oppression —
both in the patriarchal uses to which Scripture has been put
and in the androcentric fabric of the canonized texts themselves.
Recognizing this fact requires one to exercise a "hermeneutics of suspicion," which assumes that women and other marginalized people have been removed as agents from history.
Correspondingly, a "hermeneutics of proclamation" requires
that what suspicion finds in a text be named. This much of
the hermeneutics is shared by other feminisms.

Of equal importance, however, is a hermeneutics that
remembers past assertions of a "discipleship of equals," which
seeks to understand the divinely enabled powerful faith, wisdom, and leadership exercised by women in the past. Correspondingly, a feminist rhetoric integrates that "dangerous
memory" into current liberation efforts. To describe the relationship between the hermeneutics of suspicion and that of
remembrance, Schüssler Fiorenza employs a metaphor from
Adrienne Rich's description of Marie Curie's research on
radioactivity: "Her wounds came from the same source as her
power" (21). The biblical heritage, Schüssler Fiorenza claims,
is one and the same source for women's suffering and for their
deepest strength. The hermeneutics of proclamation names the
pain experienced under oppressive power; the hermeneutics
of remembrance focuses on the genuine power women have
exercised for the good, power that must be recognized because

it is needed for use now. One way in which the power residing in the text can be deployed is through "creative actualization," the liberationist practice of storytelling and "bibliodrama." Such a practice is rhetorical, not only hermeneutical; that is, it does not just explore and appreciate the meaning of texts but pays attention to the effects the discourses produce and how they produce them. It reads from a position of the special interest of feminism without doing so reductively. Creative actualization is the method most capable of doing justice to the rich dimensions of biblical texts and their historical contexts.

Lucy Hutchinson read and wrote as a liberationist. Her biblical redactions in turn reward a liberationist reading. One of the most interesting is her account of the matriarch Rebecca.[30] Hutchinson acknowledges her readers' potential concern that patriarchy can appear "harsh" when parents exercise their prerogative to choose a spouse for their child. She lets the readers of her epic know that she deeply understands and values romantic love (*Order and Disorder*, 16.260–88). In writing her husband's *Life*, she reveals that their eldest son had married the daughter of a royalist family without his father's permission, which surely would not have been granted. One purpose of this narration is to show how this young woman's inherent virtue and ability to love not only justified the marriage but also managed to win the respect and heart of her father-in-law. Hutchinson wanted her readers to understand the spirit underlying the patriarchal letter, to know that divinely given structures of governance are to be worked with freely, according to their liberating spirit, not followed slavishly. When, in her epic, she tells of Abraham's sending his servant to choose a wife for his son Isaac, she acknowledges this father's prerogative as "harsh" but insists as well on scriptural acts of remembrance that help her readers to see imaginatively the large picture ordained for human welfare and liberty that is the only context in which genuine love can develop. She explains that in the family, which is the core of society, "Since that both

the parents' godliness / To children's education is required /
He for his son a virtuous wife desired" (16.10–12). Hutchinson
portrays the reaction of Rebecca, the wife chosen for Isaac, as
a model for working with Providence. In Genesis, although
Rebecca's family requests a ten-day period for leave-taking
before her departure with Abraham's servant, Rebecca herself
decides to honor the servant's desire to depart immediately.
To actualize the meaning of this detail, Hutchinson imagines
a psychologically self-aware, wise young woman of faith:

> Not want of filial love or piety
> Made fair Rebecca here so soon agree
> Forever from her father's house to go,
> But she believed, since 'twas concluded so,
> A short stay might her pious griefs augment,
> And make her virtuous courage to relent,
> Softened with her fond mother's melting tears,
> Which might have filled her with such doubts and fears
> As would have stopped the entrance of that love
> That must the blessing of her whole life prove.   (16.183–92)

Hutchinson takes her authority to invent Rebecca's interior
experience from the Bible's mention that Rebecca's arrival
surprised Isaac by healing his grief for the loss of his own
mother, Sarah. Human love of all kinds, in Hutchinson's
vision, blesses all of life, but that blessing is not a private one
only; it involves all society and history and is governed by divine
truths that will always surprise and to whose revelations one
must remain open.

Entrusted with enormous responsibility for human welfare
as executor with Isaac of the divine covenant with Abraham,
Rebecca is recreated by Hutchinson in a way that stresses her
power to exercise right reason, that is, to discern the wisest
action and to execute that action well. For Hutchinson, this
power's exercise did not require changes in structures of
hierarchy or patriarchy (as it would in a twenty-first century
Western liberationist redaction); but it did require a vigilant

discernment and commitment to ensure that virtuous purpose was acted upon by those with governing authority. When it was not, then the faith called for one under government to exercise her special insight and power (as it would in a twenty-first century liberationist redaction). Mary Astell was to maintain that, although "the Head many times stands in need of the Inferior's Brains to manage it," nevertheless such an unwise head must be tolerated and obeyed unless he willingly accepts advice or unless Providence intervenes to place the woman above him in a hierarchy, such as Deborah or Queen Anne (*Reflections*, 62). Lucy Hutchinson, in contrast, viewed both women and men as constantly active participants with Providence. The fact that all humans are of equal spiritual worth and calling meant to her that no matter where they were placed in a hierarchical order, each person embodied ability and held responsibility for the welfare of the whole order. At the same time, for Hutchinson, the issue was not just the analytical "Brains" needed, but rather the whole complex phenomenon of right reason, which she dramatizes at length in her story of Rebecca's "framing the occasion," as she says, for her husband Isaac to make his younger son Jacob heir to his blessing.[31]

Thus, she shows Rebecca visited in her difficult pregnancy by a prophet who reveals that the younger of the twin brothers she is carrying will dominate the elder because the younger will be more fit to rule. Hutchinson then depicts Esau's behavior as reprehensible in normal human terms so that, when she narrates Rebecca's deception of her husband, which results in his giving his right of governance to his younger son Jacob, she can characterize Rebecca's action as "pious fraud whereby his zealous wife / Strove to correct the errors of his life / Who [was] governed by a partial blind affection" (18.75–77). She shows Isaac, once he is aware of what he has done, being helped by Rebecca to search back through his experience to understand how Providence had used his appetite for venison, which was closely related to his love of Esau, to delay giving this son his blessing. Painfully, in Hutchinson's redaction, Isaac comes to see that God used Isaac's own foolishness to restrain him from giving his blessing until the moment in the occasion which Rebecca had framed for him to give it to Jacob.

At the same time, Hutchinson portrays with deep feeling the grief that accompanies the next action Rebecca takes to frame an occasion: persuading Isaac to send Jacob to a foreign country, to seek a wife from her people, but also to remove him from Esau's murderous anger. For Hutchinson, this is "the saddest circumstance" of the story she has to tell (a circumstance not told in Genesis), the farewell to her son from Rebecca, who, at last, "Conquering her passions with a virtuous force, / Chased from her soul all womanish remorse." Hutchinson has Rebecca reflect that it is still in her power to engineer a situation in which Esau might relent if Jacob would surrender the right of blessing. She loves both sons and understands that Esau does not really want the birthright he in fact had given away earlier, and that, in purely human terms, she would be able to deal with his anger. However, she resolves to follow Providence unwaveringly, directing Jacob to "Fly to obtain the promises decreed" (18.291). Although the plan is for Jacob to be reunited with his parents once Esau's anger passes, as Rebecca knows it will, Jacob senses accurately that this is their final parting and inwardly mourns already the loss of his "dear and prudent mother" (18.322).

Lucy Hutchinson's writing rewards a reader with more attention than we can give it here; and the feminist liberationist approach to her writing could be developed more fully. However, in the space remaining we will turn to Milton's poetry to try a feminist liberationist reading of one of its "hard places" for feminist readers, the judgment in the Garden after the Fall.

Milton's vision for gender relations shares with Hutchinson's an ideal of the mutually creative power of women and men, made equally in the divine image, in families committed to work toward the benefit of the society that is comprised of those families. In accordance with his belief that the purpose of governance in the family is to enable governance of the whole society, Milton held that leadership in marriage should be assumed by the wife in cases where she is wiser than her husband. However, he offered no solution if the husband did not "contentedly yield" to his wife's leadership in these cases, except to allow for divorce in extreme circumstances (*Tetrachordon*, YP 2:589). It is important to name the fact that Milton did not focus on removing the systemic structures of patriarchy in the family. Likewise, it is necessary to proclaim the androcentric features of his writing that, if accepted, would reinforce patriarchy's hold on the present. But it would be self-defeating for a feminist reader, after exercising the hermeneutics of suspicion and proclamation, to stop there. Like Hutchinson, Milton also gives his readers the most important tools needed for interrogating all power structures because he requires us not only to understand who has power *over* whom, but also to examine the prior question: what is power *for?* — and to remember the freedom that is the necessary basis of "power for."[32]

Concerning Milton's portrayal of the judgment in the Garden, *The Riverside Milton* advises students, "Here if anywhere modern feminist critics and all who believe in an ideal of equality between the sexes have a strong case against Milton, who clearly believed . . . Adam's perfection outranks Eve's in the hierarchy of nature."[33] This statement assumes, realistically, that "modern feminist" readers view the human experience portrayed in this early modern epic through a kind of mathematical schema that they attribute to Milton and so map onto his poem. Milton is imagined to believe in an abstract, static and essential "hierarchy of nature" with a ranked set of "perfections" that defines the members of each sex. Utilized to interpret the words that Milton has the Son of God say to Adam before pronouncing his judgment in book 10, this map is envisioned as supplying a general set of directions for behavior, which is regulated by a command structure, as if a human governor were to command obedience like a god. In this imagined paradigm, a woman must obey a man. A man must not obey a woman. A male obeying a female's command is guilty of breaking gender hierarchy, of violating "his position in nature." Breaking this abstract gender hierarchy is then seen to be what the Son is characterizing as idolatry when he demands of Adam: "Was shee thy God." This post-Cartesian, essentialist way of looking at hierarchy, I will argue, is not Miltonic. To read *Paradise Lost* through such a lens is to read it blind. Let us try instead a liberationist reading.

Here are the Son's words:

> Was shee thy God, that her thou didst obey
> Before his voice, or was shee made thy guide,
> Superior, or but equal, that to her
> Thou didst resigne thy Manhood, and the Place
> Wherein God set thee above her made of thee,
> And for thee, whose perfection farr excell'd
> Hers in all real dignitie: Adornd
> Shee was indeed, and lovely to attract
> Thy Love, not thy Subjection, and her Gifts
> Were such as under Government well seem'd,
> Unseemly to beare rule, which was thy part
> And person, had'st thou known thy self aright.   (10.145–56)

In reading this passage, one should remember the liberationist hermeneutics Milton exercised on the Scripture that was his source. In the case of Jesus' saying on divorce, Milton advocated holding to the sense that "sounded and proclaimed liberty" in order, where necessary, "to remove . . . [a] great and sad oppression which through the strictnes of a literall interpreting" by authorities in church and state had led "to the overburdning, if not the overwhelming of many" (*Doctrine and Discipline of Divorce*, YP 2:242).

Milton's method of reading Jesus' answer to the Pharisees on divorce provides a good model for a feminist liberationist reading of Milton's own redaction of the Son's judgment of Adam, for, if taken with a strictness of literal interpreting, God's words to Adam would place a great and sad oppression on many women. According to Milton's explication of Luke, Jesus spoke his "hard saying" in response to deceitful and confused questioners, whose own turmoil was caused by their sinfulness. Jesus was, in this specific context, Milton says, giving "a sharp and vehement answer to a tempting question." Milton continues,

> [In] such cases, that we are not to repose all upon the literall terms of so many words, many instances will teach us: Wherin we may plainly discover how Christ meant not to be tak'n word for word, but like a wise Physician, administring one excesse against another to reduce us to a perfect mean: Where the Pharises were strict, there Christ seems remisse; where they were too remisse, he saw it needfull to seem most severe. (YP 2:282–83)

Schüssler Fiorenza's addition to this method would be to exercise "remembrance" not only of the internal context of the passage in question, but also of the immediate historical context of the author of the redaction, which for *Paradise Lost* certainly included anguish over the disastrous influence on England's welfare first by Charles I's submission to his queen and then by Charles II's to his mistress. Dissenters like Milton and Hutchinson felt that absolute power in the hands of a monarch who effectively turned that power over to someone with domestic power over him perverted the relation that inevitably operated between the larger state and its household estates. While noting this seventeenth century context for Milton's portrayal of Adam's fall as the failure of a governor, we will understand his vision for government itself if we turn attention to the other dimension of remembrance, the internal context the poet creates for these words.

The Son, in judgment, addresses the exorbitant confusion of the newly fallen Adam's heart, which is amply shown in the question that he puts to the Son, prompting this reply. Adam, "sore beset" by guilt, feeling that even though theoretically he should, he simply cannot shoulder all the punishment for the Fall, blames Eve. This action reveals him still to be "uxorious," reminding us that a man's "uxorious" behavior refers to a sin not of a woman but of a man who uses a woman as an excuse for his own wrong action. When he sins, he says he does so because he loves her. When he is called to repent, he holds that just as she caused his sin, so she should bear his punishment. The world's first sin, the sin that included all public and private sins that would follow in history,[34] was completed by a governor who used domestic devotion as an excuse for betraying his deepest human responsibility. Justified by "strict necessitie," which readers will recognize from their exposure to Milton's Satan as "The Tyrants plea" (4.394), the world's governor declares that his fall is the fault of womankind and that womankind is God's fault.

The wording of the Son's judgment answers Adam's failure to make a genuine confession of his sin. When we read with the awareness that the Son is not neutrally explicating a law of nature but is speaking rhetorically, performatively, "as when we bow things the contrary way, to make them come to thir naturall straightnes" (YP 2:283), we have the tools we need both to proclaim the sense that is oppressive and the sense that is liberating.

First the potential for oppression must be proclaimed; these words can easily be interpreted as saying that Adam is about to be condemned for having allowed Eve to be his "equal." However, to read the passage in this way would be to see in the original good an exercise of the power of one equal over another, which is not, within the liberationist paradigm, a faithful claim to make about the Creation, the source of human freedom and the potential source of liberation. Therefore, rejecting as inapplicable the map of a static hierarchy, we must go on to ask, "Is there a way in which we can see in this passage not 'power over' but 'power for,' the original power of creation?" We can ask, "What has 'equal' meant in Milton's other tellings of the prelapsarian vision?"

First, recall the equality of Adam's judge, the Son, who is both equal and subordinate to God and is thus a model for our perception of the combined equality and hierarchy of governor and governed, Adam and Eve. Lucy Hutchinson's phrasing of the hierarchy-within-equality of the godhead parallels Milton's. Describing the mutuality of the heavenly power as a kind of dance between the majesty of God the Father and the grace of God the Son, she says of heaven: "Here majesty and grace together meet; / The grace is glorious and the glory sweet" (*Order and Disorder*, 1.197–98). Similarly, in *Paradise Lost*, at the very moment that God the Father announces to heaven the Judgment that the human fall will incur, the Father's majesty in "the Son of God was seen / Most glorious" as he manifested "without measure Grace" (3.138–42).

Milton carefully echoes this language describing the mystery of divine hierarchy when he provides Satan's and the reader's first view of Adam and Eve, in whose "Divine" appearance the "image of thir glorious Maker shon." Although this complex passage calls for its own liberationist reading, we may note here that these prototypical humans, who hold joint "autoritie" over nonhuman creation in "true filial freedom" given them by the Creator, are to exercise this authority, like the Creator, through a kind of dance between "glorious" "Majestie" and "sweet" "Grace" (4.288–98).

When speaking with Adam about governance, then, the Son judges, in one sense, from his own archetypal experience. He draws Adam toward a recognition of betrayal of the divine paradigm with his rhetorical question, "Was shee thy God, that her thou didst obey / Before his voice." This question is an answer to Adam's accusation: "This Woman whom thou mad'st . . . so Divine . . . / Her doing seem'd to justifie the deed" (10.136–42). Its anticipated answer from a contrary Adam appears to be, "No, I was not following her action because I thought she was the all-knowing, almighty God." The Son's second rhetorical question, "was shee made thy guide," answers Adam's claim, "Her doing seem'd to justifie the deed." "Was shee made thy guide, / Superior, or but equal" is, if read from a liberationist perspective, an answer to Adam's language about his "other self, the partner of his life" and to the answer he might be tempted to give were he to persist in his boldness before his Judge: No, I never believed she was my superior; but she *was* my equal, the equal whom you commended me for seeking.

The Son's question would then be expanded: Even though she was your equal, you should not have resigned your own humanity — selfhood, agency — to comply with her request. An "equal" is not one to whom you give up your own agency; your equality was between two rational beings, both selves. To resign selfhood was to betray equality. If an equal "guides" you to resign your humanity, then that is false guiding, even though coming from an equal.

Furthermore, the Son explains, Adam resigned his "Place":

> the Place
> Wherein God set thee above her made of thee,
> And for thee, whose perfection farr excell'd
> Hers in all real dignitie: . . . her Gifts
> Were such as under Government well seem'd,
> Unseemly to beare rule, which was thy part
> And person, had'st thou known thy self aright.   (10.147–56)

Here is perhaps the most apt moment in the poem for feminist liberationist readers to recall Adrienne Rich's words about Marie Curie: "Her pain came from the same source as her power." This is a text of pain because it takes a real liberationist will to read through these words. And yet, if we do so, we attain power for women and all marginalized people.

Here we need to call upon another tenet of liberationist scriptural hermeneutics: the sense in which Scripture is foundational.

Paradise Lost, like Scripture, is not foundational in that it provides static archetypes through which we can study an everlasting picture of ideal creation. Scripture does not offer blueprints. Rather, Scripture is foundational in providing a prototype — not a pattern of what ultimate perfection will look like, but a model of how growth happens in accordance with the dynamics of the world God designed. Milton's scriptural redaction portrays the moment of first catastrophic confusion. In their falls, Eve misused a gift that they both shared but that was Adam's strongest "perfection" — the ability to identify abstract divine truths that should be operative, "bear rule," in a particular situation. Adam, in turn, misused the gift that was Eve's strongest "perfection" — the ability to focus a relationship rightly in love.

One of the revelations from Milton's telling of the Fall is that both of these divine gifts, along with all others, are in postlapsarian, historical experience shattered, scattered, and no longer necessarily identified with gender. When the Earth tilts on its axis and animals prey upon one another, husbands exert power by force over wives and kings hold power over people, quite apart from the purposes for power in society. In this condition, putting men in charge of women, or kings in charge of societies, will not reveal or return to humans the divinely shaped hierarchy they have lost.

Milton's telling of the judgment in the Garden requires us to link the words he takes from Genesis to the behavior of the Son, both Judge (using the gift that was the perfection of Adam) and Savior (using the gift that was the perfection of Eve) (10.209). Right here we are at the heart of Miltonic hierarchy, as Diane McColley and others have well explained. God disdained not to take upon him the form of a servant for humanity's sake, to cover humankind with his robe of righteousness. Like the father of a family, he clothes their nakedness (*PL* 10.215–16); like a mother, he takes their punishment on himself and dies to save their lives (10.74–75). This, Milton shows, is hierarchy in the divine model, the God-given prototype for human governance.

Where in this divine prototype is the "real dignitie" in which Adam's perfection, his ability to govern, excelled Eve's? It is present in the act of judgment performed by the Son, the great vice-gerent governor (*PL* 5.605–10). As readers knowing that the Son who adjudicates will pay the penalty exacted, we are strongly reminded in book 10, before we plunge with Adam into the history lessons of books 11 and 12, that however valuable government is, it is temporary. Eventually, even the King Divine will lay aside his scepter and God's creative power will be all in all. If we take as a symbol or paradigmatic shape of the ultimate kingdom of God not the vertical ladder or chain, but the circle of the great dance, then we can more readily see that governing, with its real and important "dignitie," is not ultimately the greatest exercise of power (*PL* 5.620–27). The power for the dance of being consists in holding the dancers together, holding all in motion in relationship to one another; it is the ability to mediate as the Son mediates. This is the ability to build a just society. It is not power of one part over another, but power for the whole. It is "mixing" proclamation of truth with "intercession sweet" (*PL* 10.228).[35]

So Milton's creative actualization of the scriptural judgment of Adam in the Garden reveals it to be a passage that embodies a "dangerous memory" of foundational justice. It very clearly shows that "power over" other subjects in governance, while a good, is not more important than "power for" calling free subjects into right relationship; it shows that there is no divinely ordained private world apart from the public good; it shows "woman" as originally gifted with this "power for"; it points to the exercise of this power at the end of time.

On the other hand, Milton has the Son simply repeat the biblical judgment of Eve that subordinates women in marriage (10.196). Although Milton's redaction of the judgment in the Garden is certainly not misogynistic, it is, unlike other parts of his epic, androcentric. His focus here is on understanding Adam's guilt in depth. Because he does not "actualize" the judgment of Eve, he allows this part of the story to point unhindered to the oppression that women have experienced throughout history — in those 100,000 tyrannical marriages lamented by Mary Astell and thoroughly acknowledged by Lucy Hutchinson herself when she treats the judgment in *Order and Disorder*.[36]

When read through the lens of feminist liberation theology, then, the call for Milton's readers is, while naming the potential for women's oppression with precision, to work for the liberation of women and all oppressed and marginalized people through the paradigm of original liberty contained in the dangerous memory that his poem reopens for use in the present historical moment.

7 • "The Ramifications of Those Ramifications"
Compounding Contexts for *Samson Agonistes*

Joseph Wittreich

"The one possibility no one has been willing to entertain (except for Samson . . .) is that there is no sense to be seen . . . , and it is this possibility that Samson thrusts in our face."
— Stanley Fish, *How Milton Works*

Milton criticism, initially drawing its leads from contexts narrowly defined and restrictive in application, is progressively taking direction from contexts compounding, steadily shifting, multiplying in number, and often eliding with one another. Stanley Fish gets it exactly right: in Milton's poetry, "context keeps expanding,"[1] not infinitely so, but so much so that it is almost as if Milton's last poems prophesy the postmodern proposition that "a multiplicity of contexts determines how influential . . . [a poem] will be."[2] The "surprise," as opposed to the "enterprise" of contextualization,[3] as far as Milton's writings are concerned, comes from watching Milton's poetry of contexts modulating into a poetry affording a proliferation of contexts for subsequent literature, sacred and secular, in so many of which instances, in active interplay, the texts and contexts, in their interdependencies, are also mutually illuminating.

Arguably the most influential of Milton's living critics, Stanley Fish has been chided for his indifference to contexts, both historical and political, by a critic who ups the ante by extending a limitation persistently acknowledged by Fish (one on which he prides himself) into areas of Fish's demonstrated expertise. According to this critic, *How Milton Works* is not only "routinely indifferent to history and politics" but "disregards context altogether — political, historical, religious, literary."[4] It is in those final exclusions — contexts, *religious, literary* — where, to this critic, *How Milton Works* seems not to work at all that it works so cunningly, both in its theoretical peregrinations and its interpretive maneuvers. Fish never loses sight of the aesthetic component of either Milton's antinomianism or Arminianism, nor of the theological and ideological connections (and disconnections) between *De Doctrina Christiana* and Milton's last poems. Milton's rebellious writings find their counterpart in Fish's provocative readings.

I. "Ambiguity . . . Retained"

> "Milton's answer is to shift the emphasis in the story from the so-called climactic act (which he renders radically mysterious) to the decision to move into the space in which that act becomes a possible one, a decision that is itself marked by a radical uncertainty."
>
> — Stanley Fish, *How Milton Works*[5]

It was still being said at the end of the nineteenth century (and it continues to be said today) that "Samson was a hero raised up by Heaven" and that, correspondingly, "Milton viewed himself . . . as raised up by Heaven."[6] Yet few who say so acknowledge, much less document, Milton's emerging suspicion of an idea that, for a while, had caught him within its embrace. Would that Milton "had considered . . . the wildness of fanaticism and enthusiasm," writes one of his eighteenth century critics.[7] In that complaint, however, the commentator crafts the bold outlines of a critique, which Milton begins in *The Tenure of Kings and Magistrates,* suppresses in *Pro Populo Anglicano Defensio,* and, eventually renewing his epics, threads through his entire tragedy. Within its scaffolding, *Samson Agonistes* may contain assumptions previously credited by Milton, but the failure of the revolution seems to have left Milton with an urgent need to reexamine those assumptions — where they lead and how to modify them, especially those that breed contempt, foster cruelty, and foment violence. Kindled not by the energy of the historical moment but by its fanaticism and frustrations, *Samson Agonistes* is a protest poem in every aspect: in its epistle, even in its generic and prosodic forms, directing "a counterblast"[8] at the Restoration, in its aesthetics and politics, as well as in the theological tenets and religious values subtending both.

During the heyday of the revolution, Milton had been quick to align Oliver Cromwell's successes with divine favor, indeed to see himself no less than Cromwell's army, as God's ally in these victories. Thus, in *Defensio Secunda,* in possession of "an inward and far surpassing light," Milton writes (as he had similarly done in his peroration to *Pro Populo Anglicano Defensio*), "If God wished those men to achieve such noble deeds, He also wished that there be other men by whom those deeds, once done, might be worthily praised and extolled, and that the truth defended by arms should also be defended by reason — the only defence truly appropriate to man" (YP 4:553; compare 4:536). Earlier, in *Elegia Quinta,* Milton imagines himself in a state of "sacred frenzy" (*CP,* 89) and then, in *Ad Patrem,* invokes those exemplary bards of former times, those apparently Samson-like bards with "flowing locks" (*CP,* 159).

Poetry and prose, at least initially, do not possess equal claims to inspiration. In *The Reason of Church-Government,* "an inward prompting which now grew daily upon me" (YP 1:810) comes upon Milton the poet, whereas in *An Apology for a Pamphlet,* with "the example of *Luther,*" Milton the polemicist is quick to challenge those who "think inspiration only the warrant thereof" when "judgement" itself may better explain polemical vehemence (YP 1:901).

Subsequently, yet before Milton celebrates Cromwell as an agent of providence, in *Eikonoklastes* he mocks Charles for laying claim to it: "Most men are too apt . . . to interpret and expound the judgements of God, and all other events of providence or chance, as makes most to the justifying of their own cause . . . ; and attribute all to the particular favour of God towards them" (YP 3:428–29). A man of violence, Charles exhibits "an excessive eagerness to be aveng'd" (YP 3:379). An agent in "horrid massacher" (YP 3:470), himself "caus[ing] the slaughter of so many thousands" (YP 3:481), Charles, as here represented by Milton, according to these remarks, may evoke the Miltonic adage that "judgement rashly given ofttimes involves the Judge himself" (YP 3:481). Indeed, Milton acts as judge when he contends that Charles was put under the power of the army "by God out of his Providence," as Milton says in *The Tenure of Kings and Magistrates* (YP 3:193), and subsequently Charles is executed, in words from *Eikonoklastes,* by "the powerful and miraculous might of God's manifest arms" (YP 3:555). In yet another transference of such rhetoric, in *Pro Populo Anglicano Defensio,* William Laud, along with Salmasius, is upbraided for "proclaim[ing] that he was archbishop 'by the providence of God'" (YP 4:481).

If *The Tenure of Kings and Magistrates* and *Eikonoklastes* are companion pieces of sorts, the first tract theorizing revolution and the second affording an apologia for the revolutionaries, the latter tract, in crucial moments, also counters the claims of the former one. Yet *The Tenure of Kings and Magistrates* is the more telling text, for even as it removes the taint of enthusiasm and zealotry from the army, which exhibited both, even as it taunts the ministers for whom "Providence . . . must be the drum, . . . the word of command, that calls them from above" and who, in "thir postures and thir motions" lay claim to both, it also cites among its authorities in the second edition the likes of Peter Martyr and Martin Luther (YP 3:243–58). For them, claims to inspiration are meaningless without the certification of divine commission and permissible only when acts proceed from a public, never a private, person — a distinction Milton had blurred in the first edition of *The Tenure of Kings and Magistrates,* only to reinstate it here.

In this prose work, still more telling is the following remark, which, without naming Samson, seems to comprehend him: "For if all human power to execute, not accidentally but intendedly, the wrathe of God upon evil doers without exception, be of God; then that power, whether ordinary, or . . . *extraordinary* so executing that intent of God, is lawfull and not to be resisted" (YP 3:198; my italics). *Eikonoklastes,* as well as *Pro Populo Anglicano Defensio,* will then credit the army with the divine instigation that *The Tenure of Kings and Magistrates* denies it. In a parallel maneuver, Milton has the protagonist of *Samson Agonistes* exclaim, "I begin to feel / Some rouzing motions in me which dispose / To something *extraordinary* my thoughts" (1381–83; my italics). But Milton will also compound uncertainty in his tragedy by pressing the questions of whether the poem's climactic action is divinely commissioned or of Samson's "own accord" (1643).

In *Pro Populo Anglicano Defensio,* Milton avers that, "chang[ing] circumstances . . . through the agency of men," God opens a path for the revolutionaries to follow: "We followed him . . . with reverence for the traces of the divine presence at every step we entered on a path surrounded by no shadows,

but rather illumined by his guidance" (YP 4:394–95, 305).
Accordingly, victories were accomplished "not without divine
inspiration" (YP 4:537). Moreover, if they were guided by
"divine inspiration," so too were Milton's defenses of their
efforts, which with "the same assistance and guidance" were
themselves divinely wrought (YP 4:537, 536). Milton, the
exemplar of a changing mind, thought in the late 1640s and
early 1650s that events could not have happened but by the
will of God. But by the late 1650s, as Cromwell would come
to do, Milton cast suspicion on such claims, arguing in *A
Treatise of Civil Power* that "no man can know at all times"
if "divine illumination . . . be in himself" (YP 7:242).

As with prophetic illumination, so with prayer. Milton's early
poetic career climaxed in the crisis lyric, *Lycidas,* a poem that
completes the poetic volume *Justa Edovardo King Naufrago*
with the heroic image of Edward King kneeling in prayer as
his ship goes down. The revolution itself began with heroic
images of Samson at prayer — with Samson as an icon for the
New Model Army and as an example of force with force tri-
umphing ("force with force / Is well ejected" [1206–07]). Yet
the revolution continues with the infamous portrait of Charles
at prayer, published as the frontispiece to *Eikon Basilike,* then
ridiculed by Milton in *Eikonoklastes* as "a masking scene" (YP
3:342–43). Not only does the revolution end with Samson having lost much of his power to inspire by force of example, hence
with Milton's finally leaving open the question of whether
Samson is (or is not) at prayer in the moments just before the
temple comes down. Milton, apparently, became increasingly
suspicious of public worship and pietistic prayer, in *Samson
Agonistes* moving back and forth from God's causing "a foun-
tain at thy prayer / From the dry ground to spring" (581–82),
to "one prayer yet remains," a prayer for "speedy death"
(649–50), to a world seemingly "deaf / To prayers" (960–61),
to the question, why do our prayers "draw a scorpion's tail
behind" (360), and ultimately to the equivocation in which

Samson is described "as one who prayed, / *Or* some great matter in his mind revolved" (1637–38; my italics).

Perhaps Milton sensed, as Heymann Steinthal would later state, that the prayer when Samson worries he may die of thirst is but "a fiction," humanizing a character, eventually all too human, when in the Book of Judges he "prays to be endowed with strength to avenge the loss of one of his eyes." When Samson dies, he "remains dead," his story then inviting the inference that not Samson but Israel is this story's "hero."[9] In an illustration to *Samson Agonistes* by Richard Westall, the Messenger, not a figure of piety but an image of horror, "is represented as imitating the attitude of Samson performing what he relates."[10] The illustration does not let us forget Milton's injunction in *Eikonoklastes:* "Privat praiers in publick, ask something of who they ask not, and that shall be thir reward" (YP 3:97). In *Samson Agonistes,* the Chorus appeals to a contrarious God that "he turn / . . . [Samson's] labours, for thou canst, to peaceful end" (708–09), yet despite its appeal cannot avert the temple catastrophe, whether or not it occurs with Samson in an attitude of prayer. Whether in its theorizing of tragedy, or in its reinterpretation of the Samson story, Milton's poem, perhaps more so than Penn ever thought, "anticipated . . . latest opinion,"[11] at once reconstituting the genre of tragedy and revising interpretation of the story he casts into it.

In *The Tenure of Kings and Magistrates* and then in *A Treatise of Civil Power* and *Samson Agonistes,* the rhetoric of inspiration, there in profusion in Milton's tragedy, is nonetheless eyeballed with suspicion. It is language coded into the preliminary matter — the "persuaded inwardly" of the Argument to *Samson Agonistes* and thereupon woven through the entire poem: "inward light" (162), "motioned . . . of God" (222), "intimate impulse" (223), "divine impulsion" and "prompting" (422), "divine instinct" (526), "work from heaven imposed" (565), "command from heaven" (1212), "part from heaven assigned" (1217), "Some rousing motions" (1382), "presage in the mind" (1387), "spirit . . . rushed on thee" (1453), "With inward eyes illuminated" (1689). Samson's entire life, its every episode (as he would have it) is a fulfillment of "divine prediction" (44). It is as if Milton is here moving toward the more mocking posture, in another century, assumed by the American President John Adams: "It will never be pretended that any person employed . . . [in national leadership] had interviews with the gods, or was in any degree under the inspiration of Heaven."[12] It can only be deplored, moreover, that, as Adams thinks, the tales, legends, and sagas often assimilated to Jewish and Christian revelation have had the effect of bloodying those religions. Indeed, what Adams implies is that it is no act of heroism but one of presumption to declare that God is on one's side, but an act of heroic humility to ask, or simply to hope, that a nation's actions put it on the side of God and not at odds with him. The prayer is not that he be on our side but that we be on his.

The Samson story, it now seems, is the tragedy of a nation mapped in the migratory journey of the tribe of Dan from the extreme southwest of Palestine to the extreme north — from Gaza (in Samson's day, an opulent city, "the outpost of Africa, the door of Asia,"[13] an intellectual and commercial center superior to any city in Palestine, a place Samson leaves in ruins), to Dan, which becomes a ruined city, with justice itself in ruins, as the Danites destroy this city, in the process turning their newly founded habitation into a place of idol worship. Moreover, in Samson's tragedy, in this national tragedy, is writ the tragedy of the world: "the breakdown of the public body," "[t]he whole world structure . . . brought down," "the overthrow of the world."[14] Such is the dire warning of the Samson story, especially as it is unfurled in Milton's poem, where the demise of an individual is irrevocably involved with the defeat of a nation. If *Samson Agonistes* commences with its protagonist imaging himself as a "Sepulcher, a moving Grave" (102), it concludes in the recognition, to adopt the words of Paulus Cassel, that the temple itself, in "a terrific crash," becomes "a vast sepulchre."[15] As the Israelites go in search of Samson's body, "Soaked in his enemies' blood" (1725), we are witnesses less to "A life heroic" (1711) than to "Blood, death, and deathful deeds" as nearly a "whole inhabitation perish[es]" (1512, 1514). The fate of Samson is thus written into the eventual fate of the Danites, which then is written into the fate of the Philistines. It may well be that Johann Gottfried Herder's grasp of the intricacies of the Samson narrative caused him to conclude that "the life of man may be considered as a miniature of the fate of nations."[16] In the Samson story, biography and history converge — apocalyptically.

II. *"Interpretive Disputes"*

> "[I]t is on the point of interpretive help that *Samson Agonistes* departs from any of the models Milton might have known . . . we find ourselves bereft of interpretive resources, impotent before the very story whose meanings were once so firmly in our grasp."
>
> — Stanley Fish, *How Milton Works*

Criticism may commence in the study of contexts for Milton's poetry, yet, in a turn of the lens, it climaxes with a glimpse at Milton's last poems as a context for history not just in Milton's time but in our own. The centrality of the past and the present to *Samson Agonistes*, it appears, has a reach beyond the poem itself. More than of their own age, Milton's last poems, as Peter Bayne suggests, are the morning of its future.[17] It is no wonder, then, that in the second decade of the last century, as he moved to assess Milton's modernity, Martin Larson got so many essential matters right: most important, that "an emancipated student of the past," Milton was "the herald of an age" that would eventually dawn; and that, increasingly apprehensive of "orthodox Christianity" as exemplified in "The Passion," and worrying over his "utter inability to think himself into that state of mind which is the essence of Christianity," Milton transgressed and transfigured both the Bible and the Christian orthodoxy founded upon it, in the process modifying Christian mythology and humanizing Christianity itself. *Paradise Lost,* though, has more "discordant or contradictory" elements than Larson thinks, which, in their turn, pave the way for *Paradise Regained* and *Samson Agonistes* — poems published together that mark new directions in Milton's thinking as well as evidence of its persisting uncertainties.[18]

By way of acknowledging that Milton wrote his last poems in the future tense, the defining poets of British Romanticism, Blake and Wordsworth, summon him to spiritual adventure. Uniting with Blake, Milton lends a hand to building "Jerusalem / In England's green & pleasant Land"; and in an apostrophe, Wordsworth declares: "Milton! thou shouldst be living at this hour: / England hath need of thee: . . . / Oh! Raise us up, return to us again."[19] The Romantics mince no words: Milton *matters* as a poet who, in *Paradise Lost* and *Paradise Regained,* is seen (most notably by the Shelleys) as the prophetic soul of the wide world, dreaming on things to come, and who, in *Samson Agonistes,* is seen as a prophetic tragedian, warning future generations of catastrophes that, if not awake to their missions, they will fail to avert.

One may think of Percy Bysshe Shelley's momentarily unheroic Prometheus, "eyeless in hate," evoking Milton's Samson, "Eyeless in *Gaza*" (*SA* 41); or of Count Cenci rejoicing in the catastrophe where "most favoring Providence was shown / Even in the manner of . . . [his young sons'] deaths":

> For Rocco
> Was kneeling at the mass, with sixteen others,
> When the Church fell and crushed him to a mummy,
> The rest escaped unhurt.[20]

The last of those lines contains a hauntingly ironic echo of the verse from *Samson Agonistes,* "The vulgar only escaped" (1659). Correspondingly, the Samson story, probably impressed upon Mary Shelley's consciousness by a recent reading of *Samson Agonistes,* is invoked by the Monster who, "torn" by "supernatural force . . . from . . . [Felix's], father," is then "dashed . . . to the ground and struck . . . violently," but who also initially resists such retaliatory gestures, even if he "could have torn . . . [Felix] limb for limb, as the lion rends the antelope." In contrast, Victor Frankenstein, "trembling with passion, tore to pieces" the female monster he was in the process of creating, causing the creature to withdraw, "with a howl of devilish despair and revenge."[21]

Mary Shelley's novel forces the question not only of who is the modern Prometheus but of who is the modern-day Samson. Is it the Creature who is thrown to the ground by Felix as Samson would do to Harapha, running upon him, "And with one buffet lay thy structure low," and "then dash thee down" (1237–40)? Or is the modern-day Samson Frankenstein who tears apart the female creature as Samson threatens to do to Dalila, "if fierce remembrance wake / My sudden rage to tear thee joint by joint" (951–52) and as formerly he had torn "the Lion, as the Lion tears the Kid" (128)? Samson is as desirous of "mortal fight" with Harapha (1175) as Frankenstein is of "mortal conflict" with the Creature.[22] In imitation of Samson, it seems, Victor Frankenstein, under the guidance of providence, "the spirits that I had invoked to aid me," and acting in accordance with a "purpose . . . assigned to me by heaven," performs as avenger and destroyer, as one of God's "ministers of vengeance,"[23] in contrast to the moment in *Paradise Lost* when "the angry Victor" recalls "His Ministers of vengeance" (*PL* 1.169–70). This vengeful god, with ministers of his wrath, is not Milton's God but, rather, as Milton's poem testifies, God as he is perceived and portrayed by Satan.

What the Shelleys drive home, as if in collaboration with Lord Byron, is that much "heterodox opinion,"[24] much audacity, is inscribed in both *Paradise Lost* and *Samson Agonistes,* the latter of which poems "Milton keeps tragic to the last."[25] As poet-historian, Milton comprehended the efficacy of analogies for the understanding of history; and thus, as much as the Bible provided him, he provides us, especially through his last poems, not just with apt analogies for but with mythic paradigms of our history, past and present: of paradise lost and eventually recovered and, in *Samson Agonistes,* of history as both a tale of tyranny and terrorism. In this regard, a remark by G. Wilson Knight still pertains: "that within his greater poetry the action . . . shape[s] itself into one remarkable prefiguration of our own gigantic, and itself archetypal, world-conflict."[26] If the point of the argument is moral condemnation or approbation, the analogies predictably gather around Milton's Satan or Messiah. Alternatively, if the objective is moral analysis, the analogies are more likely afforded by Milton's Samson as seen in different relations with all those people who, again if I may borrow words from Knight, "ruthlessly override ethical objections in obedience to an all-demanding intuition, considering themselves . . . the 'scourge of God.' "[27] Milton's last poems are less about heroes than about the problematics of heroism. Biography and history are inextricably entwined, the character of the individual and the state of the nation. Whom do we encounter in Milton's tragedy, "Shemshûm el Jebbâr, 'Samson the Hero'" — or a character like the prime minister, Levi Eshkol, remarkable for his own magnanimity, once called "Shimshon der Nebechdikker — Samson the nerd"?[28] In *Samson,* do we discover a nation in its invincibility or vulnerability, in its strength or helplessness — or a nation that is a split image, a divided entity?

At the beginning of the twentieth century, urging its "sublime dialogue" and tragic ironies upon the reader, the biblical exegete G. H. S. Walpole identified *Samson Agonistes* as a fit guide to, and ample meditation upon, Judges 16:23–31, arguing, "There is no prayer for the vindication of God's glory such as Milton fondly imagines," but in Judges, "only the natural wish for personal vengeance." In this story, by repeatedly laying claim to divine inspiration, Samson attributes all he does to God; hence, he is certain "that God will avenge Himself," but within a "history," as Walpole concludes, which "gives us no reason to believe that Samson's chief desire was to glorify God by his death." Eventually, inevitably, the contrast between Samson and Christ (owing to their respective death scenes) comes into focus. The prayer Walpole thinks is in Milton's poem is not, thus underscoring the contrast between Samson asking his God for vengeance against the Philistines and Christ asking forgiveness for his tormentors. In their respective death scenes, according to Walpole, Samson reveals "no . . . penitence, only a thirst for vengeance," in contrast with the "patience and meekness" of Christ who never, as Samson does, cries out for revenge "but only for the salvation of His enemies." In his death, Samson hopes to destroy the world that Christ would save. "Samson died as he lived," Walpole concludes, and thus a "life that might have been great was one of destruction for selfish purposes, . . . summed up in the words, 'He slew more in his death than he did in his life.'"[29]

These are contrasts, though Walpole never quite says so, that Milton's poem forces into consciousness and that emerge from the uncertainty in *Samson Agonistes* concerning whether the protagonist's final action, his destruction of the temple, is God's doing — or Samson's own. In view of seventeenth century representations of Samson as a hero of prayer, especially in the opening pages of the prayer book for the New Model Army, the uncertainty concerning Samson's prayer in Milton's poem — "he stood as one who pray'd, / *Or* some great matter in his mind revolv'd" (1637–38; my italics), the obvious excision of the supposed words of Samson's prayer from the text of Milton's poem — these details make it likely that, here in *Samson Agonistes*, Milton prosecutes a tradition of representation that the Puritan revolutionaries had promulgated earlier.

Eventually, and in greater detail than is possible here, we need to take stock of what Hans Robert Jauss would describe as the huge "hermeneutic difference between the former and the current understanding of a work," in this instance of *Samson Agonistes*, by way of "rais[ing] to consciousness the history of its reception."[30] Perhaps surprisingly, in the instance of *Samson Agonistes*, hermeneutic distance broadens rather than narrows over time. The literary past of Milton's tragedy is thus retrieved by recent criticism (seldom knowingly) as it draws past interpretations into the present and develops as well as deepens them with new contextualizations, thereby situating *Samson Agonistes* within a new conversation in which Milton's tragedy functions as a shadow text, which is more elusive than the usual context or subtext.

Lest anyone think that the interpretation here embraced is a distinctly postmodernist phenomenon, let us remember that, if the typological or regenerationist reading of *Samson Agonistes* is fixed by George Frederick Handel's *Samson: An Oratorio* (composed in 1742), "the reading" of Milton's tragedy we now associate first with John Carey and Irene Samuel was already in place, embryonically, before Milton's death, in Andrew Marvell's dedicatory poem to *Paradise Lost* and its depiction of Samson, "grop[ing] the temple's posts in spite." The trajectory of one interpretive line moves from Marvell; to Dr. Johnson, who ascribes the plaudits often bestowed on *Samson Agonistes* to "ignorance" and "bigotry"; to Shelley's Samson-like Prometheus ("eyeless in hate"); to Mary Shelley's avengers (both Frankenstein and his creature); to James Montgomery's Samson, who in his fallenness and transgression is linked to Satan within a poem, "uninviting both in its theme and the treatment of it"; and, finally, to George Gilfillan's Samson, whose hand, as he stands at the pillars, "has few flowers in it. . . . His spirit is that of Abimelech," and whose actions within the poem bare "the wrath of Heaven" and threaten "to crush wonder . . . rather than to awaken . . . admiration."[31]

What began as a commendation of Milton's ethic over that of Samson, in time, deepens into a condemnation of Milton and Samson as representatives of the same ethical system, with Peter Bayne, in the grip of what he calls "the Puritan Samson Agonistes," concluding that "[t]he spiritual depths of Christianity, the Divine power of kindness and self-sacrifice, were fully fathomed" in *none* of Milton's last poems, wherein dwells instead "the inspiration of Puritan battle."[32] Yet as if in response to Bayne, and in a gesture that returns to Marvell's condemnation of Samson, but commendation of Milton, J. Howard B. Masterman in 1897 sought to free *Samson Agonistes* from a politics of violence and religion of retaliation. Here in Milton's poem is *the tragedy of Puritanism,* which, he says, "appears as the blind and discredited champion of Divine Vengeance," now hostage to a "brute secular force" and to "religious seductions" that "might hope to strike one more blow for freedom," only to "perish in the overthrow of its enemies." The whole point of Milton's 1671 poetic volume, Masterman supposes, is to present as "a great alternative . . . the victory of patience and self-repression — the Divine overcoming of evil with good"; to choose as "the better part . . . to be patient" and, despite the penalty of disappointment, "to hope."[33] Or, put differently, the question lurking between the covers of this poetic volume is whether Milton's head was filled with the hardest and most dismal tenets of Calvinism, or whether, instead, those tenets, embedded in *Samson Agonistes* to be sure, are signatures of the atrophying world of Milton's tragedy, not of the new paradise he envisions.

It simply will not do to argue that "Heterodox views put forward in nine pages of a book [by John Carey] intended for students would probably have received little scholarly attention had Carey not also edited *Samson* in Longman's Annotated English Poets series,"[34] for those "heterodox" views were already inscribed within the critical tradition evolving from *Samson Agonistes* as early as Andrew Marvell. Moreover, because they are also a part of the Samson hermeneutic, the next question is whether, through the influence of Milton's tragedy, those same elements by the end of the nineteenth century are secured within biblical commentary pertaining to the Samson story. If influence once reached from the Bible to Milton, does it now redound from Milton's poem on to biblical exegesis?

An alternative tradition of *Samson* criticism is enabling because it presses old questions upon us, but allows for new solutions to them, in this way drawing *Samson Agonistes* out of relative seclusion, even as it releases meanings over time embedded in literary works, through new and opportune con-textualizations. One such context begins to assert itself when, instead of asking about the Bible's influence on Milton, we con-sider, alternatively, Milton's influence on the Bible; that is, the extent to which, like *Paradise Lost* and *Paradise Regained*, Milton's biblical tragedy is eventually involved in shaping a new hermeneutic, in this instance of the Samson story. What kind of presence does *Samson Agonistes* have in biblical com-mentary written subsequent to it, and what do we learn about Milton's poem from a biblical hermeneutic subtly shaped by it? The crucial century is the nineteenth, and the important years the later ones in that century, by which time it is con-ceded, "The noblest conception of . . . [Samson] in modern poetry, is that of Milton's *Samson Agonistes*." Yet this con-cession is also accompanied by uneasiness over Milton's "treat[ing] only the end of Samson's life, and notwithstanding its lofty thought and Christian fervor disfigures the beautiful simplicity of Scripture by operatic additions."[35] Milton's addi-tions signal hermeneutic trouble, even as they herald new interpretive possibilities.

Nevertheless, Milton continues to be invoked on both sides of a divided Samson hermeneutic, now as a proponent of a more dignified representation of Samson and now as an author who would deepen the tragedy of *Samson Agonistes* by revising the Judges narrative so that Manoa, by Milton's account "still alive at the time of Samson's catastrophe," is no longer spared the sorrow of Samson's final days.[36] W. A. Scott is yet another commentator of the latter half of the nineteenth century who, if critical of Milton's ambivalence toward his protagonist, nonetheless illustrates the impact of Milton's poem on an evolving Samson hermeneutic, one feature of which is that the scriptural story of Samson, and Milton's version of it, blur indistinguishably into one another. Milton is therefore a signally important authority when redactions and supplements of Scripture become both tests of the truth of the Judges history and radical complications of it.

Scott's title page epigraph — "there will I build him / A monument" (1733–1742) — is from *Samson Agonistes,* as are many of the epigraphs appended to individual chapters of this commentary, where Milton's tragedy is a regular point of reference, as well as a valuable guide through interpretive cruxes, such as when Samson is "persuaded *inwardly*" to go to the temple or when, on the evidence of "Samson's prayer," he is redeemed for heroism. Scott lets interpretive tensions sit on the surface of his commentary, for example, conceding that, taken whole, the scriptural history of Samson may discourage the invocation of him as an exemplary model: "Samson's acts are more for wonder than for our imitation."[37]

Yet that said, if Milton is chided for his failure to appreciate fully (and to admire) Samson's character, putting into his mouth as he hurls down the temple a "dying speech . . . not true to the text, nor worthy of the occasion," Scott rebukes Milton for producing a Samson insufficiently heroic, hence inadequately revealing "zeal for the divine glory" and unready to fulfill in his death the promised deliverance, "the mission for which he had been raised up."[38] Redeeming his divine commission, Samson should have redeemed both himself and his people. If not Milton's Samson, the Samson Scott envisions resembles one who, in the twentieth century, will come to be associated with William Riley Parker, F. Michael Krouse, and the whole regenerationist tradition of *Samson* criticism that, with a powerful reach into scriptural commentary, produces the regenerate Samson of James L. Crenshaw: a Samson defeated in life, triumphant in death, his tragedy metamorphosing into a divine comedy. And Crenshaw's Samson is, from his vantage point, Milton's Samson, depicted "as one who correctly perceived divine purpose behind his stirrings of passion." Yet the generic casting Crenshaw gives to the Samson story "as a tragic-comedy" is precisely the one Milton would tear from it,[39] and in such a way that commentators are forced to countenance in Samson both "savagery and recklessness."[40]

This Samson, whose history is one of "moral declension," "one of the most sad and most awful, histories in the whole Bible," is, as Christopher Wordsworth portrays him, an example of the abuse of scriptural gifts, "the miserable consequences of such misuse, and thus . . . a solemn warning." Known for his acts "of cruelty . . ., and of wanton destruction . . . , and of vindictive spite," Samson, his history "a *warning* . . . sends us to Christ" as a countermodel. As if in response to Scott's heroized Samson, including Scott's complaint about Milton's seeming ambivalence concerning Samson's heroism, Wordsworth remembers that "*Milton* . . . in his Samson Agonistes, near the end, introduces Manoah as burying . . . [Samson] and building him a monument," but in such a way as to blame Samson's miseries on his nuptial choices rather than, more broadly, on "his misuse of God's gifts, his vain-glorious self-confidence, forgetfulness of God, and disobedience to His will and word." As if in a postscript to Milton's tragedy and as an elucidation of it, Wordsworth complains that Milton is not critical enough of a "Samson . . . [who] did not leave God to work out His own vindication by lawful means, but endeavored to obtain his ends by means which involved self-destruction, for which indeed he prayed. *An unhappy end.*"[41]

If a new hermeneutic is moving into place, it is in a place partially secured by the interrogations and probings of *Samson Agonistes*. A case in point is an 1882 commentary that invokes lines from Milton's tragedy to describe Samson's death. Having already cited Milton as the representer and interpreter of Samson par excellence, J. J. Lias depicts a far more complicated Samson, often taken as a type of his country, whose story emerges as a profound critique of its culture. The Samson story *in context* is both an index to the morals of the Israelites, a mirror on the connection between apostasy and national ruin, and a protest against base ideas of God then in currency, with Samson himself revealing "a picture of human nature . . . unsubdued by the Gospel of Christ." In a commentary that resists any alignment between Samson and Christ, Lias emphasizes that Samson, who "cannot be said to have in any sense delivered Israel," is driven from beginning to end by revenge. Vengeance, according to Lias, is "the matured intention of Samson's mind": "[He] had not learned the deeper lesson: 'Vengeance is Mine . . .' The whole picture of Samson is admirably consistent with what we elsewhere learn of the man and his age."[42]

One thing is certain: by the 1880s, it was commonplace to urge that students of the Bible "would do well to refer to Milton's 'Samson Agonistes,'"[43] not merely for a glimpse of the heroic Samson but for the revelation of a Samson ambiguous, even defective, in his heroism. In 1885, *Samson Agonistes* is cited again, this time by A. R. Fausset, within a commentary which, finding that the judges themselves imperfectly realized the divine ideal, that their degeneracy ushers in earthly monarchy, also represents Samson as "a strange compound — an embodied paradox," indeed a "strange combination of paradoxes": one who is a judge but who leaves justice in seeming ruins; one who, mocking others, is himself mocked; who, though he never delivers his people, manifests the eventual possibility of doing so; and who, even if as ·"the embodied type, *"the type of Messiah, especially in his death,"* falls way short of him: "The Antitype infinitely exceeds the type: Samson prayed for vengeance, Christ prayed for the forgiveness of his murderers. Samson died to crush his foes with him; Christ died for His enemies. . . . Samson fell to rise no more; Jesus died to rise again."[44]

By the second decade of the twentieth century, Abram Smythe Palmer, threading into his commentary references to *Samson Agonistes*, presents some intriguing variations on the usual rendering of the Samson story, the new landscape of which, if I may draw upon one of Palmer's sources, resembles "the panorama of the places" from which Samson came and to which he goes, this topography "serv[ing] as text, so to speak, to . . . the artless but interesting commentaries, which checked, completed, and sometimes even contradicted one another, according to the turns of the conversation or the personal character of the speakers."[45] In the background of Palmer's commentary are the following accounts:

> At ʿAin Shemĕs there is the sanctuary of Abu Meîzar. Abu Meîzar is a nickname, meaning "the father of the woollen mantle or head-dress." One Christian feast day Abu Meîzar penetrated into the church, disguised as a monk. He seized hold of the central column sustaining the building, crying: *Ya Kudret Allah,* "O power of God," and overthrew the church, which fell in ruins and crushed the congregation.[46]

A place of ruins nearby, we are told, was similarly an arena for slaughter and massacre, where soldiers lopped off heads and left brothers slain.

Later, at "ʿAin Shemĕs, well-established as the counterpart of the Beth-Shemesh of the Bible," was discovered yet another "version of the legend of Abu Meîzar, who was also called . . . *Abu'l ʿÂzem* and Shemshûm el Jebbâr, 'Samson the hero' ":

There was once at R'meileh, which is the ancient name of 'Ain Shemĕs, a church of infidels. Abu Meîzar said to the inhabitants of Sar'a . . ., his native place: "What will you give me, if I kill the Christians and destroy their church?" "We will give you a quarter of the country," they answered him. Then Abu Meîzar entered into the church, where he found the Christians assembled for prayer, and pulled it down on top of them and him, by giving a mighty kick of the column, crying, *"Ya Rabb!"* "O Lord!" He had said previously to his compatriots at Sar'a, "Search in R'meîleh, you will find me lying on my back, and the Christians on their bellies . . ." The old people say: *"beîn Sar'a û Beît el Jemâl enkatal Shemshûm el Jebbâr,"* between Sar'a and Beît el Jemâl the hero Samson was killed.[47]

Palmer then uses these accounts to explain his own Samson, who, characterized by "grotesque and uncouth methods," "savagery and recklessness," is no enthusiast for political independence and delivery; and whose "tragedy" at the temple is one in which, glimpsing Hercules and Samson, we should also notice that "the place which the story selects for the mighty sun-hero to finish his chequered career in blood and darkness is the most western city of Palestine."[48]

Palmer continues by putting this construction on the tales just related:

A fanatic in modern times has striven to emulate the exploit of Samson. There was a Christian church at 'Ain Shemés . . . , the ancient Beth Shemesh. . . . One Abu Meîzar (otherwise known as Shemshûm el Jebbâr, "Samson the Hero," . . . forced his way into the building, seized hold of the central sustaining column, and, invoking the power of God, pulled it down, overthrowing the church, which fell in ruins and crushed the congregation of fellahin.

From his own version of this newly discovered material, Palmer concludes that, for some, the Samson story, "this equivocal section of the Book of Judges," once lifted from Scriptures, might be relegated to "folk-tale [literature] and other Apocryphal writings" and, quoting Milton on Samson quitting himself like

Samson, contends that "nothing in [Samson's] life became him more than leaving it."[49]

Palmer writes in the wake of commentators like Heinrich Graetz, who think that both "Jephthah and Samson, . . . disregarding order and discipline, brought their powers to bear, as much for evil as for good," with Samson himself faulted, indeed "censured," in Jacob's prophecy of Dan (Gen. 49:16–18) for his deployment of sneaky "stratagems and unexpected attacks," never "improving the state of affairs."[50] For just these reasons, yet another commentator concludes that "the moralizing improvement of the history in the Book of Judges is not carried beyond the story of Jephthah."[51] Samson, according to this same commentator, "while he makes havoc among the Philistines, . . . in no way appears as the champion or deliverer of Israel."[52] Indeed, as Graetz claims, the so-called "hero-judges . . ., especially Jephthah and Samson . . . evince so few of the national characteristics that they might equally well pass for Canaanites, Philistines, or Moabites. Of Samson it has been asserted that he is cast in the mould of the Syrian Hercules."[53]

His own legend a fusion of Eastern and Western mythology, his own person in our time emblematizing Israelis, Muslims, and Christians, Samson is a mirror on every side of a conflict — and a part of each side's rhetoric. In this context, what is so remarkable about *Samson Agonistes* is not Milton's giving shape to this or that reading of the Samson story but, instead, his capturing so ably the contradictions within the scriptural versions and subsequent interpretations of the tale, along with the fissures existing between the known and to-be-discovered versions of the story. That is, Milton's poem embraces a spectrum of Samsons, as does Wiseman's nineteenth century commentary, among them the "malignant savage, ever relentlessly rushing into broils and mortal combat, from the almost fiendish revengefulness of his nature." Yet like Wiseman, Milton refuses to restrict himself to any single delineation, allowing his poem to become, instead, a gallery of portraits, including (without singly endorsing) the Samson of Bishop Wordsworth, who, as we have seen above and as Wiseman is quick to acknowledge, "speaks of Samson as a man who courted self-destruction, whose last act involved a refusal to leave God to work out His own vindication by lawful means, whose dying prayer stands in sad contrast to the dying prayer of our blessed Saviour, and who can only be spoken of as having come to 'an unhappy end.' "[54] The Samson story, owing in part to Milton's intervention, is finally restored to its tragic dimensions.

III. *"Multiple Paths"*

> "Milton again evidences his disinclination to allow us a comfortable perspective on Samson's action. Does he allow us any perspective at all? Are we able to say anything about what Samson has done?"
>
> — Stanley Fish, *How Milton Works*

In the twentieth century, the regenerationist Samson is founded upon the notion that the Milton of *Samson Agonistes* has finally emerged from the chrysalis of political controversy — a very different Milton from the liberationist poet, the subversive cultural presence, in an African-American literary tradition. In his autobiography, Malcolm X numbers Milton among the eye-openers, the awakeners of the people, in part because he is introduced to Milton through the Charles W. Eliot edition, which insists upon the intimate — and mutually illuminating — relation between Milton's poetry and the history of its time. Milton's is a poetry that derives its significance from its own time even as it sheds important light upon it. Milton's is a poetry that, struggling against the outworn creeds of an atrophying religion, obliterates the pastness of the past and that, written emphatically in the present tense, strives to wrest from the present a new future. Unlike King James who, according to Malcolm X, "poetically 'fixed' the Bible . . . and . . . enslaved the world," if in the process the Bible became a "locked door" of deliberately "frustrated understanding," it was Milton, who resisting those who had twisted Christianity into an instrument of oppression, opened the locked doors of Scriptures, in the very process affording "new evidence . . . to document the Muslim teachings": "In . . . The Harvard Classics, I read . . . *Paradise Lost.* The devil, kicked out of paradise, was trying to regain possession. He was using the forces of Europe. . . . I interpreted this to show that the Europeans were motivated and led by the devil, or the personification of the devil. So Milton and Mr. Elijah Muhammad were actually saying the same thing."[55] Indeed, in the very act of unmanacling the mind, Milton, as much as Muhammad, may be said to have revealed "the interrelated meanings, and uses, of the Bible and the Quran,"[56] neither of which, as Malcolm X avows, should be used to justify cruelty and slaughter, to promote a religion of crucifixes and guns, or, as the poet William Blake objected, to hide religion in war. Still, as Michael Lieb has shown, at many points Elijah Muhammad would be at one with Keats in saying that life to Milton is death to me, especially in the emphasis that even Milton's enlightened Christianity gives to the divinity of Jesus and in its privileging of high culture over the culture of the streets.[57]

Malcolm X, on the other hand, like Milton, casts himself in the role of a prophet, but also demythologizes Christianity into the here and now and, in any comparison of Jesus and Samson, would probably emphasize that Jesus works for the betterment of mankind, not its undoing; indeed, that he sacrificed himself for the good of the human race, planting good where others had sown evil. In his own demythologizing of Scriptures, under the cover of paradise lost at the beginning of time, Milton writes of paradise lost now — *now* with the failure of the Puritan revolution; he writes of paradise recovered not on the cross but *here* in the wilderness ("*now* thou hast

regain'd lost paradise . . . / A fairer Paradise is founded *now*"
[4.606–08, 613]), even as he sees in the Samson story another
of those false apocalypses which occur when history reverses
course, turning back again into its former self; when history
has become a dead end, seemingly with no exits. Milton's last
poems, in their very juxtaposition, offer an escape, though;
hence, they are part of the resolution. In fact, Malcolm X sees
himself standing in very much the same relationship with
Martin Luther King Jr. as that struck by *Samson Agonistes* in
relation to *Paradise Regained*. Malcolm X's writings, like
Samson Agonistes, are less an embrace of wanton violence than
a representation of it, without which alternative, without
which representation, it is all the more difficult to embrace,
or yield to, the more pacifist idealisms of Martin Luther King
Jr. or of Milton in *Paradise Regained.* Strength is never enough;
for "[e]ven Samson, the world's strongest man, was destroyed"
and thus is eventually numbered with those who, "mak[ing]
heroes of themselves" by killing, do so on the grounds that this
is what God or "Allah wanted him to do."[58]

Violence in self-defense, anger and hatred as aspects of a just
war — each subtends a theology of violence and religion of
sacrifice, each complicates the world by compromising an ideology of war and peace as it authorizes retaliation and sanctions
aggression in a world where "wanton violence," as Malcolm
X explains, often overwhelms all claims to "justice," where
fighting precludes uniting in common cause and community,
where terrorists terrorize but then are themselves terrorized,
and where all hopes for paradise are *"twisted . . .* [into] pie in
the sky and heaven in the hereafter" instead of heaven "right
here . . . on *this earth . . .* in *this life."* If near the end, his
home bombed by Muslims, Malcom X came to understand that
certain Muslims would kill as long as they thought God willed
them to do so; if he came to ask, what is the Muslim religion
doing to us, where is this thirst for retaliation driving us,
Milton asks similarly, through the joint publication of *Samson*

Agonistes and *Paradise Regained,* What has Judaism done to us through the violence so often sanctioned by the story of Samson? What has Christianity done to us through the violence harbored in — and culturally promulgated — by the Crucifixion story? If Malcolm X could not pinpoint his own philosophy, Milton may have had a similarly difficult time defining his own, managing no more finally than the jostling perspectives of *Paradise Regained* and *Samson Agonistes* and the theological quagmires and ethical bramble bushes into which those poems lead us. It is, nevertheless, the politics of violence, coupled with the promise of a paradise regained, that neither Ralph Ellison nor Toni Morrison addresses in isolation from Milton, even if Ellison does so directly and Morrison only obliquely, each coming to understand with Malcolm X (and presumably Milton) that violence, chartering terror, compromises and often contravenes justice. As Malcolm X might say, Milton was providing black culture with an infusion of "intellectual vitamins."[59]

If there is (and not everyone thinks there is) an *acquist* of wisdom from Milton's tragedy, it is strongly focused by the Judges biographies, newly inflected by Milton's distinctive recasting of the Samson story, and given striking reinforcement by three different novelists (two of them African American) of the last decade — Ralph Ellison, Toni Morrison, and Philip Pullman. Each writer couples the politics of violence and prospects for recovering a lost paradise with the arduous wisdom that "those who reject the lessons of history, or who," in Ellison's words, "allow themselves to be intimidated by its rigors, are doomed to repeat its disasters."[60] In *Juneteenth*, Ellison addresses such a politics and such a promise with explicit reference to the Samson story and, it would seem, in a continuing response to Kenneth Burke's initial labeling of *Samson Agonistes*, if not as "propaganda," then as "moralistic prophecy, . . . a kind of 'literature for use,'" full of "righteous ferocity," by which violence, incorporating with suicide, effects more violence as Samson's wrathful God, authorizing his acts of destruction, also allows for their reenactment. In this reading, *Samson Agonistes*, with its "modalities of holy war" and "theocratic rage," is a "celebration," in "sullen warlike verse," by "a cantankerous old fighter-priest" of a hero who, in the course of translating political controversy into high theology, "talks of patience" but "mouths threats of revenge in the name of God."[61]

At least "*[o]n its face.*"[62] This phrase, to which we will momentarily return, is a complicating gesture in Burke's reading, allowing Ellison to worry, as Morrison also will, that the actions of such people, instead of issuing from God, are a massive force of godless nature and of cultural terrorism. Milton forces us to consider the same issue by juxtaposing Satan and the Son of *Paradise Lost* by letting the Son and Samson face one another as agents of a terror, which, checked by the Son, is unchecked by Samson. Or, as Burke would have it, in the depths of Milton's poem surface identification becomes disidentification as Milton repudiates the philosophy of retaliation, the politics of terror, by annihilating his former self, what he now construes as his satanic self, in the character of Samson.

In the end, Milton may have initially allowed for divine intervention until he became increasingly less certain of the justice, or the virtue, in wantonly exercised power better checked than fully unleashed. In the end, Milton does not confuse the Messiah of *Paradise Lost* with the Samson of his tragedy, seeing in them (as does G. Wilson Knight) a single "strength thunder[ing] down upon wrongdoers," though he does include *Paradise Regained* and *Samson Agonistes* in the same poetic volume "to elucidate the relation of New Testament ethics to international affairs"[63] and, simultaneously, in looping back to *Paradise Lost* in the final lines of *Samson Agonistes*, contrasts the Son, checking his thunder in midvolley in order to avoid destruction, with Samson who, as "cloudless thunder bolted" on the heads of the Philistines (1696), produces "Ruin, destruction at the utmost point" (1514). From this scene of devastation comes the tragic realization, as Ellison would have it, that a nation must be "conditioned to riding out the chaos of history as the eagle rides out the whirlwind."[64]

Milton is one of the figures from whom Ellison acquired his literary education concerning both the politics of literature and its interlocking aesthetics; from whom he derived the lesson that some literature perpetrates the very violence it was shored up against and propagates a theology that could prove the world's undoing. Thus, after the *Hudson Review* printed Burke's essay on *Samson Agonistes* called "The Imagery of Killing" (1948), instead of eliding suicide and the temple disaster, the Ellison of *Invisible Man* has his narrator shudder: "Whoever else I was, I was no Samson. I had no desire to destroy myself . . . ; I wanted freedom, not destruction."[65] Elsewhere, Ellison responds to Burke with the hope "that his own work, involved in sacrifice and ritualistic killing, would offer more complexity," as Milton hoped of his own, " 'the kind that giveth life and light.' "[66]

Ellison's sense of that complexity emerges in the 1999 publication of *Juneteenth* where, at the novel's intellectual center, there is this exchange between Body and Bliss:

> Say . . ., Body said, can't you hear? I said do you remember in the Bible where it tells about Samson and it says he had him a boy to lead him up to the wall so he could shake the building down?
>
>   That's right, I said.
>
>   Well answer me this, you think that little boy got killed?
>
>   *Killed*, I said; who killed him?
>
>   What I mean is, do you think old Samson forgot to tell that boy what he was fixing to do?
>
>   I cut my eyes over at Body. I didn't like the idea. Once Daddy Hickman had said: *Bliss, you must be a hero like that little lad who led blind Samson to the wall, because a great many grown folks are blind and have to be led toward the light.* . . . The question worried me and I pushed it away.

Bliss will then tell Body, "Forget about Samson, man," apparently remembering the rest of what he had been told when, earlier, he speculates to the Reverend Hickman, "We were eyeless like Samson in Gaza?" With razor sharp irony, Hickman retorts:

> Amen, Rev. Bliss, like baldheaded Samson before that nameless little lad like you came as the Good Book tells us and led him to the pillars whereupon the big house stood — Oh, you little black boys, and oh, you little brown girls, you're going to shake the building down! And then, oh, how you will build in the name of the Lord!
>
> Yes, Reverend Bliss, we were eyeless like unhappy Samson among the Philistines — and worse . . .
>
> And WORSE?
>
> Worse, Rev. Bliss, because they chopped us up into little bitty pieces . . . We were eyeless . . .
>
> . . . No eyes to see.
>
> We were truly in the dark.[67]

Bliss is here asked a question he does not want to address (what did "that little lad" know, and when did he know it?), and hidden within this question — the truth that keeps slipping away from Bliss — is an issue that Stanley Fish, almost alone among Milton's critics, comprehends as an integral part of the Samson literary tradition, wherein the boy guide "always escapes, and in one version is converted on the spot."[68] The questions Bliss (and others) have shied away from are ones that Milton addresses and answers without evasion as the Messenger, in *Samson Agonistes*, reports: "they led him / Between the pillars; he his guide requested . . . / . . . He *unsuspitious* led him" (639–35; my italics). In this usually unnoticed, but telling, emendation of the Judges story, not to mention of earlier play versions of the Samson saga, Milton, as he deepens the horror of the final catastrophe, acknowledges as Ellison seems to comprehend, that Samson is a fixture within a culture of supposed heroes who, "killing multitudes," are themselves in need of the deliverer they sought to be. Milton's point, driven home by Ellison, is that all of us, including Samson presumably, should "be interrogated not by our allies or enemies but by our conduct and by our lives"; that it is our "ideals, which interrogate us, judging us, pursuing us, in terms of that which we do or do *not* do."[69] If there is a Samson in Ellison's novel, it is a Samson (in the name of Hickman) who, betrayed by the women in his life and at times by his own people, ready to meet a lion in his path, undergoes a conversion experience founded upon what we have here described as the tragic insight of *Samson Agonistes*. If Bliss is the apostate Samson, Hickman is the true Samson compounded of "strength . . . *and the breadth of spirit.*"[70]

Apparently, the Samson story taught Milton (and later Ellison) that blood spilled in violence begets more violence, that "bloody retaliation" breeds "foolishness," and that those who see nothing and hear nothing but revenge, who "dull their senses to the killing of one group" of people, even if it be the Philistines, "dull themselves to the preciousness of all human life."[71] In the character of Samson, with his ache for vengeance, we see what to pray and not to pray for; we observe the cruelty of religious sects generally, hence what Hugo Grotius once called "the Justice of the Unjust."[72] In Milton's title character, no less than in the Samson of Judges, we behold "a portraiture . . . of the moral condition [not just of Samson but] of his people,"[73] past and present, and, simultaneously, learn that, instead of crying out against others, we must sometimes cry for our people in what Ellison would call their "feasting on revenge and sacrifice." In his words, "God never fixed the dice against anybody. . . . His way may be mysterious but he's got no grudge."[74]

As much as Ellison, Toni Morrison understood that Milton was an experimental theologian and, like Philip Pullman as well, instead of targeting Milton's poetry for critique, evokes it as a model for mounting her own critiques of God and religion,

theology and politics — a critique that, like Milton's, frets
over a god whose mission (at least in a poem like *Samson
Agonistes*) seems to be grinding people into dust over a religion which, no longer a compendium of questions, was fast
becoming a catechism of answers. In Ellison's *Juneteenth*, a
true "drama of redemption," tragic insight comes in "the blaze
of sun," in Ellison's reflections "on the moral significance of
the history we've been through."[75] In Morrison's *Paradise*, as
in *Samson Agonistes* ("O dark, dark, dark, amid the blaze of
noon" [80]), violence occurs, an imagined massacre ensues, but
in what Morrison describes as "sunlight . . . yearning for brilliance." In the words of Morrison's prophetic novel, when are
we going to learn that God does not "thunder instructions or
whisper messages into ears. Oh, no. He is a liberating God";
how are we "going to be His instrument if . . . [we] don't know
what He says"? When, finally, will we comprehend that our
theologians must stop crediting those who claim "God at their
side" in murder and rather "take aim" at such; at those who
act as God's instruments, "His voice, His retribution," and think
themselves executors of his justice, forgetting that "God's justice is His alone." We need to govern the seemingly "ungovern-
able" and "ravenous appetite for vengeance, an appetite . . . [that
we need] to understand in order to subdue."[76]

Samson, with what Pullman might call his "blood-soaked
consciousness,"[77] may be ruled by what he thinks is the justice of his anger; but, in contradistinction, anger at injustice
impels Milton to compose *Samson Agonistes* (to appropriate
language from one of Milton's letters) as an instrument for "the
sharpening rather than the blunting of . . . [our] mental edge"
as he expresses, first in prose, then in poetry, that "wisdom
exceeds strength, as much as arts of peace surpass the stratagems of war":[78] "But what is strength without a double share /
Of wisdom" (53–54). Or what is strength that does not know
its own limitations, as Ellison asks while reflecting upon both

the narrator's weakness and that of his grandfather in *Invisible Man* — a weakness through which each comprehends the oppressor's weakness. "There is a good deal of spite in the old man, as there comes to be in his grandson," so that, says Ellison, "the strategy he advises is kind of jiu jitsu of the spirit, a denial and rejection through agreement": "Samson, eyeless in Gaza, pulls the building down when his strength returns; politically weak, the grandfather has learned that conformity leads to a similar end, and so advises his children. Thus his mask of meekness conceals the wisdom of one who has learned the secret of saying the 'yes' which accomplishes the expressive 'no.'"[79] By Ellison's logic, Samson is revengeful without being resourceful, with Ellison pointing the way toward what Stanley Edgar Hyman describes as a supremely "ironic and sophisticated consciousness."[80] If Milton — or rather his Samson — falls short it is so that, as Thomas Jefferson said of John Locke, "where he stopped short, we may go on"[81] — partly by never forgetting that poetry is not hemmed in by mere representations of paradises lost and regained. In the words of one recent poet, "poetry is certainly not a 'paradise lost' nor is it a 'golden age.' On the contrary it is a question that begets another question."[82] It is a knot of questions engendering other questions, most of them marked by recalcitrance, and very few accompanied by unequivocal answers; and partly, too, by hypothesizing that, moving forward without practicing revenge, we may at last break through the gridlock of history.

Only then, when we have toppled the zealots, will heaven become a place for the living and not the dead; and then we will know, both as Morrison tells us in the last words of her novel and as Philip Pullman insists in his, that we will find our paradise in this world or not at all. In the words of Pullman, who affords an important new reception of Milton at the turn into this new millennium, "we have to build the Republic of Heaven where we are, because for [many of] us there is no elsewhere";[83] we have to regain the lost paradise not by another's but by our own initiative, not beyond but within history. And Pullman's words, just this side of the new millennium, are but an echo of Morrison's words on its other side: "How exquisitely human was the wish for permanent happiness, and how thin human imagination became trying to achieve it," people not always "shouldering the endless work they were created to do down here in [p]aradise."[84]

Did Samson shoulder his burden? That question should remain at the heart of our criticism of *Samson Agonistes* in order to ensure that it always has a heart. If not self-answering within Milton's tragedy, this and other such questions may nevertheless show Milton partially answering himself out of himself, out of those writings, their "religion . . . full of intellectual daring," especially *Paradise Regained*, with which *Samson Agonistes* is in engaging and steadily enlightening dialogue.[85] Through their coupling, through this dialectic of worldviews and opposition of ethical systems, Milton's poems of 1671 propose that, where there is an enlarging instead of a cinching of human consciousness, the attendant apocalypse of mind effects a transition in history that, stymied by one ideology, is accelerated by another. The tragic insight of the one poem effects what Ellison would probably call "the mind-jolting revolution" of the other, through which our dreams, instead of founded upon rubble, become "the blueprints and mockups of emerging realities."[86] Then, as well as now, in the searing words of the Polish poet Leon Staff, "Even more than bread we . . . need poetry, in a time when it seems that it is not needed at all."[87]

THE
TERRORIST
PLOT
● ● ●

8 • *Samson Agonistes* and the Culture of Religious Terror

David Loewenstein

1

The biblical account of Samson's devastation and vengeance does indeed seem to speak to us anew in a post-September 11 world obsessed with the horror of terrorism and haunted by colossal images of destruction. Thus, in a recent study of the "new world disorder," the rise of militant Islamic fundamentalism, and the U.S. war on terrorism, the French political scientist Gilbert Achcar specifically evokes Samson's rage and destruction of the Philistine "house" — described in Judges 16:27–30 — as he analyzes the motivation and implacable hatred of the September 11 suicide bombers: "The bombers cast down the twin pillars of the World Trade Center the way Samson does in the Bible, motivated by the same kind of hatred of the enemy and thirst for revenge." The "terrible vengeance"

of the September 11 bombers, which Achcar links with the biblical Samson and his urge to be avenged, is itself a new kind
of twenty-first century "apocalyptic terror."[1] Recently, Milton's
own dramatic version of Samson's cataclysmic destruction —
as he reduces the Philistine temple and theater to a grisly "place
of horror" with "heaps of slaughtered" (1550, 1530) and destroys
himself in the process — has been analyzed in the context of
suicide terrorism. The issue has taken on new urgency and fresh
implications since John Carey raised it directly in "A Work in
Praise of Terrorism? September 11 and *Samson Agonistes.*"[2]
Published in the *Times Literary Supplement* a year after the
tragedies of 9/11, Carey's commentary refers to Samson's
destruction of the Philistine temple and theater as a "terrorist attack" and observes, like Achcar, that "the similarities
between the biblical Samson and the hijackers are obvious. Like
them Samson sacrifices himself to achieve his ends. Like them
he destroys many innocent victims, whose lives, hopes and loves
are all quite unknown to him personally." Carey's assertions
here are intended to offer a critical response to Stanley Fish in
How Milton Works; there, Fish describes Samson's "great act"
(1389) as "a virtuous action" and "praiseworthy" — especially
"insofar as it represents [Samson's] desire to conform" to the
divine will — in a work that seems to praise terrorism, as
Carey puts it. We should note, however, that Fish never
employs the terms "terrorism" or "terrorist attack" in his
analysis of the drama. Rather, it is Carey who introduces such
highly charged language as he responds to Fish, whose "viewpoint" Carey finds "monstrous," since it seems like "a license
for any fanatic to commit atrocity" and "an incitement to terrorism" that results in "mass murder."[3] Samson "is, in effect,
a suicide bomber," Carey adds, "and like the suicide bombers
he believes that his massacre is an expression of God's will."
As I will argue, the characterization of the Miltonic Samson
as a "suicide bomber" — as though he might be compared to
the indoctrinated hijackers who brought down the World Trade

Center — seems to me highly questionable; indeed, Milton's dramatic revision of the biblical Samson's terrifying destruction downplays the very issue of suicide.

Nevertheless, as Carey asserts, in a post-9/11 world we will not be able to read Milton's drama in the same way again since "events in the real world inevitably change the way we read," and "September 11 has changed *Samson Agonistes,* because it has changed the readings we can derive from it while still celebrating it as an achievement of the human imagination." On this point I partly agree with Carey: although the horrifying events of September 11 have not in fact "changed *Samson Agonistes,*" the questions and issues we raise as we read and interpret the tragedy are more likely than ever to be colored or framed by those tragic events.[4] Nonetheless, Carey's attempt to view Milton's Samson in terms of modern-day terrorism is misleading in a variety of cultural and historical ways. We need to be more mindful about interpreting *Samson Agonistes* and issues of terrorism in culturally specific contexts — in this case, the culture and language of religious terror in mid-seventeenth century England. Otherwise, we are likely to see Milton's poem (and especially the charged issues of religious terror and the revenge it dramatizes) primarily through the distorting perspective of early twenty-first century terrorism and the anxieties it has generated. Such a reading of the terrifying destruction depicted in *Samson Agonistes,* particularly when the discourse of suicide bombing is introduced, risks the dangers of sounding anachronistic. Indeed, the terms "terrorism" and "terrorist," according to the *OED,* do not enter the English language until the time of the French Revolution and its "reign of terrorism," whereas the word "terror" — in the sense of an "action or quality of causing dread" — can be dated to at least the early sixteenth century.[5]

We might recall that Carey is a critic and editor inclined to see "the ending" of *Samson Agonistes* as "morally disgusting"; those are the words Carey uses in his first edition of Milton's shorter poems published in 1968.[6] In his post-September 11 commentary, Carey describes Milton's Samson as, "in effect, a suicide bomber," and such a provocative description, with its evocation of bloodthirsty terrorists who commit spectacular crimes against humanity, is clearly meant to reinforce a connection between Milton's Nazarite and the ruthless bombers of 9/11 with their meticulously prepared terrorist attacks. *Samson Agonistes* is a work that has been notoriously challenging to interpret. As arguably "the major site of contestation within Milton studies,"[7] it has elicited a great range of readings in the past, readings that can diverge sharply between characterizing the blind warrior Samson as a tragic hero who undergoes a process of inner regeneration and characterizing him as an imperfect man of violence whose final act of destruction Milton must surely disapprove of. Indeed, as Stanley Fish and Joseph Wittreich have reminded us in their different ways, the very issue of interpretation — in a drama full of questions in which its characters struggle to understand their ruptured, enigmatic world — remains one of the tragedy's central concerns and continues to engage its commentators.[8] Of course, interpreting *Samson Agonistes* in light of the tragic events of September 11 is more likely than ever to reinforce the view that Milton's Samson is a negative model — a deeply flawed, highly ambiguous, unregenerate figure who is not only a man of violence but now, it appears, an agent of terrorism.[9]

Yet applying our language of terrorism to Milton's Samson tests our ability to make cultural and historical discriminations; for such language, used as a critical tool, may distort more than it illuminates Milton's drama and the world of violence and holy dread it depicts. The highly charged label of "terror" is, after all, subject to a range of interpretations and diverse forms, and the language of terrorism has become such a protean rhetorical device that the term "terrorist," as Tony Judt observes, "risks becoming the mantra of our time."[10] As another recent commentator has noted about its current protean and divergent uses, "What one side in a conflict would call terror might be regarded by the other side as legitimate resistance to occupation, as well as ethnic, religious, or national oppression."[11] Indeed, the label "terrorist," I would add, has frequently been used to demonize opponents, much as the volatile term "heretic" (as Milton himself understood) was used to malign religious enemies in the early modern period or as the term "communist" was used to demonize so-called enemies in the United States during the 1950s. That is not to say that the terms "terrorist," "terrorism," or "terror" do not have their genuine uses; they obviously do. But my point is that these terms or labels are so charged in our current political and cultural discourse that they often prevent discriminating analysis of, as well as rational argument about, violent religious and political conflicts and their participants.

Milton himself was acutely aware of the dangers of employing invidious titles, especially in such volatile religious and political times as his own. In the epistle to *De Doctrina Christiana* he complains about the uses of the name "heretic" to close off debate and tarnish heterodox believers: "There are some irrational bigots," he observes,

> who, by a perversion of justice, condemn anything they consider inconsistent with conventional beliefs and give it an invidious title — "heretic" or "heresy" — without consulting the evidence of the Bible upon the point. To their way of thinking, by branding anyone out of hand with this hateful name, they silence him with one word and indeed take no further trouble. They imagine that they have struck their opponent to the ground, as with a single blow, by the impact of the name heretic alone.[12]

And so one might observe about uses of the invidious names "terrorist" or "terrorism" in our own age; for they, too, are often used indiscriminately to discredit opponents and silence more probing critical debate. By invoking the term "terrorism" to characterize Milton's Samson and his act of destruction — and by describing him specifically as a kind of "suicide bomber" — we risk misrepresenting the religious politics of Milton's drama and the poet's distinctive treatment of Samson's violent end. We may, therefore, wish to heed Milton's warning about "the name heretic" and be wary of applying terms like "terrorist" or "terrorism" to Samson.

There were, to be sure, forms of terror in Milton's England, but we need to understand and situate them in their own specific cultural, political, and religious contexts. I want, then, to consider Milton's poem in relation to the culture of religious terror in the early modern period. To what degree did he condone terror in its religious and political manifestations? To what extent can we situate *Samson Agonistes* in relation to seventeenth century terror as opposed to our own twenty-first century versions of terrorism? We need to make crucial distinctions, informed particularly by an understanding of religious terror in the tumultuous world of seventeenth century England, before branding Milton's Samson with the pejorative name "terrorist," a word unknown to Milton and his contemporaries. *Samson Agonistes*, I will suggest, owes much to the culture of seventeenth century religious terror or dread, yet that does not make Samson a terrorist in the more recent senses of that term. First, however, let us consider briefly one kind of religious and political terror Milton *did* indeed seem to support: the troubling case of Ireland and the use of terror to try to subdue its fierce resistance. In this case, the terror used by Cromwell and the New Model Army was close to one form of terrorism we are familiar with — "A policy intended to strike with terror those against whom it is adopted" (*OED*, s.v. "terrorism").

2

During the 1640s and 1650s, Milton supported a kind of state or military form of terror fueled and justified by the zealous

religious politics of the age: the use of terror against the Irish
as agents of the Antichrist. Insofar as terror "includes the use
of indiscriminate violence against civilians in order to achieve
military and political goals," it can be used not only by non-
state and underground organizations, but also "by a 'legitimate'
state apparatus."[13] Cromwell's punitive campaign to reconquer
Ireland in 1649 is one example (however rare for the English
revolutionaries) where terror was used during the Interregnum
as the fragile republic was attempting to secure its legitimacy.
The slaughter of thousands of English Protestant settlers
during the Irish Rebellion of 1641 — the "most barbarous
massacre . . . that ever the sun beheld," Cromwell called it —
warranted, it was widely believed, a vengeful and firm response
by the republic, and, only a month after the execution of the
king, a large military expedition was being prepared whose aim
Milton would vigorously defend in writing.[14] The blood guilt
of 1641 was being revenged, and the use of terror was thereby
justified as a means of sharp, swift conquest. During September
and October 1649, the New Model Army, driven by the force
of religious ideology, employed a kind of "holy ruthlessness"
against the Irish, at times slaughtering not only soldiers (including royalist ones) in garrisons but also civilians and clergy, as
the massacres during and following the sieges of Drogheda and
Wexford illustrate; some 3,500 died at Drogheda and around
2,000 at Wexford (though here there was no general massacre
of civilians).[15] On these two dreadful occasions, "the enemy,"
Cromwell wrote to John Bradshaw, "were filled . . . with much
terror";[16] or, to borrow words from *Samson Agonistes*, the
seemingly invincible Cromwell did indeed pursue "[a] dreadful way" to take his "revenge" (1591).

In a sense, Milton helped to prepare for this campaign by
means of his *Observations upon the Articles of Peace*, published
in the spring before Cromwell's New Model Army invaded
Ireland. For Milton, the crushing of Ireland by force was even
more warranted because of Charles I's "covert leaguing with

the [Irish] rebels" during the 1640s — as if Charles were engaged in treacherous satanic plots against Parliament by raising "a host of Irishmen" to foment rebellion and war against the English.[17] Subsequent references in Milton's prose to the conquest of Ireland only confirm that Milton continued to maintain his view, sometimes voiced to a wider European audience, that the conquest of Ireland was wholly justified as a holy war against the forces of the Antichrist. "In one battle," Milton boasted to European readers in the *Second Defense,* Cromwell "instantly broke the power of Hibernia" (YP 4:670), and Milton elsewhere, in *A Defense,* praised Cromwell for undertaking the war in Ireland "in full accordance with the will of God" and winning "many victories," including those at Drogheda and Wexford (4:458). Yet royalist and Catholic resistance was not quelled by the terror — or the campaign of "shock and awe"[18] — employed by Cromwell at Drogheda and Wexford, nor was Ireland won so swiftly. Cromwell had hoped that a sharp campaign of terror would quickly bring Irish resistance to an end,[19] but events eventually proved him wrong. Waterford, Clonmel, and Limerick were defended with stubborn resistance and a war of sieges and guerrilla tactics against the occupying power continued beyond Cromwell's recall in 1650.[20] Milton the controversialist, however, was helping to create and sustain a myth about Cromwell's rapid, heroic military reconquest in that savage land, and he made no apologies about a punitively severe campaign that involved the use of terror as a political and religious means to achieve that end.

Milton's polemical defense of Cromwell's Irish campaign, including its use of terror, leaves us with the uncomfortable problem of how we assess Milton's responses to that crisis in relation to his passionate defenses of religious and political freedom for which he is so often admired. We need, I believe, to confront more openly inconsistencies in Milton's religious politics where they exist. The godly revolutionary and republican writer does not always conform neatly to our perception of Milton as the eloquent spokesperson for civil and religious liberty, the author who manifests a courageous, often fierce intellectual independence and who does not hesitate to challenge political ideologies and regimes, even those of the republic and protectorate, which he has also supported. Nevertheless, Milton's militant, nationalistic Protestant responses to the Irish rebellion and Cromwell's subsequent campaign did allow for the use of military terror, for terror was a political and religious weapon in Ireland; Cromwell, for example, called the tragedy of Drogheda "a righteous judgment of God upon . . . barbarous wretches" and the slaughter at Wexford "an unexpected providence."[21] And all the evidence from Milton's writings indicates that he fully supported the New Model Army's campaign to unleash the forces of holy terror against the Irish Catholics as agents of the Antichrist.

As the troubling case of Ireland's reconquest suggests, Milton could, in specific circumstances, condone terror as a kind of political and religious weapon associated with the will and judgment of God. There is certainly no evidence to suggest that Milton — or most of his contemporaries, for that matter — ever developed reservations about Cromwell's brutal tactics, yet the terror and shock of Drogheda and Wexford have continued to reverberate to the present day.[22] Under certain circumstances, Milton did, in effect, defend a kind of terror painfully familiar to us — the use of a superior army to terrorize a population and conquer it. Yet, despite the dreadful ways Cromwell's army could execute holy revenge in Ireland, this is not quite the form of terror dramatized in *Samson Agonistes*, a poem that does not conform so easily to our modern understandings of terrorist behavior, including its religious manifestations. The drama's depiction of Samson's cataclysmic destruction instead owes much to a culture of religious terror and holy dread in mid-seventeenth century England. Its principal character — the

betrayed, blind, anguished, and enslaved warrior who resists
the Philistine attempt to compel his conscience and engage in
their "idolatrous rites" (*SA*, 1378) — does perform a spectacular act of terror in the end, yet he does not execute terrorism
in the modern way that we understand it.

3

So what, then, do we make of the case for regarding the Miltonic
Samson as a kind of "suicide bomber" who commits a "terrorist attack," to return to Carey's provocative phrases? Is
Samson genuinely comparable to a calculating suicide bomber
who intends to massacre religious and political enemies —
including innocent civilians — and who hopes to achieve a kind
of martyrdom in the dreadful process? Is *Samson Agonistes*,
with its "horrid spectacle" (1542) at the end, really "a work
in praise of terrorism," as Carey would like us to think? The
equation between Samson and a suicide bomber may give
Samson Agonistes a new urgency and significance for early-
twenty-first-century readers, especially after the near-apoca-
lyptic tragic events of September 11 and suicide bombings in
the Middle East, North Africa, Chechnya, Russia, Indonesia,
and elsewhere, attacks often fueled by a surge of religious fundamentalism. Yet the comparison also distorts as much as it
stimulates our fascination with or revulsion toward Milton's
Samson and his final terrifying act. The identification of Samson
with a modern-day suicide bomber tells us more about our own
fears and values than it does about Milton's poem and its
unique dramatization of religious terror.

For one thing, Milton seems to have wished to downplay or
diffuse the issue of Samson committing (to use Carey's words
again) "his suicide attack."[23] The Argument to the poem — a
summary of the drama, after all, in Milton's own words —
already discourages the interpretation of Samson as suicide
when it concludes by referring to "the catastrophe, what Samson

had done to the Philistines, and *by accident to himself*; wherewith the tragedy ends" (my emphasis). "By accident to himself" is, of course, the revealing phrase here. Several passages in the drama confirm the implications of the Argument's words with regard to how Samson perished: the Messenger who conveys the details of Samson's terrifying destruction and slaughter — after Manoa asks was it "Self-violence?" (1584) — observes that Samson, in decimating the Philistine aristocracy, "inevitably / Pulled down the same destruction on himself" and it was an "Inevitable cause / At once both to destroy and be destroyed" (1657–58, 1587–88), while the Chorus observes that Samson "li'st victorious / Among thy slain self-killed / *Not willingly*, but tangled in the fold, / Of dire necessity" (1663–66; emphasis added). "Self-killed / Not willingly" hardly sounds like the description of a modern-day suicide bomber. To be sure, the Chorus often proves to be unreliable and fallible in its interpretations of the drama's shocking events, as critics have frequently noted, but here its words concur with those of the Messenger and — more crucially — with Milton's summary of the drama's horrific end. *Samson Agonistes* may be an especially challenging text to interpret, but on the matter of Samson's possible suicide, Milton's Argument sends a strong signal with regard to how the drama's readers are meant to understand this controversial issue.

Moreover, as he depicts Samson taking hold of the massive pillars of the temple, Milton has clearly suppressed Samson's crucial prayer in the Book of Judges — "Let me die with the Philistines" (Judg. 16:30) — just as he has suppressed the biblical Samson's cry for personal vengeance ("that I may be at once avenged of the Philistines for my two eyes" [Judg. 16:28]), despite his acute suffering because of his blindness. Milton thus makes *Samson Agonistes* more of a drama about divine (rather than personal) vengeance and its terrifying consequences. During the English civil war, godly soldiers were expected to pray before battle, and *The Souldiers Pocket Bible*, which they customarily carried with them in their breast pockets, quoted directly from Judges 16:28, as the warrior Samson prays before wreaking destruction on the Philistines: "Then *Sampson* called unto the Lord, and said, O Lord God, I pray thee thinke upon me, O God, I beseech thee strengthen me at this time, &c."[24] The Messenger in Milton's drama reports that the blind warrior Samson stood between the massive Philistine pillars with "eyes fast fixed . . . as one who prayed, / Or some great matter in his mind revolved" (1637–38), but such scriptural details as might confirm the view of Samson as a suicide fighter praying for personal revenge for the loss of his eyes, and the terrible mental and physical affliction he has endured as a consequence, have crucially been left out by Milton.

Restoration verses by George Wither on Samson's destruction and death, written while that prophetic nonconformist poet was imprisoned in the Tower in July 1663, provide a revealing contrast with Milton's dramatic depiction. In some ways, Wither's evocation of Samson's end in *A Memorandum to London* (1665), where obedient saints "conscientiously . . . may submit / To what [God] hast ordain'd," is as close as we are likely to get in the mid-seventeenth century to the spirit of modern-day suicide bombers:

> Thy *Souldiers* will be pleas'd amid thy foes
> To die, e're any honor thou shouldst lose,
> Since *death* by them, needs never to be fear'd,
> Who know with what *life*, thou wilt reward.
> Let *Dagons* temple then be overthrown
> Though *Sampson* die, in pulling of it down:
> For, all thy Souldiers, seek their glorifying
> In *conquering*, although it be by dying.[25]

As Janel Mueller notes, Wither's passage conveys a sense of "iconoclastic fury" at a city — London — given over to wickedness and idolatry, and in that sense these lines resemble Milton's depiction of Samson's destructive end and his "desolation of a hostile city" (1561).[26] Wither's Samson is a potent figure for the fearless nonconformist who may still strike, with devastating effect, despite enduring great afflictions and insolence.

Nevertheless, the differences between Milton and Wither, in terms of their interpretations of Samson's dreadful end, are surely as notable as any similarities, and they highlight Milton's unique dramatization of the Samson story in relation to the issue of religious terror. Milton's depiction of Samson the blind nonconformist fighter, who scorns the "idolatrous rites" (1378) of the Philistines, differs in several important ways. First of all, in *Samson Agonistes,* Milton does not mention, as Wither does, the pleasure of the Lord's soldiers dying "amid [their] foes" — lines that give Samson's prayer to die with the Philistines in Judges 16:30 a positive interpretation. Nor is Milton's Samson particularly motivated or inspired by any vision of martyrdom or self-glorification by dying, that is, by knowing "with what *life*" the Lord will "reward" him or other faithful soldiers.

Nor, indeed, does the language Milton ascribes to Samson as he refers to God dispensing with him "for some important cause" (1379) suggest the analogy of a suicide bomber. Samson about to carry out "some great act" (1389) after claiming to be moved by "some rousing motions" (1382) is a Samson who goes to his end with some sense of mystery about his mission and its consequences, even within his own mind.[27] Whatever that act is, it might be "the last" (1389) of Samson's days — but Samson's precise end nevertheless remains unknown to him: "Happen what may," Samson observes to the Public Officer after issuing his biting mockery of the Philistine priests: "of me expect to hear / Nothing dishonourable, impure, unworthy / Our God, our Law, my nation, or myself, / The last of me or no I cannot warrant" (1423–26). If he is following the promptings of the Spirit — and I believe that Milton wishes us to think that he is — then Milton's Samson does not sound like a modern-day suicide bomber who has planned his terrifying, bloodthirsty revenge in a calculating manner and who relishes the slaughter of infidel women and children. Rather, Samson's opaque, tentative language, as he is led off to Dagon's temple by the officer, reminds us of the mysterious nature of God's ways and providence; for, as Fish has observed, it is based on a "provisional . . . reading of the divine will" as Samson joins those other biblical heroes of faith, namely "the worthies of Hebrews 11, who take provisional actions (going out not knowing whither they go)."[28] Providence in *Samson Agonistes* thus remains an inscrutable authority, its secret ends unfathomable to human beings, including the Lord's instruments.

Milton's Samson also does not willingly seek out the Philistine temple in order to decimate it. Here, in fact, Milton's poem has added crucially — and freely — to the Book of Judges a series of lines or dramatic exchanges that must be taken into account in any attempt to align Samson's final act with a modern terrorist attack, or to equate Samson's behavior, as Carey does, with that of a modern-day suicide bomber determined to kill as many innocent victims as possible. Indeed, Milton's addition to the Bible not only increases the dramatic tension of those moments before Samson is taken into the temple and theater of Dagon; it also has rich topical implications for *Samson Agonistes* as a polemical work of nonconformist literature during the stormy years of the Restoration. In the Bible, the enslaved Samson shows no resistance or reservations about entering Dagon's temple when called to do so by the Philistines: "And it came to pass, when their hearts were merry, that they said, Call for Samson, that he may make us sport. And they called for Samson out the prison house; and he made them sport: and they set him between the pillars" (Judg. 16:25, AV). Milton's dramatic version of the Samson story is markedly different at this point from his scriptural source. To be sure, the idea of the blind Samson making "sport" before "illustrious lords" (1328, 1318) echoes Judges, but the strained exchange between the shackled Samson and the Philistine officer who comes to collect him — that is, from line 1310 to line 1384 — does not; it is completely Milton's own invention. It is, moreover, a striking expansion of the biblical passage, for it shows, as the Bible does not, Samson's highly conscientious concerns about submitting to the "religious rites" (1320) of his idolatrous enemies and therefore engaging in a kind of ceremonial impurity. It is here that the Miltonic Samson appeals to his "conscience" (1334), a source of inner testimony, as he expresses his disdain at the Philistine attempt to turn him into a contemptuous public spectacle (since to "play before their god" is "The worst of all indignities" [1340–41]), and insists, despite the officer's demand, that he "will not come" (1332, 1342).

Milton's work dramatizes the issue of conscience in radical religious terms as his Samson firmly refuses to conform to the constraint of "outward force" and to the authority of Philistine "civil power" (1369, 1367) and religious practice, despite the suggestion, made by the Chorus, that outward conformity might at least be one way to ease the tense situation and assuage the Philistines ("Where the heart joins not, outward acts defile not" [1368]). Samson, however, refuses to allow his conscience to be usurped by another political or religious authority, as his language and arguments echo those of Milton's *Treatise of Civil Power in Ecclesiastical Causes* (February 1659), which rejects the authority of any "outward force" to constrain or compel "inward religion" (YP 7:256) and which anticipates the religious tensions of the Restoration when dissenters were regularly compelled to conform: "Commands are no constraints," Samson tells the Chorus, "If I obey them, / I do it freely" (1372–73).[29] Samson in one sense resembles the godly during the English revolution who insisted on giving themselves up to the strictest rules of holiness (Samson as a Nazarite who abhors "prostituting holy things to idols" [1358]) and on maintaining freedom from an inappropriate authority in order to submit a higher, more demanding if inscrutable authority.[30]

In addition, Milton's revision of the Bible here — particularly Samson's insistence that he "will not come" to an "abominable" temple and engage in "idol-worship" — would have had keener polemical resonance in the grim years of the Restoration, when "the contest" continued " 'Twixt God and Dagon" (461–62) and dissenters faced acute pressure to comply with the "religious rites" of the Church of England and were punished and molested for not doing so. Just a year before Milton published *Samson Agonistes,* the new Conventicle Act of 1670, famously called by Andrew Marvell "the Quintessence of arbitrary Malice,"[31] provided another example of the "use of force in religion" — both "outward and corporeal" (YP 7:241, 266) — to borrow language from *Civil Power:* it had banned groups of people meeting for religious worship outside the Church of England's services and warned against religious radicals who appealed to their conscience as a means of refusing to conform. The act, which threatened severe penalties and encouraged the use of informants to spy on nonconformists and initiate prosecutions, aimed to provide "further and more speedy remedies against the growing and dangerous practices of seditious sectaries and other disloyal persons, who under pretence of tender consciences . . . may . . . contrive insurrections (as late experience hath shown)" and who intend to pursue "any exercise of religion in other manner than according to the liturgy and practice of the Church of England."[32] In character with the persecuting Clarendon Code of the early 1660s, the 1670 act thus encouraged renewed persecution against dissenters, prompting Thomas Ellwood, Milton's Quaker student during the Restoration, to characterize it as an "unjust, unequal, unreasonable and unrighteous law" that was "rigorously prosecuted" and that created a particularly "stormy time" for Nonconformists, though "the clouds had long been gathering and threatening a tempest."[33] Samson's spurning of the Philistine "religious rites" and the command to engage in "profane" (1362) acts in Dagon's temple thus has a more urgent topical resonance for a troubled age when dissenters, who continued to insist on the free liberty of conscience, were regularly branded as "seditious" and "disloyal" for rejecting the authority and practices of the Church of England — and who continued to refuse to allow "inward religion" to be compelled, as Milton puts it in *Civil Power* (YP 7:256).

That Milton's Samson is, at first, so repelled by the idea of going to the Philistine temple and submitting to religious rites abhorrent to him makes it more likely that Milton wants his readers to see that the Nazarite is finally moved by the leadings and motions of the Spirit — those "rousing motions" — at this particularly tense moment in the drama. Of course, there is no absolute proof of this since Milton's omnipotent God never speaks in this dramatic poem (as he does in *Paradise Lost*), but then why would Milton greatly alter his scriptural source to allow Samson to express initially such a strong aversion to the idea of defiling his holy vocation as a Nazarite who must go along with the Philistine's Public Officer? As in Milton's *Civil Power*, the threat of "outward compulsions of a magistrate or his officers" and the "zeal of forcing" are juxtaposed (though here in a particularly dramatic fashion) with "the inward perswasive motions of his spirit," that "Holy Spirit within us which," Milton writes, "we ought to follow much rather then any law of man" (YP 7:260–61, 242). This passage from *Civil Power* resembles the language of the Argument of *Samson Agonistes* where Milton observes that Samson "at length persuaded inwardly that this was from God," yields "to go along with him."[34] Milton's addition to the Book of Judges at this point in the drama thus makes the analogy of Samson to a suicide bomber less than helpful: Milton's Samson neither seeks personal revenge for the loss of his eyes, nor does he eagerly seek out his enemies' place of "idol worship." Rather, he expresses at considerable length — and with a sense of revulsion strengthened by his religious scruples — his grounds for refusing to go, at first dismissing the Public Officer, to quote from the Argument, "with absolute denial to come."

There remains, in Milton's dramatic version of the story, a sense of mystery and uncertainty as Samson goes off with the Public Officer, which I have elsewhere argued can be associated with the obscure workings of providence and the Spirit in radical Puritan culture, for the godly did indeed experience a kind of provisionality associated with the leadings of the Spirit.[35] Neither Samson nor the Danites know exactly what will transpire ("How thou wilt here come off surmounts my reach" [1380], remarks the Chorus); no one has specifically directed Samson to slaughter the Philistines en masse; and Samson himself does not know for sure how it will all end as he finally acquiesces to go with the officer. As the 1671 poems suggest, Milton was particularly interested in this sort of dilemma facing the faithful or saintly hero, for even his solitary, inward-looking Jesus in *Paradise Regained* does not know where the leadings of the Spirit will take him, as he proceeds "step by step" (1.192) and is led "by some strong motion" into the pathless wilderness: "to what intent / I learn not yet, perhaps I need not know" (1.290–91). Attempts to equate Samson's responses and actions with modern terrorist behavior miss Milton's remarkable divergence from the Bible here and his highly distinctive handling of Samson's behavior at this point in the story. Such attempts also miss, as I have argued here and elsewhere, the seventeenth century radical religious implications of the Miltonic Samson and his "rousing motions," which is a crucial distinction from modern-day terrorists.

Milton's dramatic poem gives potent expression to seventeenth century anxieties about providentialism and its mysteriousness, as well as about a God of awesome power who often acts by terrifying means. A providentialist world view could lead to the banishing of self-doubt, as in the case of the New Model Army during the 1640s and 1650s, which became increasingly confident and ruthless as its godly soldiers won more victories and believed that they were performing the will of God.[36]

Thus, Cromwell, whose sense of providentialism could intersect with his sense of God as a force of holy terror, fervently believed that "God [had] put the sword into Parliament's hands, for the terror of evil-doers"; and from Ireland, where he observed that God had "manifested His severity and justice," Cromwell concluded that "a Divine Presence hath gone along with us in the late great transactions in this nation."[37] But crisis or failure could make providentialism a harsh doctrine indeed. Milton's *Samson Agonistes* dramatizes the darker, harsher side of providentialism as a shattered Samson and the Danites strive to understand the mysterious operations of providence toward a mighty deliverer whose shocking transformation from "invincible" warrior (341) — "The glory late of Israel, now the grief" (179) — seems almost beyond comprehension. "The mystery of God" (378) generates great anxiety in Milton's drama: engaged in their own process of agon, Manoa and the Chorus struggle to understand God's apparently "contrarious" (669) and harsh ways toward his chosen instrument — now enslaved, broken, and the object of derision and contempt — while Samson, whose mental torment is more acute than his physical suffering, experiences profound anguish and a keen sense of shame over the nature of his failed service to God, reproaching himself in the bitterest language: "O impotence of mind, in body strong!" (52). God's providence remains mysterious in Milton's dramatic rendition of the Samson story — we never hear the deity speaking directly to any of the characters, there is no angelical visitation to explain God's ways to Samson or to us, and fallible human beings are left to interpret, as best as they can, God's terrifying, inscrutable ways. The Israelites may observe at the end that "All is best, though we oft doubt, / What the unsearchable dispose / Of highest wisdom brings about, / And ever best found in the close" (1745–48), but such sententious maxims cannot erase the unease Milton's drama generates about the operations of providence and the terrifying acts carried out in its name.

4

Milton's God in *Samson Agonistes* is indeed a God of terror. He is a God of "living dread" (1673) who owes much, Michael Lieb observes, to biblical depictions of a God of dread who unleashes devastating powers on his enemies.[38] To Lieb's point we should add that there was also a significant discourse of religious terror in Milton's England that depicts God as an awesome power and fury whose terrible day is imminent. The turbulent religious politics of the age, and the intense religious ferment stimulated by sectarian activity, contributed significantly to the language of religious terror and gave it a renewed urgency. Such a terrifying God remained a frightening power in mid-seventeenth century England — a power that was invoked and repeatedly exploited in the writings of a wide range of godly contemporaries, some more radical in their religious persuasion than others. Furthermore, such a God of religious terror, as we might call him, hardly conforms to a "more rational conception of the nature of deity," to borrow words Lieb uses to describe the God of dread in Milton's drama.[39]

We find many examples of the language of religious terror during the 1640s and 1650s, although the language also spills over into the Restoration. Thus, in moments of apocalyptic or millenarian exuberance, Cromwell referred to the Lord as a force of terror who would astonish his enemies and act as "a severe avenger": during the second civil war, "the wonderful works of God" included "breaking the rod of the oppressor, as in the day of Midian, not with garments much rolled in blood, but by the terror of the Lord; who will . . . confound His enemies as in that day."[40] Mary Cary, author of some of the most elaborate Fifth Monarchist commentaries on the Book of Revelation and other prophetic passages, finds plenty of evidence in Scripture (including Revelation and Isaiah) for a God of fury and terror who would strike down earthly powers: her *Little Horns Doom and Downfall* and *A New and More Exact*

Mappe . . . of New Jerusalems Glory (published together in 1651) envision "the terrour of that day when the Lord shall at last be fully avenged on his enemies," including anti-Christian kings like Charles I. "Terrible and dreadful will this day be to wicked men," Cary prophesies based on her reading of Isaiah 24, as "desolations" will "come upon the inhabitants of the earth" and "multitudes shall be slain" — just as "desolation" (*SA*, 1561) comes upon the Philistines in Milton's drama. "The terribleness of this day," including the apocalyptic vengeance wrought by a God of fury upon ungodly men and powers, is also one of the principal subjects of Milton's drama, a poem inspired by the Book of Revelation as both a tragedy and work about the apocalypse.[41]

Furthermore, the militant and apocalyptic language of Quakerism during the 1650s, when this aggressively active sect was far from committed to pacifism and envisioned that the Lord was overturning the nation, evoked their own version of such an awesome God of terror. Thus, in *To the Camp of the Lord, in England* (1655), Francis Howgill conflates the agency of the reviled saints with the dreadful power and fury of the Lord; sounding the alarm of war, while urging the saints to "appear in [their] terror as an Army, and let the nations know your power," he told them to "cut down on the right hand, and slay on the left, and let not your eye pitty, nor your hande spare, but wound the lofty . . . for we have proclaimed open War."[42] As he invoked a vision of holy terror, Howgill echoed the language of a pitiless Lord in Jeremiah and Ezekiel.[43]

In Milton's culture there were also sharp reminders by the more radical godly, especially those who felt despised and scorned, that this God of holy terror would not long endure such a mockery of his saints in England. Milton's imprisoned, embittered Nazarite warrior may become "the scorn and gaze" (*SA*, 34) of his idolatrous enemies, abused as the "vilest" slave (73–74), treated as "a fool" (203), and his calamities the subject of their sport and derision. But the Lord would not "long /

Endure" the "scorn" toward himself expressed "By the idolatrous rout" engaged in their Dagonalia (*SA*, 476–77, 442–43).
Thus, the young Quaker prophet Edward Burrough wrote in
1654, "God will not be mocked, for he is terrible, and his day
is powerful and dreadful, that shall come upon the Heathen."[44]
The coming of the day of the Lord was a terrifying event that
would generate awe and amazement. Three years after the
publication of *Samson Agonistes*, a contentious William Penn,
answering an "abusive epistle" against the Quakers by orthodox Puritan divines, envisioned that "God's *Terrible Day* has-
tens upon the World," and he urged "Preparation for this Great
& Notable Day of the Lord, that the Sound of the last Amazing
Trump may not surprize us, or any of us be overtaken at
unawares."[45] The furious language of God's wrath and vengeance
and his overturning power consequently saturate early Quaker
apocalyptic writing, as well as that of other religious radicals.
Such an awesome God would terrorize his enemies and avenge
the saints who had been abused, derided, and persecuted by
them; acting contrary to the inner light, George Fox warned
"the Powers of the Earth" during the Protectorate, would set
them against "the mighty power of the Lord" so that "the terror of the Lord will persue you": "woe for ever to all *Sions*
Adversaries."[46] Thus, authorities who forced dissenters to follow the "religious rites" of the Church of England and imperiled the liberty of conscience — much as the Philistines in
Milton's drama try to compel Samson to submit to their "idolatrous rites" — could expect to be answered by the Lord of terror and dread: "Remember, ye Mighty Men of the Kingdom,
That the Great and Mighty GOD takes notice of all your
Doings," Edward Burrough warned Charles II and both houses
of Parliament in *The Case of Free Liberty of Conscience* (1661),
"and accordingly will he reward you in his Dreadful Day,
which is near to come upon all the World."[47]

Thomas Ellwood, Milton's closest Quaker connection during the 1660s, sounded in the year of the Restoration "An

Alarm to the Priests [of this generation] . . . A Message from Heaven, To forewarn them of the dreadfull day of the Lord which will suddenly overtake them."[48] Ellwood's text, *An Alarm to the Priests*, is a particularly good example of a tract that exploits, and indeed derives rhetorical vigor from, the language of religious terror in ways that are germane to *Samson Agonistes* with its terrifying God of awe and power, and with its vision of the "dreadful way" that Samson takes his "revenge" (1591). Ellwood's first piece of polemical writing, an apocalyptic text about the terrifying fury of divine judgment, wrath, and vengeance, is addressed to "the Priests of this Nation" (6), including the bishops who set themselves against the Nonconformists and the Presbyterians who set themselves "against the Lord's people here in England" (2). These priests continued to worship in their "Idol-Temples" (4) and dealt spitefully with the Lord's messengers, especially the Quakers and other radical dissenters, who were subjected, like Milton's Samson, to the most "foul indignities" (*SA*, 371) and "exposed / To daily fraud, contempt, abuse and wrong, / Within doors, or without" (75–77), including imprisonment, beatings, dismemberment, and other forms of abuse and humiliation.[49] Such hateful treatment by "inhuman foes" (*SA*, 109) of the Lord's servants only fuels the wrath of "the Lord God of Power," who promises to take "vengeance" upon the perpetrators (3).

In Milton's drama the terrifying, vengeful judgment of God includes among its victims "the well-feasted priest then soonest fired / With zeal, if aught religion seem concerned" (1419–20). Samson's ironic, derisive words here echo Milton's biting indictment in his polemical prose of the contemporary clergy, notably the Presbyterians, who "have preach't thir own bellies" and who "have kept warme a while by the affected zele of thir pulpits."[50] In Ellwood's prophetic tract, the warning of "the Lord God of power," issued through his messenger or servant (Ellwood himself), envisions "sudden destruction" and "utter desolation . . . speedily" overtaking the priests of his age

(3) — "a day of sad calamity shall suddenly overtake them" (6) — much as "destruction" comes "speedy upon" (*SA*, 1681) the Philistine priests and aristocrats in their idolatrous temple, resulting (as Manoa says) in "The desolation of a hostile city" (*SA*, 1561).[51] The "indignation and fury" of this God who, Ellwood writes, shall "break out upon [the priests], and shal utterly consume [them] from off the earth" (7) is aimed at those in England who "have drawn the people from serving the living God, and have caused them to serve strange Gods, even graven Images, . . . framed in the mould of their vain imaginations, one while they set up Episcopacy, another while Presbyterie" (6). The fall of Babylon, Ellwood's fiery tract predicts, "shall make a great noise, the sound thereof shal go through the earth, and shal strike terror . . . fear, amazement, astonishment of Spirit shall seize on all those that traffick with her" (3), much as the Philistine temple in *Samson Agonistes* — a "place abominable" devoted to "idol-worship," "idolatrous rites" (*SA*, 1359, 1365, 1378), and "superstition" (15) — is destroyed with a "hideous noise" (*SA*, 1509) and "with burst of thunder" (1651) as Samson, once again "The dread of Israel's foes" (*SA*, 342), strikes his Philistine enemies, "mortal men / Fallen into wrath divine," "with amaze" so that they are "All in a moment overwhelmed and fall'n" (*SA*, 1682–83, 1645, 1559).

One need not identify Milton specifically with any one contemporary radical religious movement or sect or writer to recognize that his *Samson Agonistes* evokes such a terrifying God who performs horrid spectacles of apocalyptic power that generate astonishment and awe — a sense of amazement among God's idolatrous enemies who have debased, emasculated, and imprisoned his blind servant and who have tried to compel him to submit to their "religious rites." Indeed, the God of "living dread" in Milton's drama — a terrifying God of revenge — assists in bringing about the catastrophe and the great reversal at the end: as the Semichorus reports, God deludes the

Philistines — "Drunk with idolatry, drunk with wine / And fat regorged of bulls and goats, / Chanting their idol" (*SA*, 1670–72) — as he sends among them "a spirit of frenzy" that "urged them on with mad desire / To call in haste for their destroyer" (1675, 1677–78). Milton's dramatic poem thus appropriates the language of religious terror and holy dread in Milton's England, but it ultimately gives the experience of religious terror a more complex expression, just as it gives the God of terror a troubling representation. The poem depicts more vividly than any contemporary tract from the period, including Ellwood's *An Alarm to the Priests*, the anxieties that lie at the heart of the culture of religious terror, with its Lord of mighty power who can test his servants in the most extreme conditions and who can swiftly decimate his enemies.

The destruction and vengeance depicted in *Samson Agonistes*, then, dramatizes a kind of awesome religious terror, which I situate in terms of the religious politics of mid-seventeenth century England and particularly its culture and language of religious terror. Yet, as unsettling as the horrific events dramatized at the end of *Samson Agonistes* may be, they do not concern terrorist activity — or "an incitement to terrorism" — in the way that we usually understand it. Nor is Milton's Samson a terrorist in the sense of his acting like a present-day suicide bomber who commits an act of calculated, indiscriminate destruction. Samson's spectacular destruction of the temple and theater of Dagon is no meticulously prepared terrorist attack. Nor is it a suicide mission, though it "inevitably" results in his death. Samson is more impulsive in his warlike behavior, and in terms of his inwardness and the prompting of the "rousing motions," he is closer in his behavior to the world of radical religious antinomianism in Milton's England.[52] But, rather than carefully plotting a slaughter of the Philistines, he feels his "rousing motions" and responds to the immediate occasion in a way that enables

Milton to dramatize, during the stormy years of the Restoration, the mystery, power, and horror of divine terror or holy dread. Moreover, insofar as *Samson Agonistes* gives dramatic expression to the intensified discourse of religious terror in seventeenth century England, it does so in a way that expresses — in vivid and emotionally raw ways — the acute tensions that Puritan providentialism could generate, as well as the sharp anxieties associated with the demanding vocation of the godly servant. In these ways, Milton's drama continues to move us as one of the most daring literary works of radical Puritan culture and, indeed, as an achievement of the human imagination.

9 • Returning the Gorgon Medusa's Gaze
Terror and Annihilation in Milton

Michael Lieb

I

In my article "How Stanley Fish Works," I address the question of Fish's outlook as it developed between the time of his now-classic *Surprised by Sin* (1967) and the publication of his brilliant but highly controversial *How Milton Works* (2001).[1] Distinguishing between the two works, I observed that "the element of anxiety" so much a part of the "harassed reader" Fish envisions in his earlier book on Milton is no longer at issue in the outlook that pervades his most recent book on Milton. If one is to speak of a reader at all, it is best done in the guise of the worshiper who aspires to be a member of the angelic choir that celebrates God on his celestial throne. Milton's *At a Solemn Music* comes immediately to mind. As Fish makes clear in *How Milton Works*, the worshiper is integral to the consortium through which the individual soul achieves perfect union both with his fellow members and with his God. This is a state in which "the individual singer" is fully "indistinguishable" from the other members of the consortium, all of whom are united as one indivisible soul as they celebrate their blessed union with the divine (312). Under these circumstances, the Miltonic reader, albeit fallen, is now afforded the opportunity to establish a renewed relationship with God. This relationship reflects a welcome self-assurance in one's ability to regain what has otherwise been irretrievably lost as a result of the Fall. One who successfully undergoes this renewal experiences the true force of what Fish calls the "inner light," a phenomenon "that is at the very 'center' of Milton's theology" (191). Milton's "entire career," Fish observes, "can be viewed as an exercise in vigilance" to remain faithful to "the authority of the inner light" as a way of understanding those profound truths "written by the spirit of God in the fleshly tables of the regenerate heart" (191).[2] Although Fish elects not to explore the traditions that constitute the "inner light," he obviously views this phenomenon as essential to the Miltonic conception of how to renew one's relationship with God. At the very least, the concept of the "inner light" (particularly as it plays into Fish's underlying thesis that "Milton works from the inside out") would appear to be essential to a true understanding of "how Milton works." For Fish, this is the "Miltonic paradigm."[3]

Given such an outlook, one might be inclined to anticipate a reading of *Samson Agonistes* that accords with the views of those critics attuned to the profound truths written by the spirit of God in the fleshly tables of the regenerate heart. As we might expect, such critics — the so-called "regenerationists" — construe the action of the drama as a movement through suffering and progressive illumination toward the "inner light." Once fully ignited, this light becomes the means by which the rebirth of the fallen strong man is ultimately realized.[4] Inspired anew by the "rouzing motions" (1382) that imbue him, Samson rises from his ashes to destroy all in his path.[5] As committed as Fish might appear to be to this version of Miltonic paradigm, such an approach is nonetheless at odds with his interpretation of *Samson Agonistes*. Vigorously opposing the regenerationists, Fish offers a reading of the drama that is not only antiregenerationist but also downright subversive. That subversive dimension emerges full force in Fish's interpretation of the final moments of the drama. There, Fish construes Samson's destruction of the temple of Dagon and its inhabitants as an act that eludes any possibility of interpretation, regenerationist or otherwise. Not only is Fish against the regenerationist agenda in his reading of *Samson*, he also is opposed to the very notion that "interpretation" itself can yield any productive meaning at this crucial annihilative juncture in the action. So we are informed that "any hint of what [that act of annihilation] *means* (if it means anything) is precisely what Samson withholds from us when he withdraws into prayer or contemplation or whatever else he may or may not be doing in the moment that constitutes the play's final and most crucial gap" (471). No doubt reinforced by the fact that we learn of the catastrophic event through a messenger who has escaped "this so horrid spectacle" (*SA*, 1542), the "spectacular" or "ocular" dimensions of the drama become a source not of seeing or knowing but of confounding all attempts to understand.

The occlusive nature of these final moments does not come unannounced. In fact, Fish argues that throughout the drama the reader is implicitly made aware of the conundrum of not knowing. It is a conundrum centered in the figure of Samson as he rails against his plight. For all his "shows" of self-denunciation and mental turmoil, Samson remains an enigma, one we are incapable of deciphering, that is, of beholding face to face. Whether it might be the unspeakable horror of Samson's fallen condition or the fear of what a direct encounter with this abject, though potentially threatening, horror might produce, we are ever prompted to keep our distance. It is the dark irony of this dilemma that the eyeless Samson thrusts into the faces of his enemies through his final act at Dagon's temple. In anticipation of this act, he challenges his enemies to witness an even greater display of strength than that which they had earlier witnessed: "As with amaze shall strike all who behold" (*SA*, 1643–45). As much as Samson gives us a devastating spectacle, he reveals *nothing* about himself. That is, Samson ultimately "shows us — nothing" (471). We may behold in our mind's eye the spectacle of Samson's bringing down the house, but we are never permitted to enter the interior of the blind man's own mind: spectacle yields no evidence.[6] For Fish, the final scene, then, is one of complete occlusion, rather than of reassuring revelation. Confounded by this "emptiness or lack" at the core of the drama, we are in no position to mount an interpretation in response to the drama's climactic moment (472). The result of this inability to interpret is that in the end there is nothing to be said about Samson, no "aquist" of wisdom. "The only wisdom to be carried away from the play," Fish maintains, "is that there is no wisdom to be carried away." The result is a kind of interpretive anarchy, one characterized most tellingly by the refrain intoned throughout the book of Judges: "Every man did that which was right in his own eyes" (473). If one is inclined to criticize such a reading by pointing out it runs counter to claims concerning the "inner light" or the prospect of taking one's place among the angelic choir before the celestial throne, so be it. As much as Fish's reading of *Samson Agonistes* appears to violate the premises that are so basic to his study as a whole, his interpretation of Milton's drama raises issues of a profound order.

Assuming there is indeed such a gap or absence at the heart of Milton's drama, there will always be those prepared to fill the gap with a "plenitude" of criticism more nearly inspired by *ad hominem* rhetoric than by a willingness to address Fish's argument on its own terms. In fact, this has been the fate of

How Milton Works, a book that has become as much the occasion of polemic as the source of constructive discourse. On the polemical front, John Carey reigns supreme.[7] In an editorial in the *Times Literary Supplement,* Carey declared that even before the horrific events of 9/11, he viewed Fish's outlook as essentially destructive, if not annihilative. By approving of Samson's final act, Fish in effect aligns himself with all those who endorse Milton's "fantasy" of wreaking vengeance upon one's enemies. Moving seamlessly from Samson to Milton, Carey goes on to declare that Milton "was a subtle-minded poet not a murderous bigot." Guilty of such "bigotry," Fish, according to Carey, proves himself willing to adopt a "monstrous" point of view, one that serves as "a license for any fanatic to commit atrocity." With the onset of 9/11, Carey became all-the-more convinced of the potential horror encoded in Fish's reading of *Samson Agonistes.* "The events of the day seem like a devilish implementation of his [Fish's] arguments," Carey observed. In Carey's reading, Fish's interpretation of Milton's drama thereby transforms the biblical strong man into a "suicide bomber, and like the suicide bombers he believes that his massacre is an expression of God's will" (15).

In the process of casting these aspersions, Carey misses the point of Fish's argument entirely. Carey's error is in associating Fish with the regenerationist point of view and then castigating Fish as one who, in the fashion of the regenerationists, looks approvingly upon Samson's massacre of the Philistines. So Carey observes, "critics have traditionally seen Samson's massacre of the Philistines as a mark of spiritual regeneration." By extension, Fish is at the forefront of this interpretive movement. As we have seen, however, it is precisely the interpretation of the regenerationists that Fish calls into question. Whereas Fish's agenda is to read the action of Milton's drama as building to a crescendo the meaning of which is elusive, Carey's reading of Fish is one in which the action of Milton's drama builds to a crescendo the meaning of which is entirely ascertainable. Fish's reading is ultimately indeterminate (frighteningly so): there is no center, nowhere to look, no meaning to be grasped, or wisdom to be gotten. Carey's understanding of the regenerationist outlook is ultimately overdetermined. Once one accedes to Samson's ultimate regeneration, there is no other path but that of annihilation. This reading not only licenses atrocity but celebrates it, indeed, sees it as the reward for the kind of spiritual regeneration that authorizes the once-fallen hero to perform as God's champion in an act of whole-sale destruction. Fish's outlook may be nihilistic or perhaps antinomian, but it is not one that claims annihilation as the inevitable outcome of regaining one's station with God.

What, then, does this say about the title of Carey's piece, "A Work in Praise of Terrorism?" By specifying the work in question and providing a context in which to focus the discourse, the subtitle of the piece ("September 11 and *Samson Agonistes*") implicitly answers the question raised by the title: "Yes, Milton's drama has been conceived in this manner, especially in light of 9/11." Carey wants to let everyone know that whoever views Milton in these terms (a view Carey attributes to Fish as the most egregious offender) must now stand trial. As we have seen, Carey prosecutes the case by taking Fish's reading of *Samson Agonistes* out of context and applies modern notions of terrorism to that reading. Such a ploy, of course, is doomed from the start. As clever and as provocative as the phrase "a work in praise of terrorism" appears to be, the application of that phrase either to Milton's drama or to Fish's reading of it simply will not do, at least in part because of what the term "terrorism" implies.

As we are all no doubt aware, "terrorism," along with such terms as "terrorist" and "terrorize," is of relatively recent vintage. According to the *OED*, "terrorism" and "terrorist" are products of the late eighteenth century, whereas "terrorize" does not appear until the early decades of the nineteenth

century. In our own time, the reality of terrorism has assumed
such renewed urgency that its meanings are constantly under
scrutiny. Terrorism has become a dreadful part of our culture.
As a global phenomenon, it has been defined variously as a sys-
tematic process of subjugation perpetrated by those who seek
to gain power, revenge loss, or maintain tyrannical control
through various destructive acts of intimidation and victim-
ization.[8] This is terrorism in its secular form, but defining the
concept in these terms leaves out at least as much as it includes.
What it leaves out is the all-important element of religion. This
point is made evident in Mark Juergensmeyer's *Terror in the
Mind of God,* which has religious violence as its theme.[9] As
important as secular terrorism might appear to be, Juergensmeyer finds that religious terrorism — that is, terrorism inspired
by religious zeal — is even more significant as a defining characteristic of modern global culture. In fact, the U.S. government has proclaimed that terrorism in the name of religion is
"the most important security challenge we face in the wake
of the Cold War."[10] Exploring the relationship between religion
and terrorism, Juergensmeyer observes that the conjunction
between the two strikes at the heart of what he calls the "religious imagination." Crucial to terrorism, violence, in turn, has
"colored religion's darker, more mysterious symbols." "Images
of death," Juergensmeyer comments, "have never been far
from the heart of religion's power to stir the imagination" (6).
That act of stirring the imagination, in turn, speaks precisely
to what Juergensmeyer terms the "Theater of Terror" (121). This
theater plays itself out both in the "real world" and in dramatic
enactments of one sort or another. As such, these acts of terrorism can be understood as "constructed events" performed in
the context of "mind-numbing, mesmerizing, theater." Correspondingly, "at center stage are the acts themselves —stunning,
abnormal, and outrageous murders carried out in a way that
graphically displays the awful power of violence — set within

grand scenarios of conflict and proclamation" (124). The horrific events of 9/11 would most certainly come under the heading of Juergensmeyer's notions of terrorism and its "theatrical" dimensions.

In a kind of quid pro quo, however, one might also suggest that the U.S. attacks on Baghdad in March 2003 represent their own form of terrorism, one in which the sudden and relentless bombardment of the enemy is undertaken to promote a reaction of shock and awe among those who are attacked. In fact, the phrase "Shock and Awe" enjoys an official standing, one underscored by the teachings of Harlan Ullman, Colin Powell's instructor at the National War College. As delineated by Ullman and others, "Shock and Awe" is the most effective way to achieve "Rapid Dominance" against the enemy. In his manifesto on the subject, Ullman declares, "the key objective of Rapid Dominance is to impose this overwhelming level of Shock and Awe" upon the enemy in order to paralyze his will and render him "totally impotent and vulnerable to our actions." Ullman invites us to recall the media representations of those who suffered Shock and Awe in earlier military campaigns. "These images and expressions of shock," Ullman observes, "transcend race, culture, and history."[11] This is terrorism at the highest "official" level. The theatrical dimension is such that the experience of Shock and Awe is conceived as a theater of battle that provides the occasion for the unsuspecting recipients of Rapid Dominance to behold the spectacle of their own demise.

II

Viewed from this perspective, *Samson Agonistes* may be looked upon as the one of the finest literary expressions not only of Juergensmeyer's Theater of Terror but also of Ullman's concept of Shock and Awe. As such, Milton's drama is a theater in which the unsuspecting Philistines are subjected to their own shock and awe as they witness the spectacle of their demise. In the process, Samson becomes the major player in this theater of terror. Whether this makes Samson a "terrorist" or what Carey calls a "suicide bomber," referring to those responsible for the barbarity of 9/11, is, of course, another matter entirely, one that requires more extensive analysis than is possible here.

Certainly, terror itself is crucial to the Miltonic point of view. In *Paradise Lost*, for example, it is especially meaningful in its association with both God and the Son. As a gesture of allegiance to his Father, the Son assumes his role as undaunted warrior. Thus, he declares to the Father, "But whom thou hat'st, I hate, and can put on / Thy terrors, as I put thy mildness on, / Image of thee in all things" (6.734–36). What is so fascinating about this declaration is not only the concept of a God that hates but the notion of a Son that views himself in the position "putting on" God's terrors: both divine hatred and divine terrors are complementary manifestations of the *imago Dei*.[12] Attiring himself in the *habitus* of hatred and terror, the Son becomes a daunting force.[13] With his ascent onto the "Chariot of Paternal Deitie" (6:750), the Son undergoes a veritable transformation, one centered in his face. "Too severe to be beheld," his face becomes that of "terrour," as well as "wrauth bent on his Enemies" (6:823–26). Milton draws upon a kind of "incarnational poetics" to embody such phenomena as terror and hatred into the figure of the Son.

In *Samson Agonistes*, the catchword is not so much "terror" as "dread," although the two can certainly be viewed as synonymous.[14] As I have explored elsewhere, the very name of God in Milton's drama is "our living Dread."[15] Just as the Son in *Paradise Lost* veritably embodies God's terror, Samson veritably embodies God's dread. I make this point in part by focusing on the language Samson uses at the onset of the catastrophe. Samson declares, "Now of my own accord such other tryal / I mean to shew you of my strength, yet greater; / As with amaze shall strike all who behold" (1643–45). Samson adopts the very locution that God himself uses as a sign of God's supreme power. The locution "of my own accord" (literally, "by myself I have sworn") assumes the form of a biblical leit-motif imbued with all the denunciatory force of the swearing of oaths by an incensed God prepared to unleash his dread upon his desperate enemies (Jer. 22:5, 49:13; compare Gen. 22:16).[16] Rather than simply seeking to be avenged for the loss of his eyes in the manner of the biblical Samson, the Miltonic Samson subsumes within himself the divine role. In the process, the Miltonic Samson becomes that inscrutable force, that *mysterium tremendum* (to use Rudolf Otto's phrase), through which all the power and all the destructive might of one known as "our living Dread" manifests himself.[17]

That Samson is capable of assuming this role may have the ring of blasphemy to some. Suppose Samson is *not* divinely inspired to talk like God and thereby to assume that most archaic role of God as "our living Dread"? Samson does, after all, pull down the same destruction on himself that he metes out to his enemies. Such objections skirt the issue. The point is that Samson is able to talk like God because he is able to act like God. Samson is thereby empowered to be triumphantly destructive in God's cause. In that cataclysmic act, all sense of Samson's "beingness" is obliterated. With this obliteration, it is now his "livingness" that matters. He has become a force, a terror, and a dread: he exists totally within the context of this new role. That is his raison d'etre. In his final moments, Samson fulfills his role as terrorist. The avatar of terrorism, he becomes "our living Dread" incarnate. This is spectacle of the most extreme sort, and, as the living embodiment of God's "dread," Samson is the vehicle of it.[18]

The reason I mention all this is that I wish to give Carey a piece of advice. In order to establish his case more convincingly, Carey might well have aimed his barbs not at Stanley Fish but at Michael Lieb. On the surface, a serene and irenic fellow but beneath, a seething cauldron of vindictiveness, Lieb delights in writing about violence, whether as holy wars in *Paradise Lost* or as *sparagmos* throughout Milton's works.[19] Accordingly, Lieb would have been a much better candidate for Carey's colasterion. Carey could have easily (and with some justification) castigated Lieb for succumbing to our baser instincts. In the case of the biblical account, at least, such instincts are made evident in Samson's outcry (as the Hebrew text relates) that he be "avenged upon the Philistines" for the loss of "one of [his] two eyes" (Judg. 16: 28). Freud would have had a field day with this one. Freudian or not, the Miltonic Samson is far more complex than that biblical fellow. Here, I believe that Fish is at his most profound.

As Fish argues, Milton's Samson does indeed defy all attempts to know, to understand, to perceive. The enigma of Samson is what underlies the Miltonic conception, one that has as much to do with God as with God's fallen emissary. This is a conception in which any attempt to penetrate the mystery of Samson will be thwarted. Just as the *deus absconditus* refuses to betray its secrets, "Samson *absconditus*" confounds all interpretive efforts to clarify.[20] By coining the phrase "Samson *absconditus*," however, I in no way seek to argue that for Fish there is any kind of union (or reunion) between God and Samson at the culminating moment of the drama. That is perhaps for the regenerationists to argue (although even here I harbor misgivings). Rather than having God and Samson unite in the "great event," the meaning of which is evident to everyone, God and Samson may be said to unite only in being simply inaccessible, "objects alike of an interpretive activity that finds no corroboration in the visible world." This too is a "union" of sorts, a union of the inaccessible, the unknowable, the enigmatic. So conceived, the relationship between Samson and God at the end of the drama is one in which Samson is looked upon "as mysterious — as difficult to read — as the God whose

disposition he refuses to appoint." For Fish, Samson's final catastrophic act overwhelms not only the Philistines but also readers, who are at a loss to know what it all means. That is why
we, along with the Philistines, are left "amazed" — that is,
"filled with panic, astonished, turned to stone." (471). I endorse
this reading up to a point, and that point is the extent to which
we are permitted to return the gaze of Samson at that final
moment of "eyes fast fixt" (1638).

This moment leads Fish to invoke the figure of the Gorgon
Medusa. With this figure at hand, he argues that the portrayal
of Samson just before he overwhelms the Philistines is one in
which Milton conflates "the terrible visage Samson now presents with the face and look of Medusa" (472). We recall from
the mythology through which this creature is forged that the
Gorgon Medusa is a monstrous figure indeed.[21] With a round,
ugly face, snakes instead of hair, a belt of boar's teeth, gigantic wings, and eyes capable of transforming into stone anyone
foolish enough to return their gaze, Medusa's visage is horrific
indeed.[22] To ballast his argument about Samson, Fish reminds
us of the Elder Brother's reference in *Comus* to "that snaky-
headed *Gorgon* sheild / That wise *Minerva* wore." With this
shield as a weapon, Minerva "freez'd her foes to congeal'd
stone," while it "dash't" "brute violence" with "sudden ado-
ration, and blank awe" (447–53).[23] Fish focuses on the "blank
awe" brought about by the Gorgon Medusa. In Fish's reading,
"blankness" is everything: it is "the emptiness or lack at the
heart of the story, the absence of an intelligibility that would
allow us to master a narrative that disables us at what is supposed to be its climactic moment." Fish alludes to Lacan as
one who has disclosed the significance of the "lack" or
"absence" that results in the act of beholding a Samson "shorn
of meaning." That significance is the fear of castration. However
"current" such a view is in Lacan, it was already voiced by Freud
in his brief but cogent "Medusa's Head" (1940). There, Freud

addresses the idea of "the horrifying decapitated head of Medusa" as specifically a fear of castration. "The terror of Medusa is thus a terror of castration," Freud concludes.[24] In his own way, the Medusa-like Samson is terrifying in the extreme, liable at any point to wreak havoc and destruction upon all who would presume to cross him, to gaze back upon that awful eyeless being.

Most important, however, is the blankness of Samson, what Milton in another context calls a "Universal blanc," that confronts him at all points.[25] Characterized by "emptiness or lack," this blankness is an "absence" that plunges us into a world of nothingness, a world in which nothing will come of nothing, a world of anarchy, of impotence, of death. I believe that this is the essence of Fish's reading of *Samson Agonistes*. An adherence to that principle is what Fish (in another context) calls "the dark side" of his interpretive convictions (565). These convictions are veritably grounded in the idea of death. In the introduction to his book, Fish sets the stage for the argument by invoking Freud's *Beyond the Pleasure Principle*. There, Fish finds the idea that "the aim of all life is death," an idea that not only underlies Freudian psychology but that is "a perfect description of Milton's thought and work." On the positive side, this view can lead to the timeless world celebrated in Milton's *At a Solemn Music*. On the negative side, it can lead to the horrific experience of the Gorgon Medusa that underscores the "blank awe" of *Samson Agonistes*. This is most certainly an unsettling yet fascinating notion of how Milton works.

Given the interpretive premises upon which the argument of *How Milton Works* is based, is it meaningful then to speak of Fish as a scholar who would endorse the idea of Samson as a terrorist? I think not. To speak of terrorism or the committing of terrorist acts is to speak of motive. For Fish, the determination of Samson's motives at the time of his act of overwhelming the Philistines is an impossible enterprise. Any attempt to discover the means of implementing such an enterprise is doomed from the start because implementation requires evidence, and all that greets us is the blankness that constitutes the most inner being of the strong man's reasons for behaving in the way that he does. For Lieb, who does see (or believes he sees) a movement in the drama to the climactic and indeed catastrophic event toward which the action leads, Samson becomes the means by which the reclaimed strong man can triumphantly carry on the work of a God whose very name is "Dread" and who freely dispenses his largess of destruction and devastation upon his enemies with a heart full of indignation and rage. Between the two Samsons (that of Fish and that of Lieb), we have two ways of understanding Milton: his most deeply held convictions and his mode of operation. The choice is ours to make, but be prepared to join the devil's party if you hook up with Lieb.

10 • "There Is Nothing He Cannot Ask"
Milton, Liberalism, and Terrorism

Stanley Fish

Preface

Since September 11, 2001, I have found myself the object of criticism from what appear at first to be different directions. From one direction I was chided (along with others) for holding certain philosophical views — labeled poststructuralist and postmodernist — that were said either to be responsible for the country's vulnerability to terrorist attack or to be corrosive of the country's resolve in the aftermath of terrorist violence. The reasoning was that since postmodernism and poststructuralism proclaim the unavailability of universally accepted standards by which actions might be evaluated, this form of thought eliminates the possibility of defending the superiority of the American way of life. According to what postmodernism tells us, some commentators complain, the terrorists' agenda and culture are in principle no better or worse than ours, and, therefore, the judgment that what they did was wrong or evil cannot be supported by reasons all rational persons would accept.

From another direction I was attacked for my reading of Milton's *Samson Agonistes*, and specifically for my contention that what Samson does in the climactic (although offstage) action of the play — tear down the Philistine temple and kill thousands of men, women, and children — must be considered praiseworthy because he believes (he cannot be sure) that it is what God wants him to do. Obviously, the link between the two criticisms of me is terrorism and especially the terrorism that takes the form of religiously inspired violence. Common to both lines of criticism is the worry that in the absence of an independent measure in relation to which judgments of right and wrong can be made, the moral life becomes a sham, for any act can be justified simply by claiming for it divine inspiration — not the devil, but God made me do it.

I. *A License for Atrocity*

In the September 6, 2002, issue of the *Times Literary Supplement* John Carey published a piece entitled "A Work in Praise of Terrorism? September 11 and *Samson Agonistes.*"[1] The essay is a complaint against what Carey takes to be the usual reading of Milton's play "as a work in praise of terrorism" and as "Milton's fantasy vengeance on his Royalist conquerors." In Carey's view, this reading turns the "subtle minded" Milton into a "murderous bigot." A better reading, he says, would pay attention to the many points in the play where Milton encourages us to question Samson's motivation and actions and render a negative judgment on them. Carey thus repeats and extends the analysis he offered in the preface to his 1968 edition of the play where he calls the act of pulling down the

Philistine temple "morally disgusting," and a "bloody act of vengeance" which, while it may be praised by the partisan Chorus and by Samson's father, is condemned "at a deeper level" by the "progression of imagery" and by much else.[2]

Carey's longtime conviction that Samson should be read as a negative model — a conviction shared by Irene Samuel, William Empson, Joseph Wittreich, Jane Melbourne, Derek Wood, and others — has been reinforced, he tells us, by the events of September 11, 2001. He explains that if we regard Samson's final action as one the play approves, then it could be said that Milton, were he alive today, would make no distinction between the Hebrew strongman and the hijackers who brought down the World Trade Center towers, or as they might say, brought down the Philistine temple of U.S. capitalism. For, as Carey points out, "the similarities between the biblical Samson and the hijackers are obvious": "Like them Samson sacrifices himself to achieve his ends. Like them he destroys many innocent victims, whose lives, hopes and loves are all quite unknown to him personally. He is, in effect, a suicide bomber, and like the suicide bombers he believes that his massacre is an expression of God's will" (15).

In this last we find the real object of Carey's ire, not Samson or even the hijackers, but the idea that acts of violence could be justified by the conviction of those who perform them that they are doing the will of God. This "viewpoint," he says, is "monstrous," and he finds a particularly monstrous instance of it in my assertion that insofar as Samson's action is an expression of "his desire to conform to [God's] will, it is a virtuous action," and that, moreover, *No other standard for evaluating it exists.* "Samson's act," I go on to say (and Carey quotes this sentence too), "is praiseworthy because he intends it to be answerable to the divine will; whether it is or not . . . he cannot know and neither can we; and in relation to the problem of judging him as a moral being, whether it is or not does not matter."[3] This line of reasoning, Carey complains, amounts to "a license for any fanatic to commit atrocity," and if "this is truly what *Samson Agonistes* teaches, should it not be withdrawn from schools and colleges . . . as an incitement to terrorism?"

Before I respond directly to Carey's challenge, I should acknowledge that there is more than a little to be said for his linking of Samson and Islamic suicide bombers. (Whether this amounts to Milton's sanctioning of terrorism is a question that depends on the prior question of just what terrorism is, a question I shall take up later.) First of all, there are passages in the play that explicitly assert that what has happened has unfolded under the direction of God. God not only approves Samson's slaughter of the Philistines; he has engineered it, says the Semichorus: "While thir hearts were jocund and sublime, / Drunk with Idolatry . . . / Chanting their Idol and preferring / Before our living Dread / . . . Among them hee a spirit of frenzy sent, / Who hurt thir minds, / And urg'd them on with mad desire / To call in haste for thir destroyer" (1669–70, 1672–73, 1675–78).[4] The key phrase is "drunk with idolatry," for it identifies those who die as persons who, quite literally, worship false Gods and who therefore have set themselves up in opposition to the true one.[5] Hence, they deserve what they get and have, in the strongest sense, brought it on themselves. Indeed, because they are spiritually dead to the living God, they are in effect already dead; they are barely human beings, for the spirit of God does not live within them.

This demonizing and dehumanizing of the enemy, as Mark Juergensmeyer remarks, are standard features of religiously justified acts of violence: the foe is turned into a satanic figure "in the scenario of cosmic war."[6] And the report that such a foe died a violent death can be welcomed with joy as Manoa and the Chorus do in gleeful anticipation of the event: "What if . . . / He now be dealing dole among his foes, / And over heaps of slaughtered walk his way?" asks the Chorus, and Manoa answers in a line that perfectly captures the frenzy and exultation of religiously inspired hate: "That were a joy presumptuous to be thought" (1527–31). Manoa later declares that there is nothing to lament (1708) — certainly not the death of thousands of Philistines — and much to celebrate, for "Samson hath quit himself / Like Samson and heroically hath finish'd / A life Heroic, on his enemies / Fully reveng'd" (1709–12).

Now, one might object — and the objection would have force — that these passages prove only that the idea of God-sanctioned violence is put forward in the play and is persuasive to some of its characters. They do not prove that the play, and by extension Milton, embraces the idea even if the Hebrew Chorus and Samson's father, partisan and limited persons after all, do. Still, it is worth noting, first, that *Samson Agonistes* does display the justification Carey so dislikes — I am doing this because I believe God wants me to — and, second, that the form the justification takes is uncannily like the form it takes in modern instances of religiously justified violence. In *Terror and Liberalism*, Paul Berman describes what he takes to be a "new kind of politics" that has "come into flower" in the last hundred years.[7] (We are concerned here with an earlier flowering.) "It was the politics of slaughter — slaughter for the sake of sacred devotion, slaughter conducted in a mood of spiritual loftiness, slaughter that led to suicide" (110). In the course of the book, Berman traces the sources of this politics and finds that one of them is the Book of Revelation, the message of which he summarizes as follows: "The subversive and polluted city dwellers of Babylon will be exterminated together with all their abominations. . . . The destruction will be horrifying. . . . Afterward, when the extermination is complete, the reign of Christ will be established and will endure 1000 years and the people of God will live in purity, submissive to God" (47).

We recognize here a crude form of the millenarianism Milton entertained and at times professed in the 1640s, a millenarianism that led Hanserd Knollys in *A Glimpse of Sion's Glory*

(1641) to proclaim, "Blessed is he that dasheth the brats of Babylon against the stones."[8] It is this spirit that Berman finds in all of the twentieth century's destructive movements — fascism, communism, radical Islam (and he might have added Christian Identitarianism and Meir Kahane's brand of militant Judaism). In each of these, he says, the story is the same: "The subversive dwellers in Babylon were always aided by Satanic forces from beyond and the Satanic forces were always pressing on the people of God from all sides" (49). Always the majority of the people of God is complacent and unaware of the imminent danger, and always the call to arms, spiritual and physical, is issued by a "revolutionary vanguard who, by embracing death, will awaken the sleeping nation" (119). ("Awake, arise, or be forever fallen.")

Berman is horrified by the politics of slaughter and he recommends in its place the kinder, gentler vision of Enlightenment Liberalism. The heart of this liberalism, he tells us, "is the recognition that all of life is not governed by a single, all-knowing and all-powerful authority — by a divine force. It was the tolerant idea that every sphere of human activity — science, technology, politics, religion, and private life — should operate independently of the others without trying to yoke everything together under a single guiding hand. It was a belief in the many instead of the one" (37). It was, in short, the belief that the private and the public spheres should be distinguished and kept separate so that in each the appropriate obligations will be honored and neither will claim supervisory scope over the other. "Render unto Caesar. . . ." Berman knows that it is precisely this doctrine that infuriates religious militants who are repelled by the idea that the obligation to do God's will can be relaxed while the business of the world is conducted by the man who, as Milton puts it in the *Areopagitica,* trades all day in his shop "without his religion."[9] But it is just such a sequestering of religion "in one corner, while the state does its business in a different corner" (79) that is necessary, Berman believes, if religious impulses are not to erode and overwhelm the commitment to public and general laws.

II. *Intentions and Consequences*

With some of the pertinent issues now foregrounded, we can bring Carey back to center stage and listen to him as he throws down the gauntlet:

> From where does [Fish] derive his certainty that "Samson's act is praiseworthy because he intends it to be answerable to the divine will"? Faced with the horror of Samson's crime, on what does he base his assertion that *"no other standard for evaluating it exists"* apart from the perpetrator's desire to perform what he takes to be God's intention? To most people common humanity supplies *"a standard for evaluating"* mass murder. Why does it not do so for Fish? (16)

The first thing to notice is that Carey's language presupposes as obvious and unchallengeable the liberal world view Berman champions; presupposes, that is, that in a civilized society, one in which religion has been safely quarantined, the only response to the death of so many is horror and condemnation. But to call Samson's act a "crime" and "mass murder" and to label the actor a "fanatic" from the beginning is to assume, without argument, everything that is in dispute both in the play — witness the exchange between Samson and Harapha on the nature of Samson's deeds — and in the criticism, which since the time of Sir Richard Jebb has been debating whether the spirit of *Samson Agonistes* is Hebraic and tribal or Hellenic and cosmopolitan. That is to say, Carey answers by fiat the question at the heart of Milton's interest here and elsewhere, the question of how one is to assess either actions or outcomes, given opposing interpretive perspectives on an event and in the absence of an uncontroversially authoritative pronouncement (an absence intensified by the condition of drama, lacking as it does a clear authorial voice).

Carey's answer to this interpretive question is simple: a lot of people whom Samson didn't know and who never harmed him died; therefore, it must be mass murder and he must be a fanatic. But Milton's answers to questions like this are never simple because he is acutely aware of the difficulty Carey slides by. We need only recall that extraordinary moment in *Paradise Lost* when, after he has heard Michael exclaim "Author of evil, unknown till thy revolt" (6.262), Satan retorts, "The strife which thou call'st evil . . . wee style / The strife of Glory" (289–90). By citing these verses, I do not mean to suggest that Milton intends us to understand that there is nothing to choose between these two accounts; rather, I think, we are intended to understand that we cannot make the choice — cannot say what kind of act the rebellion is — by simply pointing to what seem to be its empirical consequences; and we cannot do that because those consequences can be variously described ("we style it the strife of glory") and, depending on the description, the event will be given a different value. To base the judgment of an act on its consequences is to give over the responsibility of judgment to the shifting winds of the history of reception.

How, then, would Milton have us proceed if not by looking, as Carey does, to the "hideous consequences"? The answer I give, and here I am likely to be again the object of Carey's strictures, is that Milton would have us proceed by looking to the spirit within which an act is performed — to its intentional structure — rather than to what may or may not occur in its wake. My authority for this view is not my own moral or theoretical convictions and certainly not my conviction that the death of a lot of people is a good thing, but Milton's many pronouncements in his prose and poetry. One that is particular to our point is found in *The Tenure of Kings and Magistrates*, where in the course of justifying the execution of Charles I, Milton quotes with approval Sir Thomas Smith's assertion that in assessing such an act, "the vulgar judge of it according to the event, and the lerned according to the purpose of them that do it" (YP 3:221). That is to say, in a world where outcomes (but not intentions) are contingent, we should not, says Milton, justify our actions retroactively by waiting to see how they turned out and then reasoning backward to their virtue or vice, as Samson does when he decides that, given what has happened to him, the marriage to Dalila was a bad idea ("I thought it lawful from my former act"). Rather, it is a necessary and sufficient justification if the act issues from a desire to do God's will and to follow the path of obedience rather than the path of carnal impulse. (On this view of the matter, the road to hell could *not* be paved with good intentions.)

Of course, the distinction between the two paths is not always easy to discern, and one may come to doubt that it has been precisely observed either by oneself or by others; but it is, nevertheless, a real distinction and the exchange between Samson and Dalila turns on it. She says — in an anticipation bordering on parody of Don Adams's "Get Smart" tagline, "would you believe *this?*" — I did it for this reason, no, for that reason, for the reason of civil duty, for the reason of religion, because the priests urged me to, because the maxims of "wisest men" urged me to, and on and on. In response, he says, that's "hypocrisy" (872), that is, "the feigning of beliefs, feelings or virtues that one does not hold or possess." He repeats the accusation when he declares Dalila to be not "sincere" (874). It is sincerity, the intention to do good and to be true to one's deepest loyalties, that justifies, not some confected heap of tried-on and cosmetically applied reasons. (The integrity and priority of intention requires that it be as independent of worldly pressures as it is of worldly consequences.) That is why Dalila's attempt to equate her action with Jael's, who "Smote Sisera sleeping, through the Temples nail'd" (990), doesn't work in Samson's or, I believe, in Milton's eyes: Jael acted under the direction of and in service to the Lord (at least that is what is said in Judges 4:15 and following), while Dalila acted from a mixture of jealousy, ambition, and the desire to keep Samson a prisoner.[10] On the surface, the two acts — Jael's and Dalila's — may be indistinguishable; indeed, Dalila's could be said to be the less culpable given that Samson, unlike Sisera, is left alive. But the surface — the world of measurable effects, of outcomes or consequences — is not what Milton is interested in; it is in the interior recesses of the willing and intending heart that he finds the true arena of moral testing.

This same internalization of value has an aesthetic equivalent in his thought, as we can see, for example, in *Paradise Regained*, where the superiority of the Hebrew prophets to the Greek and Roman orators is attributed in part to "their majestic unaffected style" (*PR* 4.359). The question is: what is the difference between a majestic, unaffected style and a majestic affected style? The answer, Milton would say, cannot be found in a description of their respective formal features, for by that measure they will be exactly alike; one will just be the technically proficient counterfeit of the other. The true measure of the difference is interior. In one case, the words proceed from some calculated intention to deceive or impress; in the other, the words — the very same words in one sense but completely different in another — proceed "from a sincere heart" and "unbidden come into the outward gesture" (YP 1:941). And how can you tell the difference? Only if the difference is already inscribed within you. One cannot either recognize true virtue or praise it "unless he have in himself the experience and the practice of all that which is praise-worthy" (890). Whether the question is whose action, Dalila's or Jael's, is praiseworthy, or whose words are truly majestic, the answer will not be found by inspecting the outward signs. Only the intention, the unbidden and constitutive inward orientation, makes the difference, and the difference can only be recognized by one who is its (internal) bearer. It takes one to know one.

Everywhere one looks in Milton, one finds this preference (too weak a word) for the inner over the outer; everywhere one finds a refusal to mark crucial differences of judgment and evaluation on the basis of what can be observed and measured, on the basis, that is, of the letter. And this is true even if the letter is Scripture. There is, says Milton, a double scripture, "the external scripture of the written word and the internal scripture of the Holy Spirit which he . . . has engraved upon the hearts of believers"; and while "the external authority for our faith, in other words, the scriptures, is of considerable importance. . . . The pre-eminent and supreme authority, however, is the authority of the Spirit, which is internal and the individual possession of each man" (YP 6:587). Because it is an *individual* possession, you can't borrow it from another; after all, "a man may be a heretic in the truth" (*Areopagitica*, YP 2:545). And, moreover, when the prompting of the internal scripture inclines you to an action contrary to what the external scripture apparently commands, the internal scripture — the law written on the fleshly tables only you can see — always trumps. "Thus if I keep the Sabbath, in accordance with the ten commandments, when my faith prompts me to do otherwise, my precise compliance will be counted as sin," for it "is faith that justifies, not compliance with the commandments" (YP 6:639). The faith that justifies is unavailable for inspection, and therefore no man can determine from the outside whether or not you have it.

In the *Doctrine and Discipline of Divorce*, Milton employs exactly the same reasoning to argue that no one except he who has experienced it can testify to the absence of the spiritual communion that makes a marriage a marriage. "*Paulus Emilius*, beeing demanded why hee would put away his wife for no visible reason, *This shoo*, saith he, and held it out on his foot, *is a neat shoo, a new shoo, and yet none of yee know where it wrings me?* [M]uch less . . . can such a private difference be examin'd, neither ought it" (YP 2:348). The marriage that "wrings" a man is already broken, is already no marriage, and the divorce the law will not grant him is already in effect, "for he that would divorce . . . but for the law, hath in the sight of God don it already" (YP 2:348–49). Just as man is commanded to "break the Sabbath" if keeping it would be "unfruitfull either to Gods glory or the good of man," so must he not "injoyn the indissoluble keeping of a marriage found unfit" lest by doing so he "make an Idol of mariage" and "advance it above the worship of God" by making it a "transcendent command" (YP 2:276). The only command that is transcendent is the command of the Holy Spirit, of the "inward man, which not any law but conscience can evince" (YP 2:349).

Whether the question is what makes a marriage a true union, or what makes a line of poetry majestic, or what makes an action good, or what makes a law authoritative, or what makes a king legitimate, or what makes a regicide justifiable, the answer Milton gives is always the same: what is necessary is the indwelling presence of the spirit. If the things you do are done in response to that spirit — in response to faith — they are good, even if from some perspectives (perhaps the major-ity of perspectives) the result is an unhappy one. Conversely, things that are done in response to external promptings (of the kind that move Dalila) are inauthentic and therefore bad, even if from some perspectives (perhaps the majority of perspectives) the result is fortunate. The general rule is given in *A Treatise of Civil Power:* "I here mean by conscience or religion, that full perswasion whereby we are assur'd that our beleef and prac-tise, as far as we are able to apprehend and probably make appeer, is according to the will of God & his Holy Spirit within us, which we ought to follow much rather than any law of man" (YP 7:242). Note that the requirement is not that our practice is in fact in accordance with the will of God (a determination not within our power to make), but that insofar as we can "apprehend" or grasp the matter we are persuaded that it is (we may, after all, turn out to have been wrong). In short, what is asked of us is not a specific performance, but a specific intention, the intention to do God's will: We "are justified by the faith we have, not by the work we do" (YP 7:266).

III. *The Interpretive Drama*

Here, then, is the not-so-short answer to John Carey's question: where does Fish derive his certainty that Samson's act is praiseworthy because he intends it as an expression of obedience to the will of God? I derive my certainty from the writings of Milton, including the Argument of this very play where the poet describes Samson as being "persuaded inwardly" without passing judgment on the question of whether or not his inward persuasion corresponds to the truth of what God really wants him to do. I also find in those same writings a recognition of the dangers Carey correctly associates with the idea that one can justify deeds, no matter how "hideous" their consequences, by saying that they are a response to the will of God. The chief danger is that people who believe themselves to be acting in response to God's will may, in fact, be acting in response to the urgings of their own will, and may therefore clothe their commission of sin in the robe of self-righteousness. The point is made by Victoria Kahn in the context of a discussion of "reasons of state," which exceed positive law and claim the status of justified exceptions on the basis of a higher law. But, as Kahn observes, "this reference to a higher law is problematic since reason of state can be feigned to justify lowly considerations of expedience and self-interest."[11] "From the very beginning," she says, "Samson's task is to understand himself as an exception" (1078), but of course that is precisely the problem. Someone who understands himself or herself as an exception to positive law may feel licensed by that understanding to do anything he or she likes. Saint Paul poses the key question — "Shall we sin, because we are not under the law, but under grace?" (Rom. 6:14–15). Does the belief that we are under grace mean that we can do anything we like? "God forbid," says Paul, and Milton amplifies: "It is not a less perfect life that is required from Christians but, in fact, a more perfect life than was required of those who were under the law" (YP 6:535). The end for which the law was instituted — namely, "the love of God and of our neighbor" (YP 6:531) — remains; it is just that the law no longer has residence in an external code (even the code of the Scriptures) but is written on the hearts of believers where it is legible only to them. And therein lies the difficulty; for the heart on which the law is written has its own desires and in the absence of an external authority or test the task of disentangling those desires from the pious desire to do God's will is arduous, never ending, and full of anxiety.

This is a perfect description of what Samson is doing at every moment. He is, as the Chorus says (the Chorus is not always wrong), "laboring" his mind (1298). That is, he is trying to figure out the relationship between his present situation and God's will, and he is trying to determine whether and in what circumstances he might once again be an instrument of that will. The drama of the play is thus an interior one; the drama, as many have said, is interpretive, and the interpretive stakes are as high as they get, eternal life or spiritual death.[12] The big question — and everyone in the play has a go at answering it — is how can one identify the true path to obedience amid all the conflicting agendas, guides, rationales, and rationalizations? The action of the play, at least as I describe it, consists of the discovery, made again and again by characters and readers alike, that the world's visible signs do not provide an authoritative answer to that question in the form of a recipe or a test or an algorithm.[13]

This is all I mean by the judgment that so incenses Carey: the judgment that, insofar as Samson's act is the outward gesture of his interior desire to do God's will, "it is a virtuous action" and "no other standard for evaluating it exists." I should add — although I wouldn't have thought it necessary — that no other standard exists *in the play.* Carey seems to think that by giving this account of what Samson does, I endorse it and endorse too the reason — "me hungering . . . to do my Father's will" (*PR,* 2.259) — I assign to it. But I endorse nothing except my reading — I am doing literary criticism, not morality — and the basis of that reading is not any personal view I might have about religiously inspired violence, now or then, but the repeated de-authorization *in the play* of every external sign — of every other standard — that might serve as a guide to interpretive certainty. Interpretive certainty (or at least interpretive confidence) could be achieved if a relationship of cause and effect could be established between the return of Samson's strength, the rejection of Dalila's several appeals, the recovery of his spirits in the form of some "rousing motions," the pulling down of the temple, and, most importantly, the return of God's favor (which assumes it has been lost, an assumption Samson makes but not one the play ratifies). But while the elements requisite for the determination of a cause and effect relationship are present in the play — Samson's strength does return, he does resist Dalila, he does experience rousing motions, he does pull down the temple — they are not arranged (as they are in other versions of the story) in a way that encourages or allows us to draw a straight line from them to the return of God's favor. It is not that there are no answers to the question "What is the meaning of what happens at the temple?"; it is, rather, that there are too many answers — given by the Chorus, by Manoa, by Harapha, by Dalila (not, however, by Samson) — and that not one of them is unambiguously confirmed.

This refusal to provide interpretive guidance leaves readers and critics where it leaves the characters, arguing about the significance of Samson's actions present, past, and future and finding no independent and visible measure by which they could be assessed. In his exchange with Dalila, Samson's measure is sincerity, or purity of intention, something one can claim, but hardly demonstrate. In the exchange with Harapha, the Philistine giant plays the role of John Carey by confronting Samson with the empirical measure of visible (and hideous) consequences. What God, he asks, will accept a champion who is "A murderer, a revolter and a robber" (*SA* 1180)? "How dost thou prove me these?" (1181), Samson replies, and the giant answers by pointing to specific acts: you did this, and then that, and then committed this other outrage, all while you were "subject to our lords" (1182). Samson first responds by invoking the traditional argument that deeds, otherwise suspect, are allowable in times of war — "force with force / Is well ejected when the conquered can" (1206–07) — but then he turns to his true and stronger (in the sense of more deeply believed) position: "I was no private but a person raised / With strength sufficient and command from Heav'n" (1211–12). Or, in other words, what you call robbery, murder, and revolt, I style as the effects of obedience to God. It is because I do these things in response to heaven's command that they are justified, and no other standard for evaluating them exists.

IV. *Antinomianism*

Of course, the fact that the account Samson gives of the motive for his actions perfectly accords with mine does not render that account the right one or the one Milton would approve. It does, however, allow us to give a name to Samson: he is an antinomian, as, I believe, Milton was also. That is, he prefers to any outward justification of his actions the internal justification of the Spirit of God working within him (with due allowance always for the difficulty of telling the difference between that spirit and promptings less noble). "From the Middle Ages on," says Norman Burns, "the antinomianism implicit in the law breaking of Old Testament heroes was usually tamed by asserting that they acted on divine commands."[14] Burns is convinced, as I am, that Milton "reconceived the character of Samson found in the Book of Judges and . . . presented Samson . . . as an antinomian hero of faith" (28).[15]

To be sure, calling Samson an antinomian does not clear him of the charge of terrorism, for there remains the possibility that "antinomian" is just another word for terrorist. This is certainly the view of J. MacBride Sterret, who in a dictionary of theology describes antinomianism as the doctrine of "extreme fanatics who deny subjection to any law other than the subjective caprices of the empirical individual," and goes on to say that "all moral sophists are antinomians, all who pervert the principle that the end justifies the means into a disregard for established moral laws, so that some personal or finite end be attained." Sterret's distress at the argument implicit in antinomianism — I do it under the command of the Spirit — is more than matched by the anonymous author of "An Answer to a Book Entitled 'The Doctrine and Discipline of Divorce'" (1644), who complains that if Milton's view of divorce were accepted, "it would be an occasion to the corrupt heart of man without any just cause at all, merely to satisfy his lust, to pretend causes of divorce." "Who sees not," he exclaims, "how many thousands of lustfull and libidinous men would be parting from their Wives every week?,"[16] a question answered amusingly in 1646 by Thomas Edwards when he reports a conversation with a Mistris Attaway who, after having read *Doctrine and Discipline*, "hath practised it in running away with another womans husband."[17] This is how it is, says the anonymous respondent to Milton's tract, with those who go around doing anything they like and justifying it by saying, "We live in Christ, and Christ doth all for us; we are Christed with Christ and Godded with God."[18]

Obviously, "antinomian," like "terrorist," is not a name one gives oneself, and indeed in this same *Doctrine and Discipline of Divorce,* Milton lumps the doctrine with anabaptism and other *"fanatick* dreams" (YP 2:278). Nevertheless, by all the signs, Milton is an antinomian, although, as we have seen, his version of antinomianism, far from relaxing the requirements of morality, tightens them and makes them more difficult to live up to. What links antinomianism with terrorism, at least on the surface, is the doctrine (decried by Sterret) that the end justifies the means, the doctrine that no action is to be recoiled from if God commands it, or (and here is where all the interpretive troubles come back in) you are persuaded inwardly that God commands it. Milton, says Joan Bennett, agreed with the Ranter Laurence Clarkson that "there is no single commandment that literally and absolutely must not be broken" in the service of faith, although those not informed by that faith or informed by another will see what you do differently.[19] Milton himself "advocated in the regicide tracts what royalists called murder, in the divorce tracts what clergy called adultery" (*Reviving Liberty,* 110), just as, she might have added, Harapha would call what Samson is about to do, were he to know about it in advance, mass murder and atrocity by suicide.

The antinomian hero stakes everything on a faith that no sign in the external world confirms, a faith that many signs in the external world point away from. That is why, as Bennett observes, the paradigmatic antinomian hero, one to whose example Milton often returns, is Abraham, the first in the catalog of the heroes of faith in Hebrews 11, who is resolved to kill his son because God has told him to. Bennett quotes Christopher Fry's version of the story in which Isaac asks, "Is there nothing he may not ask of thee" and Abraham answers "nothing":

> This is the illumination of antinomian Christian liberty: There is nothing he may not ask. . . . At stake is not whether one suffers or dies, but whether one suffers in faith, trusting, as Abraham does, that the seeming contradiction of a law is accounted for

by the highest purpose of the whole law, God's love. Abraham . . .
is prepared to kill his son, not in spite of the fact that he loves
Isaac, but *because* he loves him. This is the purest antinomianism. (*Reviving Liberty,* 156)

If so, it is easy to see why many want nothing to do with it.
While the argument may have a theological cogency — were
Abraham to disobey God for the sake of Isaac, he would make
Isaac into an idol or "transcendent command" by preferring
him to the Creator — the price of its cogency may seem too
high, a licensing of the license performed by those who need
only say I act according to the inner promptings of the Spirit.
Going down that path legitimizes people who, hearkening to
inner voices or to rousing motions, commit what certainly looks
like mass murder. Would it not be better, one might ask, to
put to one side the question — unavailable to a *public* answer —
of what God commands and settle (if that is the word) for what
is commanded by the imperative to live in peace and (possible) prosperity with one's neighbors, an imperative that requires
obedience to procedural and published rules no matter what
inner messages one believes oneself to have received from on
high? To that question, liberalism, the political philosophy that
honors the procedural means above the substantive end and
preaches the priority of the right over the good, will answer
yes in thunder and will supplement that answer with a side-
long glance at negative examples such as Samson and Jim
Jones, who illustrate the danger of following the light of conscience wherever it leads. Samson, or perhaps the more reflective
Milton, might reply that there are worse things than death and
that the destruction of cities or civilizations informed by the
spirit of Sodom and Gomorrah is a necessary prelude to the
building of a better, purer world. One might even argue that
in destroying or extirpating evil, the faithful hero follows or
anticipates the example of Christ, who will, says Milton,

> dissolve
> Satan with his perverted World, then raise
> From the conflagrant mass, purg'd and refin'd,
> New Heavens and new Earth, Ages of endless date
> Founded in righteousness and peace and love,
> To bring forth fruits, Joy and Eternal Bliss.   (*PL*, 12.546–51)

V. *The Question of Terrorism*

There we must leave the question of what law we are to follow and by what signs we are to know it in the confidence that
(a) there will be no end of answers to it; (b) that no answer will
be independently authorized; and that (therefore) (c) interpretive challenges of the kind put to Samson will always be with
us. But perhaps we can take one last stab at the question or
questions that brought us here. Is the Samson of *Samson
Agonistes* a terrorist? Is Milton a terrorist? Is Stanley Fish a
terrorist? Well, to take the last first: Stanley Fish is a literary
critic (a worse thing in some eyes than being a terrorist), and
while the readings he gives of literary texts, including this one,
may be right or wrong, no reading he gives commits him to
terrorism or to becoming an apologist for terrorists, or to any
other political or moral stance, for that matter. (There is, as I
have argued elsewhere, no relationship whatsoever between
one's performance as a literary critic and one's performance
in any other area of life.)[20]

That said, what about Samson and Milton? Are they terrorists? They are certainly, on my account, antinomians, but
does this make them terrorists? Well, it depends on what you
take the hallmarks of terrorism to be. If terrorism is the willingness to violate civil law in the name of a higher commitment,
Samson and Milton (as Charles I would attest) are terrorists,
as is the Abraham who is willing to sacrifice Isaac, and the Jael
who smote Sisera sleeping through the temples nailed, and the
Martin Luther King, Jr., who urged his followers to break laws
he and they considered oppressive.

But this answer settles the question too easily by identifying as a terrorist anyone who cares more for the end than the means. If this is what terrorists are, there are an awful lot of them — every proponent of affirmative action, for example, is one — and the word would seem to have lost its edge when it is taken to refer to activities recognized by everyone as being beyond the pale. The current literature tries to give the word "terrorist" back its edge by associating it with the performance of violence in a certain mode. For Mark Juergensmeyer, terrorist acts are "public acts of destruction, committed without a clear military objective, that arouse a widespread sense of fear."[21] In a similar vein, Jessica Stern defines terrorism "as an act or threat of violence against noncombatants with the objective of exacting revenge, intimidating or otherwise influencing an audience."[22] But that covers the bombing of Dresden, the destruction of Hiroshima and Nagasaki, the invasion of Afghanistan, and the Nuremberg trials. Defined that way, terrorism is simply the name you give to whatever your enemies do, and you can apply it, as Secretary of Education Paige has, to the members of the National Education Association.

If we want the word "terrorism" to stand for something recognized as such by all parties, we shall have to reserve it for a form of activity that no one would want to claim because it would be repugnant even as a sanctified means. The way to do this is to remember that, strictly speaking, terrorism is the name of a military tactic, one that is to be distinguished from more traditional tactics in which gathered armies fight pitched battles according to the rules of the Geneva Convention. Terrorism, as we now know too well, involves hit-and-run skirmishes, covert operations, activity that is intermittent and therefore productive of surprise and anxiety, and theatrical excess. (This is not a complete list, but it will do.) Those who employ these tactics do so in the name of a cause that supposedly justifies them, and it follows that what they are committed to is not the tactics but the cause. The militants interviewed and discussed by Berman, Juergensmeyer, and Stern explain what they do in just those terms: It is because we are dedicated to the work we have been called to, they say, that we must perform these actions. Terrorism is not for us a career choice, but a means to an end. No one says, I just love violence and inflicting pain and I'll go anywhere and do anything just to get that rush.

But suppose there were someone like that, someone who killed women and children, burned cities, spread plague because he liked to, because it was what he did, because it was what he was. That would be a terrorist, pure and simple, someone for whom the tactics we call terrorism were not a means in the service of a larger goal, but the goal itself. In Milton's work, there is only one such being, and he identifies himself in this line from *Paradise Lost:* "Only in destroying [do] I find ease" (9.129). Satan is the arch-terrorist, inflicting pain and inspiring fear because that's what keeps him going, and he does have disciples — wanton serial killers, despots who love the cruel exercise of power more than they love its results, anyone devoted to destruction as an end in itself. This does not describe either Milton or his Samson, either of whom may be many things — regicide, misogynist, elitist, bully, boor — but they are not terrorists. This does not mean, however, that it is safe to have them walking around in the world. In the course of a conversation with Mir Aimal Kansi, who is in prison for having opened fire on commuters waiting to enter the headquarters of the CIA, Jessica Stern discovers that he has a master's degree in literature. "What kind of literature?" she asks. The "poetry of Milton," he replies (179). Score one for John Carey.[23]

Notes

Notes to Preface

1. See Stanley Fish, *How Milton Works* (Cambridge, Mass.: Harvard University Press, 2001).

2. Stanley Fish, *Surprised by Sin: The Reader in "Paradise Lost"* (London: Macmillan Press, 1967). This book has been reissued in a second edition with a new preface (Cambridge, Mass.: Harvard University Press, 1997).

Notes to Introduction / Cable

1. Emily Eakin, "The Latest Theory Is That Theory Doesn't Matter," *The New York Times*, April 19, 2003.

2. John Milton, *Tetrachordon*, in Frank Allen Patterson, *The Student's Milton* (New York: Appleton-Century-Crofts, 1930; reprint, 1961), 675.

3. Stanley Fish, "Make 'Em Cry," *Chronicle of Higher Education*, March 5, 2004.

4. Stanley Fish, "The War on Higher Education," *Chronicle of Higher Education*, November 26, 2003.

5. John Carey, "A Work in Praise of Terrorism?" *Times Literary Supplement* 6 (September 2002): 15.

6. Feisal G. Mohamed, "Reading Samson in a New American Century" (paper delivered March 12, 2004, at the International Milton Congress, Duquesne University); revised and updated in *Milton Studies*, vol. 46, ed. Albert C. Labriola (Pittsburgh: University of Pittsburgh Press, 2006).

7. Stanley Fish, *There's No Such Thing as Free Speech* (Oxford: Oxford University Press, 1994), 23.

8. Stanley Fish, "The Same Old Song," *Chronicle of Higher Education*, July 11, 2003.

9. John Milton, *Areopagitica*, in Patterson, *The Student's Milton*, 741.

Notes to Chapter 1 / Grossman

1. Fish's own account of this occasion, which included papers by Victoria Silver and William Kolbrenner as well as myself, and a response by Fish, has been printed as the epilogue to *How Milton Works* (Cambridge: Belknap Press of Harvard University Press, 2001), 561–73.

2. Joel Fineman, "The Significance of Literature: The Importance of Being Earnest," delivered at the 1979 MLA convention in connection with a forum on the "Self in Writing" and published with notes added in *October* 15 (1980): 79–90. The published version was intended to preview a chapter on Wilde in a book unfortunately prevented by Fineman's early death. I quote it as reprinted in the posthumous *The Subjectivity Effect in Western Literary Tradition* (Cambridge, Mass.: The MIT Press, 1991), 32–42. The quoted passages are extracted from 39 n. 5; page numbers hereafter cited in the text.

3. Coincidences accumulate: of course Augustine is not only famously hooked by a text of Saint Paul's epistle, but also a very earnest reader of the destined implications of fish, which he draws both from what he sees as the entirely nontrivial, anagrammatic doubling of the Greek *ixthys* and the name of the Son and from the order of creation and the characteristics of the creatures of the sea. See especially *Confessions*, 13.24, and *The City of God against the Pagans*, 18.13.

4. See, for example, Shakespeare's characterization of "lust" as "a swallowed bait," in sonnet 129, which Katherine Duncan-Jones glosses with a reference to Cleopatra's "fancy of catching fish: 'And as I draw them up, / I'll think them every one an Antony, / And say, Ah, ha! Y'are caught'" (*Antony and Cleopatra*, 2.5.12–14), *Shakespeare's Sonnets*, ed. Katherine Duncan-Jones, The Arden Shakespeare (London: Thomas Nelson, 1997), Sonnet 129, line 7 and note. The crossing of the erotic and spiritual metaphors receives an ironic turn in Angelo's remark after his first interview with Isabella, "O cunning enemy, that, to catch a saint, / With saints dost bait thy hook!" *Measure for Measure*, ed. J. W. Lever, The Arden Shakespeare (London: Methuen, 1965), 2.2.180–81.

5. William Shakespeare, *Troilus and Cressida*, ed Kenneth Palmer, The Arden Edition (London: Methuen, 1982), 5.2.141–45: "O madness of discourse, / That cause sets up with and against itself! / Bifold authority! Where reason can revolt / Without perdition, and loss assume all reason / Without revolt."

6. Yet the eye trolling the *OED* for "troilism" first falls on an obsolete verb: "to troil": "to dupe, beguile, deceive," which might lead one to conclude that this second word indeed derived from Troilus and

provided another homophone to mediate Troilus's triangle and Lodge's, but the *OED* derives the word, rather mysteriously, from Old French *troillier*, which, as far as I can tell, refers to the operation of a kind of wine press. See *Le Robert Dictionnaire de la Langue Français*, 2nd ed., s.v. *treuiller.*

7. Slavoj Žižek, *Enjoy Your Symptom! Jacques Lacan in Hollywood and Out* (London: Routledge, 1992): "I have always found extremely repulsive the common practice of sharing the main dishes in a Chinese restaurant. So when, recently, I gave expression to this repulsion and insisted on finishing my plate alone, I became the victim of an ironic 'wild psychoanalysis' on the part of my table neighbor: is not this repulsion of mine, this resistance to sharing a meal, a symbolic form of the fear of *sharing a partner*, i.e., of sexual promiscuity? The first answer that came to my mind, of course, was a variation on de Quincey's caution against the 'art of murder' — the true horror is not sexual promiscuity but sharing a Chinese dish: 'How many people have entered the way of perdition with some innocent gangbang, which at the time was of no great importance to them, and ended by sharing the main dishes in a Chinese restaurant!' "

8. Lacan, *Ecrits: A Selection*, trans. Alan Sheridan (New York: Norton, 1977), ix.

9. An "informed reader" like Stanley Fish will immediately recognize that Lacan was anticipated in this insight by John Milton, whose God remarks about the about-to-fall Adam and Eve, "They trespass, authors to themselves in all / Both what they judge and what they choose; / for so I formed them free, and free they must remain, / Till they enthrall themselves" (*PL* 3.122–25). From *John Milton: The Complete Poems*, ed. John Leonard (New York: Penguin Books, 1998). Subsequent citations of Milton are to this edition.

10. Stanley Fish, *Is There a Text in This Class? The Authority of Interpretive Communities* (Cambridge: Harvard, 1980).

11. An appended note begins, "Again we cannot develop the point adequately" and goes on to sketch a brief reading list in psychoanalysis along which the claim could be pursued (42 n. 8). Readers familiar with his work will note, however, that Fineman had offered a substantive and detailed argument along similar lines in his book on Shakespeare's sonnets: *Shakespeare's Perjured Eye: The Invention of Poetic Subjectivity in the Sonnets* (Berkeley and Los Angeles: University of California Press, 1986); hereafter cited by page number in the text.

12. See Jacques Lacan, *The Seminar of Jacques Lacan, Book VII, The Ethics of Psychoanalysis, 1959–1960*, ed. Jacques-Alain Miller, trans. Dennis Porter (New York: Norton, 1992), 71. See also 101–05. The German term is taken from Freud's article on *Verneinung* [Negation] (1925).

13. Stanley Fish, *Self-Consuming Artifacts: The Experience of Seventeenth-Century Literature* (Berkeley and Los Angeles: University of

California Press, 1972), 3; hereafter cited by page number in the text.

14. *The Fly*, directed by Kurt Neumann, screenplay by James Clavell, based on a short story by George Langelaan. Twentieth-Century Fox, 1958. The film was remade by David Cronenberg in 1986; Cronenberg's version retains the trans-mat mishap, but sophisticates the science: molecular exchange results in a mutating hybrid who appears human at first but progressively develops fly characteristics over time.

15. Duncan-Jones, *Shakespeare's Sonnets*, Sonnet 138.

16. Stanley Fish, "Theory's Hope," "The Future of Criticism: A Critical Inquiry Symposium," *Critical Inquiry* 30 (2004): 375–76.

17. I make this argument at length in *The Story of All Things: Writing the Self in English Renaissance Narrative Poetry* (Durham: Duke University Press, 1998) see esp. 107–26. Freud was hardly unaware of the literary critical character of his new science when he coined the term "Oedipus complex."

18. By his own account, this naming had an adventitious origin, when as a beginning teacher he was asked to teach the Milton course of an absent colleague.

19. For a succinct and useful account of the development of the theories of transference, see the entry for "transference" in J. Laplanche and J.-B. Pontalis, *The Language of Psychoanalysis*, trans. Donald Nicholson-Smith (New York: Norton, 1973).

20. *The Interpretation of Dreams*, in *The Standard Edition of the Edition of the Complete Psychological Works of Sigmund Freud*, trans. James and Alix Strachey, 24 vols. (London: Hogarth, 1953–73), 5:562. This edition is hereafter cited as *SE* in the text, followed by volume and page number.

21. Freud, *Fragment of an Analysis of a Case of Hysteria*, in *SE* 7:65 n. 1.

22. Jacques Lacan, *Ecrits*, 156–59. Lacan follows the distinction between metonymy as a figure of contiguity and metaphor as a figure of resemblance made by Roman Jakobson in Roman Jacobson and Morris Halle, *Fundamentals of Language*, rev. ed. (The Hague: Mouton, 1975), 72–76.

23. A structurally similar reversal of the normative occurs in the "dinner" scene in Luis Buñel's film *Le Fantôme de la Liberté* (1974), when the guests, who are sitting on commodes around what appears to be a formal dinner table, excuse themselves one by one to go into the bathroom, where they lock the door before eating solitary and private dinners. The transferential relation (in either direction) between the social and private bodily function, here displaced from the sexual to the excretory, recalls Freud's remark on the anatomical contingency of the association: "inter faeces et urinam nascimur."

24. Freud nods in this direction when he includes "secondary revision" [*sekundäre Bearbeitung*] among the distorting mechanisms of the dream-work. According to Freud, this redrafting of the dream to make

it more coherent and intelligible is most active as the dreamer nears wakefulness and is completed only as the dream is recounted.

25. The example becomes less willfully outlandish when we recall that Milton's close associate, Marvell, found occasion to imagine his poetic persona raped by fruits and flowers ("The Garden") and crucified by briars ("Upon Appleton House").

26. William Shakespeare, *Hamlet*, ed. Harold Jenkins (London: Methuen, 1982), 3.4.8–9.

27. Freud, "The Dynamics of Transference," in *SE* 12:97–108.

28. "Remembering, Repeating and Working-Through," in *SE* 12:145–56. On transference and repetition, see also *Beyond the Pleasure Principle*, in *SE* 18:18–23. The process of binding emotion through unconscious repetition underlies the classic readings by Freud and Jones of *Hamlet* as a reenactment of unresolved Oedipal passions. In *The Interpretation of Dreams*, Freud remarks that "Hamlet is capable of doing anything — except take vengeance on the man who did away with his father and took that father's place with his mother, the man who shows him the repressed wishes of his own childhood realized. Thus the loathing which should drive him on to revenge is replaced by self-reproaches, by scruples of conscience, which remind him that he himself is literally no better than the sinner whom he is to punish" (*SE* 4:265). See also *Introductory Lectures on Psychoanalysis*, XXI: "But let us now turn from the direct observation of children to the analytic examination of adults who have become neurotic. What help does analysis give towards a further knowledge of the Oedipus Complex? . . . Analysis . . . shows that each of these neurotics has himself been an Oedipus or, what comes to the same thing, has, as a reaction to the complex, become a Hamlet" (*SE* 16:335).

29. Aristotle, *Poetics*, book 6, para. 1; Milton, *Samson Agonistes*, line 1759; see also Jacques Lacan, "The Tragic Dimension of Psychoanalytic Experience," in *The Seminar of Jacques Lacan, Book VIII*, 289–325.

30. John Rumrich, *Milton Unbound: Controversy and Reinterpretation* (Cambridge: Cambridge University Press, 1996).

31. T. S. Eliot, having imperiously divided himself into critic and poet, is a particularly fascinating figure in this respect. One need only read aloud the more orotund periods of the *Four Quartets* to sense what is at stake for the poet in the critic's representation, in a 1936 essay, of Milton as lacking "a visual imagination" and authoring a language that insinuates itself into the ears of subsequent poets to become "an influence against which we still have to struggle." In some of its phases a countertransferential reading might suggest that Eliot transfers onto Milton the resentment of the paternal deity that he labors so hard to invoke and that Milton cannot avoid. But in a different phase I would want to discover how my own subjective economy is in play in this construction of Eliot as the subject of *resentiment*. Eliot's 1947 "retraction" reaffirms his conviction that "the contemporary situation reaffirms that Milton is a

master whom we should avoid." See "Milton I" and "Milton II," in *On Poetry and Poets* (London: Faber & Faber, 1957), 138–45, 146–61; quoted phrases at 139, 151.

32. Fish, *How Milton Works*, 432–42.

33. *Freaks*, directed by Tod Browning, written by Al Boasberg, Willis Goldbeck, Leon Gordon, and Edgar Allan Woolf, based on the novel *Spurs*, by Clarence Aron Robbins (MGM, 1932).

Notes to Chapter 2 / Lewalski

1. See, for example, essays in *Milton Studies*, vol. 38, *The Writer in His Works*, ed. Albert C. Labriola and Michael Lieb (Pittsburgh: University of Pittsburgh Press, 2000); Marshall Grossman, *"Authors to Themselves": Milton and the Revelation of History* (Cambridge: Cambridge University Press, 1987); Stephen B. Dobranski, *Milton, Authorship, and the Book Trade* (Cambridge: Cambridge University Press, 1999).

2. Stanley Fish, *How Milton Works* (Cambridge, Mass.: Harvard University Press, 2001).

3. From the preface to book 2, *The Reason of Church-Government*, in *Complete Prose Works of John Milton*, 8 vols., ed. Don M. Wolfe et al. (New Haven: Yale University Press, 1953–82), 1:823. Citations of Milton's prose in text and notes are from this edition, abbreviated YP.

4. He specified several "graver subjects" he hoped to write about: hymns of the heavenly gods, sacred poems of creation and nature's marvels, and especially "Kings and Queens and *Hero's old, / Such as the wise* Demodocus once told / In solemn Songs at King *Alcinous* feast." Written in July or August 1628 as part of Milton's composition for a vacation exercise at Cambridge, the poem was first printed in Milton's *Poems, Etc. Upon Several Occasions* (London, 1673), and is quoted from that edition.

5. Unless otherwise indicated, Milton's early poems are quoted from *Poems of Mr. John Milton, Both English and Latin* (London, 1645). Book and line numbers for Milton's poems and translations of his Latin poems are supplied from *John Milton: Complete Poems and Major Prose*, ed. Merritt Y. Hughes (Indianapolis: Odyssey-MacMillan, 1957).

6. "O mihi si mea sors talem concedat amicum / Phoebaeos decorasse viros qui tam bene norit, / Si quando indigenas revocabo in carmine reges, / Arturumque etiam sub terris bella moventem; / Aut dicam invictae sociali foedere mensae, / Magnanimos Heroas" (ll. 78–83).

7. Manso wrote a biography of Tasso and erected a funeral monument to Marino. See Stella P. Revard, *Milton and the Tangles of Neaera's Hair: The Making of the 1645 Poems* (Columbia, Mo.: University of Missouri Press, 1997), 215–24; and Barbara K. Lewalski, *The Life of John Milton: A Critical Biography*, rev. ed. (London: Blackwell, 2003), 111–14.

8. Peter Lindenbaum, "John Milton and the Republican Mode of Literary Production," *The Yearbook of Literary Studies: Politics, Patronage, and Literature in England, 1558–1658* 21 (1991): 121–36.

9. Quotations in text and notes from *Paradise Lost* are from *Paradise Lost. A Poem. In Twelve Books* (London, 1674).

10. See Lewalski, *Life of John Milton*, 245–54, 284–85.

11. Sharon Achinstein, *Milton and the Revolutionary Reader* (Princeton, N.J.: Princeton University Press, 1994), 3–70.

12. Ibid., 24–33. See also Joad Raymond, *The Invention of the Newspaper: English Newsbooks, 1641–1660* (Oxford: Clarendon Press, 1996).

13. See Nicholas von Maltzhan, *Milton's History of Britain: Republican Historiography in the English Revolution* (Oxford: Clarendon Press, 1991); and Lewalski, *Life of Milton*, 216–22, 346–49.

14. See David Loewenstein, "The Revenge of the Saint: Radical Religious Culture and the Politics of *Paradise Regained*," *Literature and History* 3 (1994): 63–89.

15. Citations from *Paradise Regained* and *Samson Agonistes* are taken from the first edition, *Paradise Regain'd. A Poem in IV Books. To which is added Samson Agonistes* (London, 1674).

16. See Barbara K. Lewalski, "Milton's *Samson* and the 'New Acquist of True [Political] Experience,'" in *Milton Studies*, vol. 24, ed. James D. Simmonds (Pittsburgh: University of Pittsburgh Press, 1988), 233–51.

17. The actual author was John Gauden, who set forth the circumstances in a letter to Clarendon on January 21, 1660 [1661], and received as reward the bishopric of Worcester. Some contemporary respondents to the *Eikon Basilike* suspected his authorship at the time. See Lewalski, *Life of Milton*, 247–48, 410, 671 n. 48.

18. He also invokes the legal definition whereby a publisher or printer is held responsible for a work along with its author or in his place if he is unknown, asserting, "he who published that *Cry* must be considered its author" (701).

19. Douglas Trevor, *The Poetics of Melancholy in Early Modern England* (Cambridge: Cambridge University Press, 2004), 164–71.

20. The preface to Milton's *Artis Logicae Plenior Institutio, Ad Petri Rami Methodum concinnata, Adjecta est Praxis Analytica & Petri Rami vita* (London, 1672), states that for the ease of students he abridges in one continuous (219-page) volume Ramus's famous *Dialecticae libri duo* (1572) and explanatory materials from others' commentaries (chiefly George Downame's 800-page commentary), "except where I disagree with what these commentaries say" (YP 8:208–10).

21. Ben Jonson, *Timber; or, Discoveries*, in *Works*, 11 vols., ed. C. H. Herford and Percy and Evelyn Simpson (Oxford: Clarendon Press, 1925–52), 638.

22. *A Variorum Commentary on the Poems of John Milton*, ed. A. S. P. Woodhouse and Douglas Bush (New York: Columbia University Press, 1972), 2:2.544–65.

23. *Samson Agonistes*, preface, p. 3. The epigraph reads: "Aristot. Poet. Cap. 6. Tragoedia mimesis, praxeos spondaias, etc. Tragoedia est imitatio actionis seriae, &c. Per misericordiam & metum perficiens talium affectuum lustrationem." Milton, of course, means the reader to recall the entire definition: "Tragedy is, then, a representation [mimesis] of an action that is heroic and complete, and of a certain magnitude — by means of language embellished with all kinds of ornament, each used separately in the different parts of the play; it represents men in action and does not use narrative; and through pity and fear it effects relief to those and similar emotions." See *The Poetics* 6.1, in *Aristotle*, vol. 23, trans. W. Hamilton Fyfe (Cambridge, Mass.: Harvard University Press, 1973), 24–25.

24. See the Nativity ode, 27–28: "And joyn thy voice unto the Angel Quire, / From out his secret Altar toucht with hallow'd fire"; *Elegy VI*, 77: "Diis etinem sacer est vates, divumque sacerdos" [For truly the bard is sacred to the gods and is their priest]; and *Ad Patrem* 24–26: "Carmine seposisti retegunt arcana futuri / Phoebades, & tremulae pallentes ora Sibyllae; / Camina sacrificus sollennes pangit ad aras" [By Song Apollo's priestesses and the trembling Sibyl, with blanched features, lay bare the mysteries of the far-away future. Songs are composed by the sacrificing priest at the altar].

25. See *Of Reformation* (YP 1:558–60); *Animadversions* (YP 1:722–23); and the *Apology for Smectymnuus* (YP 1:868–69, 899–901, 916, 946–47).

26. In the second edition of *The Doctrine and Discipline of Divorce*, Milton claims he has recovered "a most necessary, most charitable, and yet most injur'd Statute of *Moses*" buried "under the rubbish of Canonicall ignorance: as once the whole law was . . . in *Josiahs* time" (YP 2:224). See Jason Rosenblatt, *Torah and Law in "Paradise Lost"* (Princeton, N.J.: Princeton University Press, 1994), 98.

27. Jonathan Richardson, *Explanatory Notes and Remarks on Milton's "Paradise Lost" . . . With a Life of the Author*, in *The Early Lives of Milton*, ed. Helen Darbishire (London: Constable, 1932), 291.

Notes to Chapter 3 / Patterson

This essay was delivered as a plenary lecture at the International Milton Symposium, Beaufort, South Carolina, on June 8, 2002. I am delighted to be able to publish it in a volume honoring Stanley Fish, who taught me how to write in a more human and colloquial way.

1. For Milton's poetry and verse letters, see John Milton, *Complete Poems and Major Prose*, ed. Merritt Y. Hughes (Indianapolis: Odyssey-

MacMillan, 1957); for Milton's prose tracts written in Latin, see the *Works of John Milton*, 18 vols. in 21, ed. Frank Allen Patterson et al. (New York: Columbia University Press, 1931–42), hereafter cited as CM; and for Milton's English prose tracts, see *Complete Prose Works of John Milton*, 8 vols., ed. Don M. Wolfe et al. (New Haven: Yale University Press, 1953–82), hereafter cited as YP. My practice of rendering Milton's negatives in boldface is selective, focusing on those I believe bear particular cognitive or theoretical weight.

2. Marvell, *Poems and Letters*, 2 vols., ed. H. M. Margoliouth, rev. ed. edited by Pierre Legouis (Oxford, 1971), 1:46.

3. *The Divine Week and Works of . . . Du Bartas*, 2 vols., trans. Joshua Sylvester, ed. Susan Snyder (Oxford, 1979).

4. Leonard noted this as a puzzle in his edition, but he was also kind enough to call it to my attention in personal correspondence.

Notes to Chapter 4 / Labriola

1. To my knowledge, two commentators have acknowledged that the Son is begotten as an angel in *Paradise Lost*. The first acknowledgment, in *The Poems of John Milton*, ed. John Carey and Alastair Fowler (London: Longman, 1968), 727, is a one-sentence note to *Paradise Lost*, 5.842–45: "Abdiel appears to regard the Messiah's kingship over the angels as a kind of incarnation, involving the setting aside of divinity; just as his human incarnation in Jesus will, at a later state of the divine emanation." The second is my own essay, " 'Thy Humiliation Shall Exalt': The Christology of *Paradise Lost*," in *Milton Studies*, vol. 15, ed. James D. Simmonds (Pittsburgh: University of Pittsburgh Press, 1981), 29–42.

2. For commentary on Christ as an angel, see *De Doctrina Christiana* (the theological treatise putatively by Milton), in *The Works of John Milton*, 18 vols. in 21, ed. Frank Allen Patterson et al. (New York: Columbia University Press, 1933), 14:286–89. For the Caedmonian works in the Junius manuscript (*Genesis A, Genesis B*, and *Christ and Satan*) that bear on Milton's portrayal of the Son as an angel, see *The Caedmon Poems*, trans. Charles W. Kennedy (London: Routledge, 1916). See also my comparative study of the Junius manuscript and Milton's epic, "The Begetting and Exaltation of the Son: The Junius Manuscript and Milton's *Paradise Lost*," in *Milton's Legacy*, ed. Charles W. Durham and Kristin A. Pruitt (Selinsgrove, Pa.: Susquehanna University Press, 2005), 22–32. In the present essay, I will not pursue the topic that the Son is the angel of the Lord or the angel of Yahweh. I pursue that topic in a forthcoming essay, "Jewish Christianity in Milton's *Paradise Lost:* The Son as the Angel of the Lord." For discussion of the Son as the angel of the Lord, see Jean Daniélou, *The Development of Christian Doctrine before the Council Nicaea: The Theology of Jewish Christianity*, trans. John A. Baker

(London: Aarton, Longman & Todd, 1964), vol. 1, esp. chap. 4, "The Trinity and Angelology," 117–46, and chap. 5, "The Son of God," 147–72. 3. Though I will examine the ontological relationship of the Father and the Son in *Paradise Lost,* I will do so by reference to The Martyrdom and Ascension of Isaiah. My argument concerning the Son's status as a divine person is not situated in the context of ongoing commentary on Milton's orthodox trinitarianism, Arianism, or subordinationism. For me to become involved in such controversy would divert attention from my focus, which is a comparative study of the Son and his descensions from divinity to become an angel, then to be incarnate.

3. *The Old Testament Pseudepigrapha,* ed. James H. Charlesworth (Garden City, N.Y.: Doubleday, 1985), 172. The Martyrdom and Ascension of Isaiah is quoted from this edition, cited by page number. For a discussion of the Martyrdom and Ascension of Isaiah as a confluence of Jewish-Christian thinking, see Michael Lieb, *The Visionary Mode: Biblical Prophecy, Hermeneutics, and Cultural Change* (Ithaca, N.Y.: Cornell University Press, 1991), 190–201.

4. Milton's poetry is quoted from *John Milton: Complete Poems and Major Prose,* ed. Merritt Y. Hughes (New York: The Odyssey Press, 1957).

5. For a brilliant explanation of why Satan "thought himself impaired," see Stanley Fish, *How Milton Works* (Cambridge: Harvard University Press, 2001), 511–18.

Notes to Chapter 5 / Revard

1. See, for example, John Peter, *A Critique of "Paradise Lost"* (London: Longman, 1960): "What is more curious is that the whole battle anticipated with such excitement and described with such attention, should prove to be a fiasco, a sort of sham-fight, and pointless as it is noisy" (78). A. J. A. Waldock, *"Paradise Lost" and Its Critics* (Cambridge: Cambridge University Press, 1947), comments that the battle enlivens with the Son's entrance: "The narrative [of book 6] makes a brave show, but only towards the end, with the entry of the Son, does real life come into it: it acquires new zest then, the verse itself seems invigorated, and we are swept to a superb close" (111).

2. See Satan's sun-bright chariot at 6.100–103, 338. Other chariots are mentioned at 1.311; 2.887; 3.394, 522; 6.211, 358, 390, 711. Fowler describes Messiah's chariot as a "triumphal chariot," which contrasts with Satan's "counterfeit" chariot and his ascent into it, a factitive claim to sovereignty. *Paradise Lost,* ed. Alastair Fowler (London: Longman, 1971), 345n. Citations to Milton's works, unless otherwise noted, are to John Milton, *Complete Poems and Major Prose,* ed. Merritt Y. Hughes (New York: Odyssey Press, 1957).

3. For Thyer's commentary on Hesiod and the citation of the principal classical sources from Homer and Virgil, see *Notes to Book VI,*

"Paradise Lost." With Notes of various Authors, ed. Thomas Newton (London, 1749).

4. See G. Wilson Knight, *The Chariot of Wrath: The Message of John Milton to Democracy at War* (London: Faber and Faber, 1942), 158. In *Professional Correctness: Literary Studies and Political Change* (Oxford: Clarendon Press, 1995). Michael Lieb also discusses Knight's concept of the chariot in *Children of Ezekiel: Aliens, UFOs, the Crisis of Race, and the Advent of End Time* (Durham, N.C.: Duke University Press, 1998).

5. Milton's principal source for the vision of God in a machine is Ezekiel 1:4–28 and its fragmentary parallels in Exodus 24:10, Isaiah 6:2, Daniel 7:9, Psalms 18:10, and Revelation 4:6–8. Both Hume and Newton cite Ezekiel as the source for the description of the chariot in *Paradise Lost,* 6.749–59. See Newton, *Notes to Book VI;* Patrick Hume, *The Poetical Works of Mr. John Milton* (London, 1695). Also see Thomas Keightley, *An Account of the Life, Opinions, and Writings of John Milton, With an Introduction to "Paradise Lost"* (London, 1855), 474–79, a detailed treatment of the chariot and its cherubic bearers in Ezekiel as well as related passages in Psalms, Daniel, Revelation, and Isaiah.

6. Denis Saurat, *Milton, Man and Thinker* (London: Jonathan Cape, 1925), asserts that Milton knew the Zohar and the Kabbalah, but does not investigate his use of the Merkabah in *Paradise Lost.* Harris Fletcher, *Milton's Rabbinical Readings* (Urbana: University of Illinois Press, 1930), asserts that Milton knew rabbinical sources, but does not discuss the Merkabah. Jason Rosenblatt, *Torah and Law in "Paradise Lost"* (Princeton: Princeton University Press, 1994), reviews the question of Milton's knowledge of Hebrew texts and cites the criticism of Fletcher's and Saurat's assertions (82–85). Golda Werman, *Milton and Midrash.* (Washington, D.C.: Catholic University of America Press, 1995), also criticizes Saurat's and Fletcher's views about Milton's Hebraic studies. She believes that Milton used Latin translations rather than the original Hebrew in many of his investigations, though he could and certainly did read the Hebrew Bible (2–7, 27–41).

7. J. H. Adamson, "The War in Heaven: Milton's Version of the *Merkabah," Journal of English and Germanic Philology* 57 (1958): 690–703, reprinted in *Bright Essence: Studies in Milton's Theology,* ed. W. B. Hunter, C. A. Patrides, and J. H. Adamson (Salt Lake City: University of Utah Press, 1971), 103–14. I cite the version in *Bright Essence.*

8. Milton was involved in rabbinical readings in the 1640s and he certainly could have come to a knowledge of the Kabbalah without More's prompting.

For a discussion of Milton's chariot, see Michael Lieb, *Poetics of the Holy* (Chapel Hill: University of North Carolina Press, 1981); "Milton's Chariot of Paternal Deity as a Reformation Conceit," *Journal of Religion* 65 (1985): 359–77; Lieb, *The Visionary Mode: Biblical Prophecy, Hermeneutics, and Cultural Change* (Ithaca, N.Y.: Cornell University

Press, 1991); Lieb, *Children of Ezekiel*; "Encoding the Occult: Milton and the Traditions of *Merkabah* Speculation in the Renaissance," *Milton Studies* 37 (Pittsburgh: University of Pitts-burgh Press, 1999), 42–88.

9. For More's life, see Robert Ward, *The Life of Henry More*, ed. Sarah Hutton, Cecil Courtney, Michelle Courtney, Robert Crocker, and A. Rupert Hull (Dordrecht: Kluwer, 2000). Ward was a younger contemporary of More, having been admitted to Christ's College in 1674. He was not More's pupil, but More accepted him as his sizar and gave him an advowson in 1685. Also see Robert Crocker, "Henry More: A Biographical Essay," in *Henry More, Tercentenary Studies*, ed. Sarah Hutton (Dordrecht: Kluwer, 1989). An abridged version of Ward's life was printed in 1911. Also see Robert Crocker, *Henry More, 1614–1687: A Biography of the Cambridge Platonist* (Dordrecht: Kluwer, 2003).

10. Anne Conway was a confidante with whom More maintained a lively correspondence before and after the Restoration, discussing with her a good many of his philosophical and theological views. See *The Conway Letters, The Correspondence of Anne, Viscountess Conway, Henry More, and their Friends, 1642–1684*, ed. Marjorie Hope Nicolson (London: Humphrey Milford for Oxford University Press, 1930). Sarah Hutton has recently re-edited the letters.

11. More allegedly was concerned during the Commonwealth era that he might lose what little preferment he had at Cambridge because he refused to affirm the Covenant. After the Restoration, More refused the deanery of Christchurch, the provostship of Dublin College, and the deanery of St. Patrick's and other such preferments (Ward, *The Life of Henry More*, 43–45, 98).

12. For commentary on More's interest in and reactions to Descartes, as well as his scientific interests, see Stephen M. Fallon, *Milton among the Philosophers: Poetry and Materialism in Seventeenth-Century England* (Ithaca, N.Y.: Cornell University Press, 1991), 50–78. Fallon also gives considerable attention to Anne Conway and her philosophical inquiries into materialism, which were collected and published post-humously in 1690 (119–33).

13. Henry More, *Conjectura Cabbalistica* (London, 1653).

14. See Marjorie H. Nicolson, "Milton and the *Conjectura Cabalistica*," *Philological Quarterly* 6 (1927): 1–2.

15. *The Divine Dialogues* (London, 1668) was More's first extensive use of the Merkabah in his work. He refines and expands his work on the Merkabah in the two treatises that appeared in a work on the Zohar by Christian Knorr von Rosenroth, which included essays and transla-tions by various hands. See *Visionis Ezekieliticae sive Mercavae Expositio, Ex Principiis Philosophiae Pythagoricae Praecipuisque Theosophiae Judaicae Reliquiis Concinnata* and *Catechismus Cabbalisticus*, in

Kabbala Denudata, Seu Doctrina Hebraeorum Transcendentalis et Metaphysica atque Theologica Opus Antiquissimae Philosophiae Barbaricae variis speciminibus refertissimum (Frankfurt, 1677), 1.2: 223–73, 274–92. These two works are reprinted in *Opera Omnia* (London, 1679).

16. See Richard H. Popkin, "The Spiritualistic Cosmologies of Henry More and Anne Conway," in *Henry More, Tercentenary Studies*, 105.

17. Adamson, *Bright Essence*, 108.

18. The versions of *The Immortality of the Soul* that More printed in 1659 and 1662 do not contain references to the Merkabah. When he translated his English works into Latin for the *Opera Omnia* (1679), More added notes (scholia) to *The Immortality of the Soul*, which made direct connections to the Kabbalah, including the note to book 3, chapter 10, which Adamson, *Bright Essence*, cites (see 3.426). The notes, including the one in question, were translated into English for the version of *The Immortality of the Soul*, included in More's posthumous *Collection of Philosophical Works* (London, 1712), 306. Adamson cites the note from the posthumous edition of 1712, apparently assuming it was also contained in the 1659 edition of *The Immortality of the Soul.*

19. More's *Divine Dialogues* were completed by 1666, though not published until 1668 because of alterations to the text demanded by the censor, probably in *The Two Last Dialogues*, which were published first.

20. More remained from the 1650s until the end of his life an opponent of the Quakers and the Fifth Monarchists. See, for example, his comments in the "Preface to the Reader," in *An Explanation of The grand Mystery of Godliness* (London, 1660), xi–xii.

21. In the preface to *An Explanation*, More affirms his belief in Mede's interpretation of Revelation (xxii–xxiii).

22. See Joseph Mede, "Comment," *The Key of the Revelation*, trans. Richard More (London, 1643), part 2. *Complete Prose Works of John Milton*, 8 vols., ed. Don M. Wolfe et al. (New Haven: Yale University Press, 1953–82), 6:623–24; hereafter designated as YP. For a comparison of Mede's and Milton's millenarianism, see my essay, "Milton and Millenarianism," in *Milton and the Ends of Time*, ed. Juliet Cummins (Cambridge: Cambridge University Press, 2003), 54–55.

23. Only with the accession of the Catholic James II did More feel constrained politically both because of his millenarianism and his anti-Catholic views. See Ward, *The Life of Henry More*, 107–08.

24. John Carter, *The Wheel turned by a voice from the throne of Glory* (London, 1647), 59.

25. Peter Sterry, *The Comming Forth of Christ In the Power of his Death* (London, 1650), 8, 11–12, 26. Also see my discussion of Sterry in *The War in Heaven* (Ithaca, N.Y.: Cornell University Press, 1980), 257–60.

26. See "To the Reader," *An Explanation of The grand Mystery of*

Godliness: "But to the eternal laud and praise of our infinitely-merciful God, whose eye of Providence ever watches over his Church, when things were most desperate, he was pleased to answer the prayers and well-meant endeavours of his faithful servants with not onely hopes but enjoyments more sudden and more ample then could then be imagined, in restoring our Gracious Soveraign *CHARLES the Second.* . . . For those works of so great sound, and of no less import, namely the *Millennium*, the *Reign of the Saints,* the *New Jerusalem,* and the like, to them that are not very wild or ignorant can signifie nothing else but the recovery of the Church to her ancient Apostolick Purity." More attributes the honor of recovering "that pure and Apostolick Church" to the newly restored Charles II (xii–xiii).

27. See, for example, More, "Preface to the Reader," *An Exposition of the Seven Epistles to the Seven Churches* (London, 1669). Also see the preface to his exposition of Revelation, in *Apocalypsis Apocalypseos* (London, 1680).

28. According to Ward, More thought government "exceeding Happy" when the people willingly obeyed and princes sincerely sought the welfare of the people. He thought monarchy the best form of government and bewailed "the late Troublesome and calamitous Times" of the Commonwealth (Ward, *The Life of Henry More*, 113–14).

29. See Aharon Lichtenstein, *Henry More: The Rational Theology of a Cambridge Platonist* (Cambridge, Mass.: Harvard University Press, 1962), 9, 133. Also see John Spurr, " 'Latitudinarianism' and the Restoration Church," *The Historical Journal* 31 (1988): 61–82.

30. In a letter to Anne Conway, cited by Spurr, " 'Latitudinarianism' and the Restoration Church," More objects to the latitudian name, but goes on to say that "it were the interest both of the King and of the Church if [such persons, that is, latitudinarians] were multiplyde into hundred of thousands" (63).

31. In book 4, More's principal interlocutor, Philotheus, defends toleration of both Calvinist and Antinomian views within Reformed Christianity for the interest of unity within Protestantism. He argues that all those who possess "the Apostolick Faith entire, without any Idolatrous superstition, who murther no man for his Conscience, and make the infallible Word of God it self the Object of their Profession" belong to the Kingdom of God. Therefore, their different convictions about other matters of belief should be tolerated (*Divine Dialogues*, 2:66). *Divine Dialogues* (London, 1668) are hereafter cited by volume and page number. Like More, Milton, in *Of True Religion* (London, 1673), affirms that true religion depends on two principles: on an implicit faith and a reliance on the Word of God only. "If all Protestants would hold to these two Principles, they would avoid and cut off many debates and Contentions, Schism, and Persecutions, which too oft have been among them" (4–5).

32. See, for example, *An Exposition of the Seven Epistles to the Seven Churches; Together with A Brief Discourse of Idolatry; with Application to the Church of Rome* (London, 1669). In "Epistle Dedicatory," More states that "the Church of *Rome* was openly declared to be that *Babylon the Great* . . . the Pope with his Clergie to be that notorious Antichrist" (sig. A5ᵛ). More dedicates the tract to John Robartes, whom Charles II had recently appointed lord lieutenant of Ireland and who was a member of Charles II's privy council. More commends Robartes for his "adherence to the Apostolick Faith and just Interest of Reformed Christendome" (sig. A4ʳ).

33. See *The Correspondence of Anne, Viscountess Conway,* 294. More himself has one of his interlocutors declare that good Christians are also good subjects of the State (*Divine Dialogues,* 1:63).

34. The first three dialogues, which were published together, concern the nature and attributes of God, the providence of God, and providence as it pertains to the customs of man in the world. The last two dialogues (4 and 5), also published together, pertain to the kingdom of God within us and without and of God's special providence over his church from the beginning to the end of things. The two final dialogues will be my particular focus, particularly dialogue 5, which deals with the vision of Ezekiel.

35. The seven men who take part in the *Dialogues* meet in Cuphophron's garden on successive days during the summer. Cuphophron, the zealous Platonist and Cartesian, is probably Anne Conway's husband, Edward Conway, to whom More dedicated *The Immortality of the Soul.* Sophron, the sober man, may be Dr. George Rust, another Cambridge associate of More; Hylobares, the witty materialist, is probably the young John Locke. See M. F. Howard, introduction to *The Life of the Learned and Pious Henry More* (London, 1911), 13–19. The description of the characters of the seven men is taken from the *Dialogues.* The identification of the men with More's acquaintances is approximate, and some characters are under dispute or may be composite sketches. Cuphophron, for example, has also been connected with Joseph Glanvil, another Cambridge man and friend to More.

36. See Crocker, "Henry More: A Biographical Essay," 15n.

37. The four beasts (man, lion, ox, eagle) of Revelation 4:7 were often compared to the four-faced chayyoth or cherubim of Ezekiel's chariot (1:10), and their four-foldedness equated. More comments: "Here the Lamps are distinguishable from the four Beasts: but in *Ezekiel's* Cherub-Chariot the living Creatures themselves are resembled to *Lamps,* because that Vision represented also the actual Kingdome of Angels. But yet the Beasts here are described almost just in the same manner the Cherubims are in *Ezekiel's* Vision, which denotes the *Angelicalness* of this last and best state of the Church" (2.305). He also says that the four Beasts are the "*Hieroglyphick*" of that "Communialty" of God's people on earth (2.303).

38. Euistor leads the discussion at this point, pointing out that Luther supported the lawful authority of the princes of Germany against the Emperor and that Calvin respected the law and did not expel the Bishop of Geneva. Moreover, Protestants and Catholics joined against Spanish tyranny in the United Provinces (*Divine Dialogues*, 2:80–90). Philotheus contends, moreover, "Every Secular Prince, nay, every private man, has a commission from Heaven to cast off the yoke of *Rome*, as being that *Mysticall Babylon* mentioned in the *Apocalypse*" (*Divine Dialogues*, 2:91).

39. In the Latin treatise, *Visionis Ezekieliticae sive Mercavae Expositio*, in *Kabbala Denudata*, 1.2.238, More alludes to the different methodology that he used in *Divine Dialogues*, explaining that he had already offered in *Divine Dialogues* an ethico-political interpretation of Ezekiel's vision and that he was now offering a metaphysical and theosophical.

40. In *Visionis Ezekieliticae sive Mercavae Expositio* (ibid., 1.2.243–45), More explains the interconnectedness of the four worlds, which correspond among the kabbalists, he explains, to the four-foldedness of the cherubim. The highest of these worlds is the Aziluthic (of Emanation); the next two the Briathic (of Creation) and the Jezirathic (of Formation) and the lowest or terrestial, the Asiathic (of Faction). Ezekiel's vision describes the highest of these worlds — the Angelical or Aziluthic, which through the agency of the Messias, the rider of the chariot, will ultimately be brought to earth.

41. The eyes of the chariot are likewise providential, "watching over the terrestrial Regions, and carrying all things on according to their own purpose" (2.288). The fire and light of the chariot symbolize "the Spirit thoroughly penetrating and possessing" it (2.283). The chariot possesses "one common mind and one motion as it is in the Angelicall Kingdome," for the wings of the Cherubim touch "*one another; and whither the Spirit was to goe, thither they went*" (2.308).

42. In *Visionis Ezekieliticae sive Mercavae Expositio*, More connects the four animals of Revelation to the four worlds of the Kabbalah, the eagle representing the highest or the Aziluthic world (ibid., 1.2.250–53).

43. More reads the word "amber" kabbalistically, its number signifying the title of the Son. See Adamson, *Bright Essence*, 111. See More, *Divine Dialogues*, 2:296–97; *Visionis Ezekieliticae*, 1.2.260–64. In *Visionis Ezekieliticae*, 1.2.240–41, and in *Catechismus Cabbalisticus* (1.2.274–77), More identifies Jehovah, the God of Israel, with the second person of the Trinity, the Logos, who is presented as the vision of the man on the throne in Ezekiel, or as he calls him, the Soul of the Messias, before he took on carnal form as Jesus Christ. At the millennium Jew and Gentile will be drawn into the kingdom that Christ rules with his saints on earth (*Divine Dialogues*, 2:311). Also see *Catechismus Cabbalisticus*, 1.2.291–92. Both *Visionis Ezekieliticae* (1.2.270–72) and *Catechismus Cabbalisticus* (1.2.280–91) conclude with descriptions of the triumph of Messias's kingdom and the institution of his millennial reign.

44. Nicolson, *The Correspondence of Anne, Viscountess Conway,* notes that More's *Dialogues* were popular in their time, with the exception of books 4 and 5, which were criticized; see 292n.

45. In Revelation 4:2–5, the throne is ringed with a rainbow and out of it proceeds lightning and thunders. In Ezekiel 1:26, the likeness of a sapphire throne, inlaid with amber, appears above the firmament over the heads of the animals and on it sat the likeness of a man, readily identified by Christian commentators as Christ.

Notes to Chapter 6 / Bennett

1. Sandra Gilbert and Susan Gubar, *The Madwoman in the Attic: The Woman Writer and the Nineteenth-Century Literary Imagination* (New Haven: Yale University Press, 1979), 21. In the quarter century following Gilbert's challenge, Milton's works became a site visited by emerging varieties of feminism offering analyses of gender and patriarchy, and opening the literary canon to women authors. Christine Froula's "When Eve Reads Milton: Undoing the Canonical Economy," *Critical Inquiry* 10 (1983): 321–47; reprinted in *John Milton,* ed. Annabel Patterson (London: Longman, 1992), has been widely used in classroom teaching to represent a feminist approach.

2. Diane Kelsey McColley, *Milton's Eve* (Urbana, Ill.: University of Illinois Press, 1983).

3. See Maureen Quilligan, *Milton's Spenser: The Politics of Reading* (Ithaca, N.Y.: Cornell University Press, 1983), for example, 224–26.

4. Hilda L. Smith, "Introduction: Women, Intellect, and Politics: Their Intersection in Seventeenth-Century England," in *Women Writers and the Early Modern British Political Tradition* (Cambridge: Cambridge University Press, 1998), 6–7.

5. For a challenging formulation of a difference between patriarchal gender subordination and capitalist sexism, see Ivan Illich, *Gender* (New York: Pantheon Books, 1982), chaps. 1 and 2. In focusing on this question, I do not mean to say that the issues important to liberal feminism are inherently the most important ones, only that they are the issues most widely present in classrooms where Milton's poetry is taught. Two scholars, in addition to McColley, who treat feminist issues in Milton in ways that I find very rewarding are Catherine Gimelli Martin, *The Ruins of Allegory: "Paradise Lost" and the Metamorphosis of Epic Convention* (Durham, N.C.: Duke University Press, 1998), and Victoria Silver, *Imperfect Sense: The Predicament of Milton's Irony* (Princeton, N.J.: Princeton University Press, 2001).

6. Joseph Wittreich, *Feminist Milton* (Ithaca, N.Y.: Cornell University Press, 1987), and Sharon Achinstein, "'Pleasure by Description': Elizabeth Singer Rowe's Enlightened Milton," in *Milton and the Grounds of Contention,* ed. Mark R. Kelley, Michael Lieb and John T. Shawcross

(Pittsburgh: Duquesne University Press, 2003), 64–87, demonstrate that women readers and writers of the late seventeenth and eighteenth centuries experienced Milton not at all as a bogey but as a source for the liberation of their own voices. Mihoko Suzuki, *Subordinate Subjects: Gender, the Political Nation, and Literary Form in England, 1588–1688* (Burlington, Vt.: Ashgate, 2003), explores the influence of pamphlet literature on seventeenth century women's writing and offers a current bibliography of secondary works with which anyone interested in charting a genealogy of feminism should be familiar.

7. Mary Astell, *Some Reflections upon Marriage,* in *Astell: Political Writings,* ed. Patricia Springborg (Cambridge: Cambridge University Press, 1996), 36; hereafter cited in the text by page number. For treatments of Astell's life and work, see *The First English Feminist: Reflections upon Marriage and Other Writings by Mary Astell,* ed. Bridget Hill (New York: St. Martin's Press, 1986), and Ruth Perry, *The Celebrated Mary Astell: An Early English Feminist* (Chicago: University of Chicago Press, 1986).

8. Joan K. Kinnaird, "Mary Astell and the Conservative Contribution to English Feminism," *The Journal of British Studies* 19 (1979): 64.

9. Astell, *A Fair Way with the Dissenters and Their Patrons,* in Springborg, *Astel.*

10. Patricia Springborg, "Mary Astell (1666–1731), Critic of Locke," *American Political Science Review* 89 (1995): 622.

11. Catherine Gallagher, "Embracing the Absolute: The Politics of the Female Subject in Seventeenth-Century England," *Genders* 1 (1988): 37.

12. Until David Norbrook established Lucy Hutchinson's authorship of *Order and Disorder* and published a modern edition in 2001, the extent of Hutchinson's writing had not been recognized. See *Order and Disorder,* ed. David Norbrook (Oxford: Blackwell, 2001), hereafter cited in the text by page number, as well as Norbrook's "Lucy Hutchinson's 'Elegies' and the Situation of the Republican Woman Writer (with Text)," *English Literary Renaissance* 27 (1997): 468–521, "Margaret Cavendish and Lucy Hutchinson: Identity, Ideology and Politics," *In-Between: Essays and Studies in Literary Criticism* 9 (2000): 179–203, and "John Milton, Lucy Hutchinson and the Republican Biblical Epic," in Kelley, Lieb, and Shawcross, *Milton and the Grounds of Contention* (Pittsburgh: Duquesne University Press, 2003): 37–63.

13. *The Life of Mrs. Lucy Hutchinson, Written by Herself: A Fragment* in *Memoirs of the Life of Colonel Hutchinson with a fragment of autobiography,* ed. N. H. Keeble (London: J. M. Dent, 1995), 26.

14. Norbrook, "Margaret Cavendish and Lucy Hutchinson," 197, emphasizing a point made by Margaret Ezell, notes that manuscript circulation was, in the Restoration period, a form of publication.

15. Keeble, introduction to Hutchinson, *Life,* 243–44.

16. Norbrook, "Margaret Cavendish and Lucy Hutchinson," 196–97.

17. John Milton, *A Readie and Easie Way to Establish a Free Commonwealth* (1660), in *The Complete Prose Works of John Milton*, 8 vols., ed. Don M. Wolfe et al. (New Haven: Yale University Press, 1953–82), 7:443. Quotations from Milton's prose works are taken from this edition, hereafter cited as YP.

18. For a discussion of right reason, also called *recta ratio* and phronesis, see my *Reviving Liberty: Radical Christian Humanism in Milton's Great Poems* (Cambridge, Mass.: Harvard University Press, 1989), chap. 4 and throughout. See also Robert Hoopes, *Right Reason in the English Renaissance* (Cambridge, Mass.: Harvard University Press, 1962).

19. "Prudence" is the Latin-based word that describes judgments and actions rooted in "phronesis" or "right reason."

20. This explanation, given confidently to the reader of the *Memoirs*, is the same explanation that Milton probes intensely when he creates a discussion between the angel Raphael, who holds Hutchinson's theology without complication, and Adam, who must learn what it means to put such a theory into praxis (*PL* 8.520–640).

21. Gilbert affirms Charlotte Brontë's Shirley, who sees Eve in this passage as modeled on Milton's cook or dairy maid, "Eve-as-little-woman," the Victorian housewife (193–94).

22. "Dangerous memory" is a term used in liberation theology; see José Míguez Bonino, *Toward a Christian Political Ethics* (Philadelphia: Fortress Press, 1983), 105.

23. Hutchinson's life offers intriguing parallels with Milton's. Like him, she was considered a prodigy by her devoted parents, who "spared no cost to improve her." Bilingual from birth in French and English, by the age of four she could read English thoroughly and was taken along to sermons, which an unusual memory allowed her to recite and discuss afterward with adults. At Latin, she outstripped her older brothers, who themselves had "a great deal of wit" (150). By seven, she considered most of the subjects taught by her eight tutors to be trivial and read her own choices of books deep into the night, even though her mother was concerned, as Milton's parents' servants had been, that this habit would damage the child's health. Of highest importance to Hutchinson from her earliest days was the study of "the knowledge of God." However, once she had been careful to instruct her mother's maids in serious discourse, she "thought it no sin to learn or hear witty songs and amorous sonnets or poems, and twenty things of that kind" wherein she was, like the young Milton, very apt. Like Milton, she devoted the civil war years to writing and taking actions that put her literary and personal gifts at the service of the revolutionary cause. After the Restoration, she composed a long biblical epic, which, like her prose work, is filled with expressions of her revolutionary commitments.

24. Norbrook, "Margaret Cavendish and Lucy Hutchinson," 198.

25. Ibid., xiv.

26. Barbara K. Lewalski, *The Life of John Milton: A Critical Biography* (Oxford: Blackwell, 2000), 337.

27. Norbrook, "Margaret Cavendish and Lucy Hutchinson," 203.

28. José Míguez Bonino, interviewed by Elsa Tamez in *Against Machismo,* ed. and trans. John Eagleson (Oak Park, Ill.: Meyer Stone Books, 1987), 57. Epigraph to this section is from Bonino, *Toward a Christian Political Ethics* (Philadelphia: Fortress Press, 1983), 105.

29. All quotations of Schüssler Fiorenza are from *But She Said: Feminist Practices of Biblical Interpretation* (Boston: Beacon Press, 1992).

30. Astell's use of Rebecca in her array of proofs for the Bible's approval of women contrasts strikingly with Hutchinson's. Whereas Hutchinson sees in Rebecca a woman of fine judgment deeply involved in working with Providence and creatively draws forth her story, Astell is simply looking for divine approval of women who successfully overrule husbands; she feels less confident in Rebecca's case than in Deborah's, but insists "you must at least grant that she paid greater deference to the Divine Revelation, and for this Reason at least, had a Right to oppose her Husband's Design" (23).

31. For students unable to understand how predestinarian Calvinist theology, such as that of Lucy Hutchinson and most of the Puritan revolutionaries, could coexist with humanist belief and praxis, this story provides a clear example.

32. For a discussion of the challenges inhering in the use of this distinction by feminist theology between "power over" and "power for," see Schüssler Fiorenza, *But She Said,* 72–73.

33. Roy Flannagan, *The Riverside Milton* (Boston: Houghton Mifflin, 1998), 628 n. 61. Quotations of Milton's poetry are taken from this edition.

34. The *Christian Doctrine* characterizes the original sin as including in that one act all possible sins (YP 6:383–84).

35. This dance is a central liberationist metaphor for Schüssler Fiorenza (*But She Said,* 52). Stanley Fish offers a helpful reflection on the Miltonic dance metaphor in *How Milton Works* (Cambridge, Mass.: Harvard University Press, 2001), 179–82.

36. Lucy Hutchinson includes in her reflections on the Fall much of the lesson that Milton's Adam receives from the angel Michael in book 11. Recounting the judgment of Eve, she proclaims that even in the best postlapsarian marriages there is for the woman a loss of liberty in addition to all the suffering that comes with pregnancy, labor, births, childrearing, sickness, and death (5.127–80). Also, however, she remembers and proclaims the immense human power for channeling divine grace.

Notes to Chapter 7 / Wittreich

1. Fish, *How Milton Works*, 117.

2. Marjorie Perloff, quoting Bob Perelman, "The Marginalization of Poetry," in *Twenty-First-Century Modernism: The New Poetics* (London: 2002), 42.

3. For this distinction, see Janel Mueller, "Contextualizing Milton's Nascent Republicanism," in *Of Poetry and Politics: New Essays on Milton and His World*, ed. P. G. Stanwood (Binghamton, N.Y.: Medieval and Renaissance Texts and Studies, 1995), 264.

4. John K. Leonard, "Did Milton Go to the Devil's Party?" *The New York Review of Books* 49, no. 12 (July 18, 2002): 31.

5. Fish, *How Milton Works*, 452 (for section title) and 464 (for section epigraph). Alan Rudrum pleads with Fish "to resolve difficulties rather than create them," at once exposing Rudrum's own unwillingness to do the mediatorial work of a new Milton criticism even as, with blinders still secure, Rudrum sharpens the ideological divide in Milton criticism, which is owing in part to the divide, historically, in the Samson hermeneutic itself. See Alan Rudrum, "Review Article: Milton Scholarship and the Agon over *Samson Agonistes*," *Huntington Library Quarterly* 65, nos. 3–4 (2002): 469.

6. Thomas Keightley, *An Account of the Life, Opinions, and Writings of John Milton, with an Introduction to "Paradise Lost"* (London: Chapman and Hall, 1855), 322.

7. John Upton, as cited by Francis Blackburne, "An Answer to Some Criticisms on Milton's *Paradise Lost*," *Memoirs of Thomas Hollis*, 2 vols. (London, 1780), 2:624. For recent scrutiny of Milton's attitudes toward divine motions and commissions, see Abraham Stoll, "Milton Stages Cherbury: Revelation and Polytheism in *Samson Agonistes*," in *Altering Eyes: New Perspectives on "Samson Agonistes*," ed. Mark R. Kelley and Joseph Wittreich (Newark, Del.: University of Delaware Press, 2002), 281–306; and Joseph Wittreich, *Shifting Contexts: Reinterpreting "Samson Agonistes"* (Pittsburgh: Duquesne University Press, 2002), esp. 268–78.

8. I appropriate this phrase from A. J. Grieve, ed., *Samson Agonistes* (London: J. M. Dent, 1904), vi.

9. Heymann Steinthal, "The Legend of Samson," quoted in Ignaz Goldziher, *Mythology among the Hebrews and Its Historical Development*, trans. Russell Martineau (London: Longman and Green, 1877), 402, 446. Paul Carus, *The Story of Samson and Its Place in the Religious Development of Mankind* (Chicago: Open Court, 1907), notes that Steinthal resists the idea (as developed by Gustav Roskoff) that Samson is a hero of prayer, Roskoff's chief evidence for which is that "the spirit of Yahweh comes over Samson and gives him heroic strength to accomplish his deeds" (5). Compare Roskoff, *Die Simsonssage nach ihren Entstehung, Form und Bedeutung, und der Heracles Mythus* (Leipzig: E. Bredt, 1860), 45. On

Milton's shifting idea of prayer, see Sharon Achinstein, "*Samson Agonistes*," in *A Companion to Milton*, ed. Thomas N. Corns (Oxford: Blackwell, 2001), 415–16.

10. As remarked by John Penn, *Critical, Poetical and Dramatic Works*, 2 vols. (London: Hatchard, 1796, 1798), 2:260–61. The Richard Westall illustration is reproduced by William Hayley, *The Poetical Works of John Milton. With a Life of the Author*, 3 vols. (London: W. Bulmer, 1797), vol. 3, opposite 67.

11. Penn, *Critical, Poetical, and Dramatic Works*, 2:222.

12. John Adams, "A Defence of the Constitutions of Government of the United States of America — (1787–1788)," in *The American Enlightenment: The Shaping of the American Experiment and a Free Society*, ed. Adrienne Koch (New York: G. Braziller, 1965), 258.

13. See Abram Leon Sachar, *A History of the Jews*, 5th ed. (New York: Knopf, 1965), 30; compare *The New Testament Study Bible: Revelation*, ed. Ralph W. Harris et al. (Springfield, Mo.: Complete Biblical Library, 1990), 115.

14. J. T. et al., *The Spirit of Judgment: Readings and Addresses* (London: Stow Hill Bible and Tract Depot, 1932), 124.

15. Paulus Cassel, *The Book of Judges*, trans. P. H. Streenstra (New York: Charles Scribner, 1872), 224.

16. Johann Gottfried Herder, *Oriental Dialogues: Containing the Conversations of Eugenius and Alciphron on the . . . Sacred Poetry of the Hebrews* (London, 1801), 322.

17. Peter Bayne, *The Chief Actors in the Puritan Revolution* (London, 1878), [299].

18. Martin A. Larson, *The Modernity of Milton: A Theological and Philosophical Interpretation* (Chicago: University of Chicago Press, 1927), viii, 171, 264.

19. See the prefatory lyric to Blake's *Milton* and Wordsworth's sonnet, "London, 1802," in *The Romantics on Milton: Formal Essays and Critical Asides*, ed. Joseph Wittreich (Cleveland: Press of Case Western Reserve University, 1970), 39, 111, respectively.

20. Percy Bysshe Shelley, *Prometheus Unbound* and *The Cenci*, in *Shelley's Poetry and Prose*, ed. Donald H. Reiman and Sharon B. Powers (New York: Norton, 1977), 136 (1.7) and 250 (1.3.58–61), respectively.

21. Mary Shelley, *Frankenstein*, ed. Maurice Hindle (Harmondsworth: Penguin, 1985), 176, 207.

22. Ibid., 242.

23. Ibid., 243, 254–55, 242, 248; compare 240, 241, 244, 251.

24. Quoted from *Byron's Letters and Journals: The Complete and Unexpurgated Text of All the Letters*, 13 vols., ed. Leslie A. Marchand (London: J. Murray, 1973–94), 9:60.

25. See J. Macmillan Brown, who is also quoted by Lawrence John

Zillman, as saying that *Samson Agonistes* "is really the tragedy not of Samson but of John Milton"; see *Shelley's "Prometheus Unbound": A Variorum Edition*, rev ed., ed. Lawrence John Zillman (Seattle: University of Washington Press, 1960), 70. Zillman reports that the editors of *Poet Lore* (1897) engage Milton and Shelley under the following topics: "Grounds for Identifying the Samson with the Prometheus Story; the Lack of Correspondence of Milton's *Samson Agonistes* with the Prometheus Story" (79). See especially the section, "The Prometheus Stories as Treated by Aeschylus, Shelley, Goethe, Milton" (589–606) and, within that section, the subtopics of "Grounds for Identifying the Samson with the Prometheus Myth" (595), "The Lack of Correspondence of Milton's *Samson Agonistes* with the Prometheus Story" (595–96), "The Characterization of the Heroes of Aeschylus, Shelley, Goethe, Milton, and Byron," (600–602), "The Underlying Philosophy of the Poems" (600–606), all in *Poet Lore: A Quarterly Magazine of Letters*, ed. Carlotte Porter and Helen A. Clarke, n.s. 1, no. 9, 4 (October–December 1897).

26. G. Wilson Knight, *Chariot of Wrath: The Message of John Milton to Democracy at* War (London: Faber and Faber, 1942), 83.

27. Ibid., 39.

28. See Abram Smythe Palmer, *The Samson Saga and Its Place in Comparative Religion* (London: Isaac Pitman, 1913), 188; and Edward Rothstein, "Shelf Life: Six Days of Confusion That Rearranged World Politics," *New York Times*, July 6, 2002, B9, who, in his Samson citation, is misquoting Levi Eshkol as his words are reported by Michael B. Oren, *Six Days of War: June 1967 and the Making of the Modern Middle East* (Oxford: Oxford University Press, 2002), 18; see also 317.

29. G. H. S. Walpole, *Handbooks to Judges and Ruth* (London: Rivingtons, 1901), 157–58, 159–60 (compare 158), 100.

30. Hans Robert Jauss, *Toward an Aesthetic of Reception*, trans. Timothy Bahti (Minneapolis: University of Minnesota Press, 1982), 28. Rudrum, "Review Article," complains that "the fundamental problem of most revisionist criticism" is that "it outlines what significance the poem might have for modern readers and then imputes it back to Milton as his meaning" (479). On the contrary, revisionist criticism is now mapping the reception of literary works, which typically inscribes competing interpretive traditions, with those traditions, then, vastly complicated by the interplay of literary criticism (pertaining to *Samson Agonistes*) and biblical hermeneutics (for the Samson story). Traditional Milton criticism is reluctant to examine its roots and thus often denies (as does Rudrum) its own history. Witness where variorum projects of the last century and of our own commence, hence the centuries of commentary they necessarily ignore.

31. See, respectively, Andrew Marvell, "On Mr. Milton's *Paradise Lost*," in *Andrew Marvell: The Complete Poems*, ed. Elizabeth Story Donno

(Harmondsworth: Penguin, 1972), 192 (see esp. lines 5–10); Samuel Johnson, "The Rambler No. 139. Tuesday, July 16, 1751," as excerpted by Ralph E. Hone, ed., *John Milton's "Samson Agonistes": The Poem and Materials for Analysis* (San Francisco, Calif.: Chandler, 1966), 103; Percy Bysshe Shelley, *Prometheus Unbound,* in Reiman and Powers, *Shelley's Poetry and Prose,* 136 (1.7); Mary Shelley, *Frankenstein,* passim; James Montgomery, *The Poetical Works of John Milton with a Memoir,* 2 vols. (London: Bohn, 1843), xlviii; George Gilfillan, "Critical Estimate of the Genius and Poetical Works of John Milton," in *Milton's Poetical Works: With Life, Critical Dissertation, and Explanatory Notes,* 2 vols., ed. Charles Cowan Clarke (Edinburgh: James Nichol, 1853), 2:xxx. Of Marvell's poem, it needs to be remembered that he is marking not Milton's identity with, but distinction from, Samson; and of Johnson's remarks, that his harsh words come on the heels of his observation (in "The Rambler, No. 139") that Samson "declares himself moved by a secret impulse to comply, and utters some dark presages of a great event to be brought to pass by his agency, under the direction of Providence" (102) and, later (in "The Rambler, No. 140. Saturday, July 20, 1751") that his severest censure is for "the solemn introduction of the Phœnix . . . which is . . . incongruous to the personage to whom it is ascribed," hence the poet's "grossest errour" (104).

32. Bayne, *The Chief Actors,* 345.

33. J. Howard B. Masterman, *The Age of Milton* (London: G. Bell and Sons, 1897), 72. Compare J. H. Hexter, *Reappraisals in History,* 2nd ed. (Chicago: University of Chicago Press, 1979), 248.

34. Rudrum, "Review Article," 466. Why a book addressed to "students" should be treated so dismissively needs explanation, particularly in view of the fact that the book in question is addressed to "the ordinary man . . . the intelligent reader"; see John Carey, *Milton* (London: Evans Brothers, 1969), 5.

35. Cassel, *The Book of Judges,* 225.

36. Ibid., 208, 225.

37. W. A. Scott, *The Giant Judge; or, The Story of Samson, the Hebrew Hercules,* 2nd ed. (San Francisco, 1858), 301, 305–06, 309, 253.

38. Ibid., 309–10.

39. See William Riley Parker, *Milton's Debt to Greek Tragedy in "Samson Agonistes"* (Baltimore: Johns Hopkins University Press, 1937); F. Michael Krouse, *Milton's Samson and the Christian Tradition* (Princeton, N.J.: Princeton University Press, 1949); and James L. Crenshaw, *Samson: A Secret Betrayed, a Vow Ignored* (London: S.P.C.K., 1979), the last of whom, while recognizing the negative features in Samson's character, also contends that, in Milton's rendering of it, Samson is depicted as driven by divine impulse (83, 129, but also 88–89, 94, 95, 96, 143). In "Samson," the section entitled "Postcanonical Readings of the Story,"

The Anchor Bible Dictionary, 6 vols., ed. David Noel Freedman (New York: Doubleday, 1992), James L. Crenshaw concludes, "In Milton's eyes," Samson's "defeat was only a temporary tragedy" (5:954). This is not to say that there are no representations of what is supposed to be Milton's heroic Samson in the nineteenth century; see, for example, Anonymous, "The Samson-Saga and the Myth of Herakles," *The Westminister and Foreign Quarterly Review* 121 (April 1884): 317, 324–25.

40. See the anonymous essay, "Samson: Was He Man or Myth?" *The Thinker: A Review* 4 (July–December 1893): 294.

41. Christopher Wordsworth, *The Holy Bible, in the Authorized Version,* 6 vols. (London: Rivingtons, 1875–76), 2:134, 139, 133, 137, 140, 144, 143–44 (my italics).

42. See J. J. Lias, *The Book of Judges* (Cambridge: Cambridge University Press, 1882), 9, 25, 155, 165, 175. See also Lawrence Levermore, *Talks on the Book of Judges* (London: Morgan and Scott, [1910]), who ends his own commentary with what he calls Milton's "thrilling lament" in *Samson Agonistes* (96).

43. Lewis Hughes, *Analysis of the Book of Judges with Notes Critical, Historical, and Geographical* (London: J. Heywood, 1884), 118.

44. See A. R. Fausset, *A Critical and Expository Commentary on the Book of Judges* (London: J. Nisbet, 1885), 4, 245, 250, 261, 262–63.

45. See Charles Simon Clermont-Ganneau, "Tour from Jerusalem to Jaffa and the Country of Samson," in *Archeological Researches in Palestine during the Years 1873–74,* 2 vols., trans. Aubrey Stewart (London: Committee of the Palestine Exploration Fund, 1897, 1899), 2:204.

46. Ibid., 2:205.

47. Ibid., 2: 205, 207, 209–10. C. F. Burney, ed., *The Book of Judges with Introduction and Notes* (London, 1918), 392, reports that "the place name Beth-shemesh, 'Temple of the Sun,' [is] in the immediate neighborhood of the scene of that hero's [i. e., Samson's] exploits."

48. Palmer, *The Samson Saga,* 7, 187.

49. Ibid., 188, 232, 187.

50. Heinrich Graetz, *History of the Jews,* 6 vols., trans. Bella Löwy (Philadelphia: Jewish Publication Society of America, 1891–98), 1:64, 66.

51. George Foot Moore, *The Literature of the Old Testament* (New York: Henry Holt, 1913), 88. If Moore is right in his conjecture that the original redactor "left out the adventure with Delilah and Samson's tragic end" (85), then Milton's tragedy takes on even more emphatically the character of a scriptural supplement.

52. George Foot Moore, *A Critical and Exegetical Commentary on Judges* (1895; reprint, Edinburgh: Charles Scribner's Sons, 1976), 313.

53. Graetz, *History of the Jews,* 5:715

54. Luke H. Wiseman, *Men of Faith; or, Sketches from the Book of Judges* (London: Hedder & Stoughton, 1870), 281, 284.

55. Malcolm X, with Alex Haley, *The Autobiography of Malcolm X* (1964; reprint, New York: Grove Press, 1966), 185, 205–06, 185–86.

56. Ibid., 210.

57. Michael Lieb, *Children of Ezekiel: Aliens, UFOS, the Crisis of Race, and the Advent of End Time* (Durham, N.C.: Duke University Press, 1998), 155–56.

58. Malcolm X, *Autobiography*, 366, 200–201.

59. Ibid., 201, 391.

60. Ralph Ellison, *Juneteenth: A Novel*, ed. John F. Callahan (New York: Random House, 1999), 19.

61. Originally published under the title, "The Imagery of Killing," *Hudson Review* 1, no. 2 (Summer 1948): 151–67, Kenneth Burke's essay is reprinted under the title, "The 'Use' of Milton's Samson," in *A Grammar of Motives and a Rhetoric of Motives* (Cleveland: Meridian Books, 1962), 527–44. For the quotations, see 528, 529, 541, 533, 527, 529, 527.

62. Ibid., 527 (my italics).

63. Knight, *Chariot of Wrath*, 100, 115; compare 101–07.

64. Ellison, *Juneteenth*, 17.

65. Ellison, *Invisible Man* (1953; reprint, New York: Signet, 1964), 212.

66. As reported by Lawrence Jackson, *Ralph Ellison: Emergence of Genius* (New York: John Wiley, 2002), 390.

67. Ellison, *Juneteenth*, 228–29, 121–23.

68. Fish, *How Milton Works*, 450.

69. Ellison, *Juneteenth*, 235 (compare 357), 14, 17.

70. Ibid., 309 (my italics).

71. Ibid., 285, 284.

72. Hugo Grotius, *Of the Rights of War and Peace . . . in Which Are Explained the Laws and Claims of Nature and Nations*, 3 vols., trans. John Morrice et al. (London: D. Brown, T. Ward and W. Meares, 1715), 2:465.

73. Wiseman, *Men of Faith*, 279.

74. Ellison, *Juneteenth*, 296, 310.

75. Ibid., 322, 368.

76. Morrison, *Paradise*, 285, 273, 87, 18, 87, 160.

77. Philip Pullman, *His Dark Materials, Book III: The Amber Spyglass* (New York: Knopf, 2000), 408.

78. See Milton's Letter 21: To Emeric Bigot (March 24, 1656), in *The Works of John Milton*, 18 vols., ed. Frank Allen Patterson (New York: Columbia University Press, 1931–38), 12:87, and *Defensio Secunda*, 8:107.

79. Ralph Ellison, "Change the Joke and Slip the Yoke," *Partisan Review* 25, no. 2 (Spring 1958): 220.

80. See Stanley Edgar Hyman, commenting on Ellison's *Invisible Man*, in "The Negro Writer in America: An Exchange," ibid., 210.

81. Thomas Jefferson, "Notes on Locke and Shaftsbury," in *The Papers of Thomas Jefferson*, 29 vols., ed. Julian P. Boyd et al. (Princeton, N.J.: Princeton University Press, 1950–2002), 1:548.

82. Adonis (Ali Ahmad Said), *The Pages of Day and Night*, trans. Samuel Hazo (Evanston, Ill.: Northwestern University Press, 2000), xiv.

83. Pullman, *The Amber Spyglass*, 363.

84. Morrison, *Paradise*, 306, 318. Morrison wanted the last word of her novel (in contrast with its first word) to be lowercased, and it is in subsequent editions of the book.

85. I borrow this phrase from *Milton: "Samson Agonistes,"* ed. F. T. Prince (Oxford: Oxford University Press, 1957), 16. Arguing that Samson's Naziriteship is a temporary, not permanent, condition — a period of retirement and contemplation before a return to action — Peter Martyr asserts an analogy between the Samson story and the tale of Jesus tempted, each of them retreating to the mountain at nighttime and, in daytime, returning to their people; see *Most Fruitfull & Learned Comentaries* (London: John Day, 1564), f203v. This analogy is, however, thwarted by Milton's tragedy. Therein lies the tragedy of Samson as it is inscribed in Milton's poem that bears his name.

86. Ellison, *Juneteenth*, 14, 17.

87. As quoted by Azar Nafisi, "Words of War," *The New York Times*, Thursday, March 27, 2003, A23.

Notes to Chapter 8 / Loewenstein

1. Gilbert Achcar, *The Clash of Barbarians: September 11 and the Making of the New World Order*, trans. Peter Drucker (New York: Monthly Review Press, 2002), 61–62, 81–85.

2. John Carey, "A Work in Praise of Terrorism? September 11 and *Samson Agonistes*," *The Times Literary Supplement*, September 6, 2002, 15–16.

3. Carey is responding specifically to *How Milton Works* (Cambridge, Mass.: Harvard University Press, 2001), 426, 428.

4. On the question of whether or not the events of September 11 have "changed" Milton's drama, see Stanley Fish's essay in this volume.

5. *OED*, s.v. "terrorism" and "terrorist"; s.v. "terror," *OED* 2.

6. *Milton: Complete Shorter Poems*, ed. John Carey (London: Longman, 1971), 333. Quotations from Milton's poetry are from this edition.

7. See the introduction to *Altering Eyes: New Perspectives on Samson Agonistes*, ed. Mark R. Kelley and Joseph Wittreich (Cranbury, N.J.: Associated University Presses, 2002), 2; the full introduction (11–29) provides an acute assessment of the critical debates and positions in Milton studies since 1969 when John Carey asserted that *Samson Agonistes* "is not a drama of inner regeneration"; see Carey, *Milton* (London: Evans

Brothers, 1969), 145. Carey was soon followed by Irene Samuel's inter-
pretation of the unregenerate Samson: "*Samson Agonistes* as Tragedy,"
in *Calm of Mind: Tercentenary Essays on "Paradise Regained" and
"Samson Agonistes,"* ed. Joseph A. Wittreich, Jr. (Cleveland: Case Western
Reserve Press, 1971), 237–57. Some (but by no means all) of the critical
debates and disagreements are summarized and discussed in Alan Rudrum,
"Milton Scholarship and the *Agon* over *Samson Agonistes*," *Huntington
Library Quarterly* 65 (2002): 465–88.

8. See especially Joseph Wittreich, *Interpreting "Samson Agonistes"*
(Princeton: Princeton University Press, 1986), and *Shifting Contexts:
Reinterpreting "Samson Agonistes"* (Pittsburgh: Duquesne University
Press, 2003), as well as the essays in Kelley and Wittreich, *Altering Eyes*.
For Fish, see "Question and Answer in *Samson Agonistes*," *Critical
Quarterly* 11 (1969): 237–64 (incorporated into *How Milton Works*, chap.
12); "Spectacle and Evidence in *Samson Agonistes*," *Critical Inquiry* 15
(1989): 556–86 (incorporated into *How Milton Works*, chap. 13).

9. In addition to criticism of Carey and Samuel cited in note 7, the
works by Wittreich cited in note 8 have tended to emphasize this negative view of Samson's violence, making him "a figure of dubious heroism" (*Interpreting Samson Agonistes*, 327). In contrast to this critical
perspective, Michael Lieb stresses that the drama is "a work of harsh and
uncompromising violence, indeed, a work that exults in violence"; see
"'Our Living Dread': The God of *Samson Agonistes*," in *Milton Studies*
33, *The Miltonic Samson*, ed. Albert C. Labriola and Michael Lieb
(Pittsburgh: University of Pittsburgh Press, 1997), 4, while Samson (in
both Milton's *Defensio Prima* and the drama) may be seen "as a model
of heroism"; see Lieb, *Milton and the Culture of Violence* (Ithaca, N.Y.:
Cornell University Press, 1994), 235; see also 237–63. For my own view
of the drama as a spectacle of violence, see *Milton and the Drama of
History: Historical Vision, Iconoclasm, and the Literary Imagination*
(Cambridge: Cambridge University Press, 1990), chap. 6.

10. Tony Judt, "The Road to Nowhere," *The New York Review of Books*
49, no. 8 (May 9, 2002): 4.

11. Baruch Kimmerling, *Politicide: Ariel Sharon's War against the
Palestinians* (London: Verso, 2003), 73.

12. *De Doctrina Christiana*, in *Complete Prose Works of John Milton*,
8 vols., ed. Don M. Wolfe et al. (New Haven: Yale University Press,
1953–82), 6:123; hereafter designated as YP and followed by volume and
page number.

13. Kimmerling, *Politicide*, 73–74.

14. Cromwell, *Writings and Speeches of Oliver Cromwell*, 4 vols., ed.
W. C. Abbott (Cambridge, Mass.: Harvard University Press, 1937–47), 2:198;
Ian Gentles, *The New Model Army in England, Ireland and Scotland,
1645–1653* (Oxford: Blackwell, 1992), chap. 11, esp. 350.

15. On "holy ruthlessness," see Gentles, *The New Model Army*, 115–16. For the number of killed at Drogheda and Wexford, see Gentles, 361, 367; and Austin Woolrych, *England in Revolution, 1625–1660* (Oxford: Oxford University Press, 2002), 469–70.

16. See Cromwell's letter of September 16, 1649, to Bradshaw, president of the Council of State and the recipient of Milton's copious praise in the *Second Defense: Writings and Speeches of Oliver Cromwell,* 2:124.

17. See John Milton, *The Readie and Easie Way* and *A Defence of the People of England,* YP 7:410, 4:430–31.

18. For Michael Lieb's use of this term in relation to *Samson Agonistes* where the Philistines are subjected to "shock and awe," see his essay in this volume. The phrase could be applied just as easily to Cromwell's campaign of terror to destroy Irish resistance.

19. "Truly I believe this bitterness will save much effusion of blood, through the goodness of God," Cromwell wrote to John Bradshaw: *Writings and Speeches of Oliver Cromwell,* 2:124. See also 2:127 (Cromwell's letter to William Lenthall).

20. Gentles, *The New Model Army,* 368–82; Toby Barnard, "Irish Images of Cromwell," in *Images of Cromwell: Essays for and by Roger Howell, Jr.,* ed. R. C. Richardson (Manchester: Manchester University Press, 1993), 181–82. Woolrych, *Britain in Revolution,* 471–72, however, notes that the terror struck by Cromwell in his first two operations did "for a time" weaken resistance to him.

21. *Writings and Speeches of Oliver Cromwell,* 2:127, 142.

22. See John Morrill, "Cromwell and His Contemporaries," in *Oliver Cromwell and the English Revolution* (London: Longman, 1990), 267; Gentles, *The New Model Army,* 362.

23. Carey, "September 11 and *Samson Agonistes,*" 15.

24. *The Souldiers Pocket Bible* (London, 1643), 4. See also Gentles, *The Model Army,* 94. Mark Houlahan, "Spin Controlling Apocalypse in *Samson Agonistes,*" in *Milton Studies* 31, ed. Albert C. Labriola (Pittsburgh: University of Pittsburgh Press, 1994), 3–5, also notes the importance of *The Souldiers Pocket Bible* for the soldiers of the parliamentarian army, but the context for his discussion is the use of a pocket Bible by soldiers during the 1991 Gulf War. The title page of the 1643 *Pocket Bible* includes the imprimatur of Edmund Calamy, one of the antiepiscopal Smectymnuans defended by Milton the zealous controversialist.

25. George Wither, "A Single Sacrifice," in *A Memorandum to London* (London, 1665), 58, 60.

26. Janel Mueller, "The Figure and the Ground: Samson as a Hero of London Nonconformity, 1662–1667," in *Milton and the Terms of Liberty,* ed. Graham Parry and Joad Raymond (Woodbridge: Boydell & Brewer, 2002), 141.

27. Carey's suggestion that Samson's "rousing motions" "may signal his purely human excitement about a glimpsed opportunity" overlooks the opaqueness of Samson's language here; nor does it adequately take account of Samson's disgust at the very idea of going to the Philistine temple ("A Work in Praise of Terrorism?" 15).

28. Fish, *How Milton Works*, 426, 417.

29. On issues of Restoration dissent and Milton, see also Sharon Achinstein, "*Samson Agonistes* and the Drama of Dissent," in *Milton Studies* 33, 144–50, revised and incorporated into her *Literature and Dissent in Milton's England* (Cambridge: Cambridge University Press, 2003), 138–47. I place greater emphasis on *Civil Power* and the 1670 Conventicle Act as a means of understanding the polemical implications of this distinctive episode in *Samson Agonistes*.

30. See J. C. Davis, "Religion and the Struggle for Freedom in the English Revolution," *Historical Journal* 35, no. 3 (1992): 523–24.

31. *The Poems and Letters of Andrew Marvell*, 2 vols., ed. H. M. Margoliouth, 3rd ed., rev. Pierre Legouis and E. E. Duncan-Jones (Oxford: Clarendon Press, 1971), 2:314.

32. *The Stuart Constitution: Documents and Commentary*, 2nd ed., ed. J. P. Kenyon (Cambridge: Cambridge University Press, 1986), 356.

33. *The Life of Thomas Ellwood*, ed. C. G. Crump (London: Methuen, 1900), 169–70. William Penn, *The Continued Cry of the Oppressed for Justice* (London, 1675), lamented "the great OPPRESSIONS and CRU-ELTIES" brought on by the new Conventicle Act (7–15). For *Paradise Regained* as a radical religious poem in the context of the 1670 Conventicle Act, see my afterword ("The Time is Come") to *Milton and the Ends of Time*, ed. Juliet Cummins (Cambridge: Cambridge University Press, 2003), esp. 245–47.

34. Milton, *Complete Shorter Poems*, 344.

35. David Loewenstein, *Representing Revolution in Milton and His Contemporaries: Religion, Politics, and Polemics in Radical Puritanism* (Cambridge: Cambridge University Press, 2001), 276–81. Although I discuss this issue from a different context and perspective, I agree with Fish, who notes "an uncertainty as to the connections between the events in the world of man and the will of God" (*How Milton Works*, 414; compare 417).

36. Gentles, *The New Model Army*, 107, 115–16.

37. *Writings and Speeches of Oliver Cromwell*, 1:377, 2:186. The language of providentialism runs throughout Cromwell's writings. The politics of providence is treated more broadly in the period in Blair Worden, "Providence and Politics in Cromwellian England," *Past and Present* 109 (1985): 55–99.

38. Lieb, "The God of *Samson Agonistes*," 3–26. See also Lieb's essay in this volume.

39. Ibid., 20.

40. *Writings and Speeches of Oliver Cromwell*, 1:653, 619; Cromwell refers here to God's dealings with the Midianites in Numbers 21.

41. Mary Cary, *The Little Horns Doom and Downfall; or, A Scripture-Prophesie of King James, and King Charles*, and *A New and More Exact Mappe or Description of New Jerusalems Glory* (London, 1651), 184–97 (where other scriptural texts include Isaiah 30:30, 34:8, 66:15; Joel 2:31; 2 Peter 3:7); the preface of *Samson Agonistes*, where Milton singles out David Pareus's 1618 commentary (translated in 1644) on the Book of Revelation as a tragedy. In the second edition of *The Resurrection of the Witnesses, and Englands Fall* (London, 1653), Cary comments on the apocalyptic struggles of the saints who, since 1645 (the year the New Model Army was created), had created "terror and amazement" in "all their enemies, overcomming those that have made War against them in these three Nations of *England*, *Scotland*, and *Ireland*" ("To the Reader," sig. Bv). On Milton's drama and apocalypticism, see also Barbara K. Lewalski, "*Samson Agonistes* and the 'Tragedy' of the Apocalypse," *PMLA* 85 (1970): 1050–62.

42. Francis Howgill, *To the Camp of the Lord, in England* ([London, 1655]), 8–9.

43. See, for example, Jeremiah 13:14 ("I will not pity, nor spare, nor have mercy, but destroy them"; compare Jer. 21:7); Ezekiel 8:18 ("Therefore will I also deal in fury: mine eye shall not spare, neither will I have pity"; compare Ezek. 5:11, 7:9, 9:5, 10).

44. Edward Burrough, *A Warning from the Lord to the Inhabitants of Underbarrow* (1654), in *The Memorable Works of a Son of Thunder and Consolation: Namely, That True Prophet, and Faithful Servant of God* (London, 1672), 3.

45. William Penn, *A Just Rebuke to One and Twenty Learned and Reverend Divines* ([London], 1674), 32.

46. George Fox, *A Message from the Lord, to the Parliament of England* (London, 1654), title page, 2.

47. Burrough, *Works*, 820.

48. Thomas Ellwood, *An Alarm to the Priests; or, A Message from Heaven* (London, 1660), 1. Subsequent page references to Ellwood's work are noted parenthetically in my text.

49. See Ellwood, *An Alarm*, where the Lord says, "you . . . would have none of my reproof; but have dealt despightfully with my messengers, beating and stoning some, imprisoning some, dismembering some, and slaying others" (3).

50. See the digression in Milton's *History of Britain*, YP 5:449.

51. Or, as the Quaker prophetess Dorothy White, *A Lamentation Unto this Nation* (London, 1660), warned the nation the same year, "the Approach of the *Great* and *Terrible Day* cometh, and that very swiftly"

as the God of scourge pours out "his wrath without *mixture*" upon the ungodly (5, 8).

52. See Norman T. Burns, "'Then Stood Up Phinehas': Milton's Antinomianism, and Samson's," in *Milton Studies* 33 (1996), 27–46; Loewenstein, *Representing Revolution*, chap. 9. See also Fish's essay in this volume.

Notes to Chapter 9 / Lieb

1. Michael Lieb, "How Stanley Fish Works," *Journal of Religion* 82 (April 2002): 253. Stanley Fish, *How Milton Works* (Cambridge, Mass.: Harvard University Press, 2001); *Surprised by Sin: The Reader in "Paradise Lost,"* 2nd ed. (1967; reprint, Cambridge, Mass.: Harvard University Press, 1998). References to Fish's works in my text are indicated by page number. References to Milton's poetry in my text are to *The Complete Poetry of John Milton*, ed. John T. Shawcross, 2nd rev. ed. (Garden City: Doubleday, 1971). References to Milton's prose by volume and page number in my text are to *The Complete Prose Works of John Milton*, 8 vols. in 10, gen. ed. Don M. Wolfe et al. (New Haven: Yale University Press, 1953–82), hereafter designated YP. Corresponding references to the original Latin (and on occasion to the English translations) are to *The Works of John Milton*, 18 vols. in 21, ed. Frank Allen Patterson et al. (New York: Columbia University Press, 1931–38), hereafter designated CM.

2. When one encounters the phrase "inner light," such figures as George Fox and the Quakers come to mind. For these so-called "Children of Light," the inner light is a manifestation of divine revelation bestowed upon the faithful as a sign of God's grace. As a result of such a bestowal, the faithful are renewed and illuminated. Available only to those fully capable of understanding the nature of the gift, this signature of divine grace is crucial to all that the Quakers represent.

3. "The Miltonic Paradigm" is the heading to the first part of Fish's book (21).

4. The classic statement of this interpretive outlook is voiced by Mary Ann Radzinowicz, in her pioneering book *Toward "Samson Agonistes"* (Princeton: Princeton University Press, 1978), and the classic argument against it is undertaken by Joseph Wittreich, in his own pioneering works, most notably, *Interpreting "Samson Agonistes"* (Princeton, N.J.: Princeton Uni-versity Press, 1986), as well as his more recent publications, among them, *Shifting Contexts: Reinterpreting "Samson Agonistes"* (Pittsburgh: Duquesne University Press, 2002). The battle between the regenerationists and the nonregenerationists has a longstanding history. Responding to this tradition, John T. Shawcross draws upon the *De Doctrina Christiana* (1.17) to argue that the accurate term is "renovation," not "regeneration." See Shawcross, "Misreading Milton," in *Milton Studies* 33, *The Miltonic*

Samson, ed. Albert C. Labriola and Michael Lieb (Pittsburgh: University of Pittsburgh Press, 1996), esp. 192–93. See also Albert C. Labriola, "Divine Urgency as a Motive for Conduct in *Samson Agonistes," Philological Quarterly* 50 (1971): 99–107.

5. Compare the prefatory statement, "The Argument": "at length perswaded inwardly that this was from God." The statement suggests Milton's own "take" on the whole matter of how the "rouzing motions" are to be viewed.

6. I allude, of course, to Fish's "Spectacle and Evidence in *Samson Agonistes," Critical Inquiry* 15 (1989): 556–86. This article is incorporated into chapter 13 of Fish's *How Milton Works.*

7. John Carey, "A work in praise of terrorism? September 11 and *Samson Agonistes," TLS,* September 6, 2002, pp. 15–16. References to this article in my text are by page number. See also Carey's earlier review "The Devil in the Detail," *Sunday Times,* June 24, 2001.

8. See the definition of terrorism advanced in the *OED,* s.v. Because of its emphasis on the secular, this definition is finally inadequate.

9. Mark Juergensmeyer, *Terror in the Mind of God: The Global Rise of Religious Violence,* 3rd rev. ed. (Berkeley and Los Angeles: University of California Press, 2003), 5–7. References in my text are to this edition. See also Jessica Stern, *Terrorism in the Name of God: Why Religious Militants Kill* (New York: HarperCollins, 2003). According to Stern, there are two characteristics of terrorism that are crucial for distinguishing it from other forms of violence. "First, terrorism is aimed at noncombatants. . . . Second, terrorists use violence for dramatic purpose: instilling fear in the target audience is often more important than the physical result. This deliberative creation of dread is what distinguishes terrorism from simple murder or assault" (xx).

10. See Juergensmeyer, *Terror in the Mind of God,* 6. Juergensmeyer's conclusion is based on Warren Christopher, "Fighting Terrorism: Challenges for Peacemakers," address to the Washington Institute for Near East Policy, May 21, 1996; reprinted in Warren Christopher, *In the Stream of History: Shaping Foreign Policy for a New Era* (Stanford: Stanford University Press, 1998), 446.

11. Harlan Ullman et al., *Shock and Awe: Achieving Rapid Dominance,* Institute for National Strategic Studies ([Washington, D.C.]: NDU Press Book, [1996]), [9, 13].

12. For the idea of a God that hates, see my " 'Hate in Heav'n': Milton and the *Odium Dei," English Literary History* 53 (1986): 519–39. This essay is now available in my book, *Theological Milton: Deity, Discourse and Heresy in the Miltonic Canon* (Pittsburgh: Duquesne University Press, 2006), 261–78.

13. In this regard, see my "Milton and the Kenotic Christology: Its Literary Bearing," *English Literary History* 37 (1970): 342–60.

14. In *Samson Agonistes*, the word "terror" is invoked significantly in connection with katharsis, which Milton defines as the act of "raising pity and fear, *or terror*" (italics mine) in order "to purge the mind of those and such like passions." Here, "terror" assumes an "Aristotelian" cast: its bearing is aesthetic as much as it is psychological, a fact emphasized by the citations from the *Poetics* on the title page of Milton's drama, not to mention at the very outset of the preface to *Samson*. Although Aristotle's *Poetics* does not mention "terror" in connection with "pity" and "fear," Milton does not hesitate to place "terror" in apposition to "fear" as a way of focusing and intensifying the mimetic implications of the cathartic experience. In its ties with katharsis, then, terror, might become for Milton an essential element in the experience of the tragic. See the headnote to *Samson Agonistes*, titled "Of That Sort of Dramatic Poem Which Is Call'd Tragedy" (Shawcross, *The Complete Poetry of John Milton*, 573). Among other studies of the subject, see Martin Mueller, "Pathos and Katharsis in *Samson Agonistes*," *English Literary History* 31 (1964): 156–74; and John M. Steadman, "Passions Well Imitated: Rhetoric and Poetics in the Preface to *Samson Agonistes*," in *Calm of Mind: Tercentenary Essays on "Paradise Regained" and "Samson Agonistes"* (Cleveland: Case Western Reserve, 1971), 175–207. For Aristotle's discussion of katharsis, see his *Poetics* (section 1, part 6), *Aristotle, Horace, Longinus*, ed. T. S. Dorsch (Baltimore: Penguin Books, 1965): "by means of pity and fear bringing about the purgation of such emotions" (39). "Terror" as a synonym for "fear" is not mentioned.

15. Michael Lieb, " 'Our Living Dread': The God of *Samson Agonistes*," *Milton Studies* 33 (1996), 3–25. This essay is now available in my *Theological Milton*, 184–209.

16. The term "accord" is interesting here as well. If the phrase "my own accord" suggests the idea of initiating an action on one's own authority, the word "accord" draws upon the Latin sense of "to the heart," an etymology that points up the significance of uniting with God or in unison with God: "heart-to-heart."

17. See Otto's now-classic *The Idea of the Holy: An Inquiry into the Non-Rational Factor in the Idea of the Divine and Its Relation to the Rational*, trans. John W. Harvey (London: Oxford University Press, 1928), passim. There is an entire range of words in the Hebrew Bible to explain the idea of a God whose name is "dread." The word that comes immediately to mind in this context is *pakhad* (Job 4:13–14, and so on). Corresponding terms are relevant, among them, *khatat* (Gen. 35:5, Ezek. 32:23–32, and so on). As he embodies the meanings that underlie these terms, Samson emerges as both minister and scourge of God.

18. This is precisely the kind of outlook that underlies what might be called "the terrorist frame of mind." As we have come to know it,

terrorism manifests itself in the unpredictable yet horrific behavior of those bent on *jihad*. Thus perpetrated in the name of God, terrorism assumes the aura of the "religious" or "holy" enactment of self-sacrifice (literally) to a divine cause. In that act of self-sacrifice, the obliteration of the self becomes the ultimate sign of faith. Once again, Juergensmeyer is helpful here. Sacrifice (from *sacrificium*), Juergensmeyer reminds us, is "that which makes holy." As such, the annihilative acts of the terrorists are "performed in a religious context that transforms the killing into something positive" (170–71). This transformative aspect is in keeping with the spectacle it is intended to generate. In his exploration of the "Theater of Terror," Juergensmeyer maintains, "the very adjectives used to describe acts of religious terrorism — symbolic, dramatic, theatrical — suggest that we look at them not as tactics but as *performative violence*. The spectacular assaults of September 11, 2001, were not only tragic acts of violence; they were also spectacular theater" (126). Spectacle is at the very heart of what the terrorist psyche is all about.

19. For the idea of holy wars in Milton, see Lieb, *Poetics of the Holy: A Reading of "Paradise Lost"* (Chapel Hill: University of North Carolina Press, 1981), esp. 246–312. For the idea of *sparagmos* in Milton, see Lieb, *Milton and the Culture of Violence* (Ithaca, N.Y.: Cornell University Press, 1994).

20. The Chorus itself seems committed to this view, as it declares: "All is best, though we oft doubt, / What th'unsearchable dispose / Of highest wisdom brings about" (1745–48).

21. *The Oxford Classical Dictionary* (Oxford: Clarendon Press, 1970), 472.

22. On the notion of the Gorgon Medusa's face, see the excellent study of Julia M. Walker, *Medusa's Mirrors: Spenser, Shakespeare, Milton, and the Metamorphosis of the Female Self* (Newark: University of Delaware Press, 1998), which offers its own gender-oriented reading of Medusa. Walker comments that the Gorgon Medusa actually "has no face." Between her beautiful body and her beautiful hair, "there is nothing" (48). That "nothing" might well be said to resonate with Fish's reading of *Samson*.

23. According to the editors of *A Variorum Commentary on the Poems of John Milton*, 4 vols. to date, gen. ed. Merritt Y. Hughes (New York: Columbia University Press, 1970–75), 2:914, "Medusa, one of the three Gorgons, whose face turned beholders to stone, had her head cut off by Perseus, the seducer of Andromeda. Because, in the chaste Minerva's temple, Medusa had been ravished by Neptune, the goddess had 'changed the Gorgon's locks to ugly snakes. And now to frighten her fear-numbed foes, she still wears that snaky head upon her breast,' i.e., on her shield." References to the Gorgon Medusa appear throughout Milton's works. See,

for example, Milton's account of hell in *Paradise Lost* as a place in which "*Medusa* with *Gorgonian* terror" threatens any who would transgress Hell's laws (2:610–11).

24. Sigmund Freud, *The Standard Edition of the Complete Psychological Works of Sigmund Freud*, 24 vol., trans. James Stratchey (London: Hogarth Press, 1962–74), 18:273–74.

25. The phrase "universal Blank" alludes to the proem to book 3 of *Paradise Lost* (47).

Notes to Chapter 10 / Fish

1. John Carey, "A Work in Praise of Terrorism? September 11 and *Samson Agonistes*," *Times Literary Supplement*, September 6, 2002, 15–16.

2. John Carey and Alastair Fowler, eds., *John Milton, Poems* (London: Longmans, 1968), 335, 341.

3. Stanley Fish, *How Milton Works* (Cambridge, Mass.: Harvard University Press, 2001), 426, 428.

4. Quotations of Milton's poetry are from *Complete Poems and Major Prose*, ed. Merritt Y. Hughes (New York: Macmillan, 1957).

5. This is the view held by Michael Lieb: "Through a misplaced allegiance to an idol that ultimately fails them, they are destroyed by . . . a power whose impact they never for a moment expected to encounter." See "Our Living Dread: The God of *Samson Agonistes*," in *Milton Studies* 33, *The Miltonic Samson*, ed. Albert C. Labriola and Michael Lieb (Pittsburgh: University of Pittsburgh Press, 1996), 13.

6. Mark Juergensmeyer, *Terror in the Mind of God: The Global Rise of Religious Violence* (Berkeley and Los Angeles: University of California Press, 2000), 173.

7. Paul Berman, *Terror and Liberalism* (New York: Norton, 2003), 110.

8. Hanserd Knollys, "A Glimpse of Sion's Glory": *Puritanism and Liberty*, 2nd ed., ed. A. S. P. Woodhouse (Chicago: University of Chicago Press, 1950), 233.

9. *The Complete Prose Works of John Milton*, 8 vols., ed. Don M. Wolfe et al. (New Haven: Yale University Press, 1953–82), hereafter designated YP and cited parenthetically by volume and page number in the text.

10. See on this point Alan Rudrum, "Milton Scholarship and the *Agon* over *Samson Agonistes*," *Huntington Library Quarterly* 65 (2002): 478. "Dalila's pleas of, 'Civil duty, religion, and public good' . . . serve to define the nature of an idolatrous state, in which religious duty represents no more than the wishes of the priests and elders of her tribe." See also David Gay, *The Endless Kingdom* (Newark: University of Delaware Press, 2002), 137: "[Samson] is, Milton suggests, 'persuaded inwardly that this was from God,' . . . Dalila, in contrast, is continually pressured by voices outside of her."

11. Victoria Kahn, "Political Theology and Reason of State in *Samson Agonistes*," *South Atlantic Quarterly* 95 (Fall 1996): 1068.

12. See Anne K. Krook, "The Hermeneutics of Opposition in *Paradise Regained* and *Samson Agonistes*," *SEL* 36 (1966): 129–47; Victoria Kahn, "Political Theology"; Gay, *The Endless Kingdom*, 99–184; John Shawcross, *The Uncertain World of "Samson Agonistes"* (Cambridge: D. S. Brewer, 2001). Interpretive conflict, as an organizing theme, is, I would argue, the key to answering the question of just how *Paradise Regained* and *Samson Agonistes* are related to each another. Are the figures of Samson and Christ to be linked by typology, or opposed as bad and good examples, respectively? It seems to me that the two productions share a single plot even though the differences of genre might tend to obscure the basic similarity. In both the poem and the play, the hero is presented (by one character in *Paradise Regained* and by many in *Samson Agonistes*) with a succession of motives and reasons for action — wealth, military success, art, domestic ease, pride, despair, quietism, nationalism, political reform, the responsibility of leadership — and in both the hero rejects these reasons and motives in favor of the trumping reason that one must strive to be faithful to God without forcing or limiting ("appointing") his will. The value of the actions each takes is measured by the actions refused, actions that would nominate alternative loyalties and alternative obligations. The actions refused are specific and knowable in their likely effects; the actions taken find no immediate confirmation in the world, but stand as testimony to the substance of things hoped for and the evidence of things not seen. Samson and Christ are alike heroes of faith despite the enormous differences of personality and affect. The fact that one performs a spectacular but problematic act, while the other is problematic in his refusal to act should not lead us to think of them as opposing figures; rather, they jointly illustrate the truth that faithful action — action taken in response to God's will, however imperfectly known — can take any form, including the form of just saying no.

13. See Fish, chapter 13, "The Temptation of Intelligibility," *How Milton Works*, 447–55.

14. Norman Burns, "Milton's Antinomianism, and Samson's," in *Milton Studies* 33 (1996), 29.

15. On the question of Milton's antinomianism, see Joan Bennett, "Milton's Antinomianism and the Separation Scene in *Paradise Lost*," *Reviving Liberty: Radical Christian Unionism in Milton's Great Poems* (Cambridge, Mass.: Harvard University Press, 1989); and Alan Rudrum, "Milton Scholarship and the *Agon* over *Samson Agonistes*," *Huntington Library Quarterly* 65 (2002): 484: "Milton's radicalism was generally antinomian."

16. "An Answer to a Book Intitled 'The Doctrine and Discipline of Divorce'" (1644), reprinted in W. R. Parker, *Milton's Contemporary Reputation* (Columbus: Ohio State University Press, 1940), 8.

17. Thomas Edwards quoted in Parker, *Milton's Contemporary Reputation*, 77.

18. "An Answer to a Book," in ibid., 36.

19. Bennett, *Reviving Liberty*, 110

20. Stanley Fish, *Professional Correctness: Literary Studies and Political Change* (New York: Oxford University Press, 1995).

21. Juergensmeyer, *Terror in the Mind of God*, 5.

22. Jessica Stern, *Terror in the Name of God: Why Religious Militants Kill* (New York: Harper Collins, 2003), xx.

23. One of the things John Carey says in his *TLS* essay is that *Samson Agonistes* has changed since September 11, 2001. That cannot be true. What is true is that in the aftermath of September 11, arguments, already in full career, about the meaning of *Samson Agonistes* — and especially arguments as to whether Samson's act was meant to be approved or condemned — acquired a new relevance as readers came quickly to see parallels between the moment the play dramatizes and the moment the nation had just lived through. But this new relevance, while it may have added spice and even a contemporary urgency to the search for Milton's meaning, could not have altered the object of that search. If a text were to alter with every change in the circumstance of its reception, the work could not be said to have a meaning, but rather would have as many meanings as there are circumstances and receivers, would have, in effect, infinite meanings. And if that were the case, *disagreement* about the text's meaning would be impossible, and literary criticism would not progress beyond the assertion and counterassertion of "it means this to me" and "maybe so, but it means something else to me." The very activity in which Carey engages — criticizing my account of Milton's meaning — commits him to believing that *Samson Agonistes* does have a meaning and that it is our business as critics to figure out what it is.

Selected Publications By and About Stanley Fish

Books and Collections Focusing on Stanley Fish's Work

Veeser, H. Aram, ed. *The Stanley Fish Reader*. Oxford: Blackwell, 1999.
Donnelly, Phillip J. *Rhetorical Faith: The Literary Hermeneutics of Stanley Fish*. Victoria, B.C.: English Literary Studies, University of Victoria, 2000.
Owen, J. Judd. *Religion and the Demise of Liberal Rationalism: The Foundational Crisis of the Separation of Church and State*. Chicago: University of Chicago Press, 2001.
Olson, Gary. *Justifying Belief: Stanley Fish and the Work of Rhetoric*. Albany: State University of New York Press, 2002.
Olson, Gary, and Lynne Worsham, editors. *Postmodern Sophistry: Stanley Fish and the Critical Enterprise*. Albany: State University of New York Press, 2004.

Selected Publications by Stanley Fish

Books

John Skelton's Poetry. New Haven: Yale University Press, 1965.
Surprised by Sin: The Reader in "Paradise Lost." London: Macmillan, 1967.
Seventeenth-Century Prose: Modern Essays in Criticism. Edited by Stanley Fish. Oxford: Oxford University Press, 1971.

Self-Consuming Artifacts: The Experience of Seventeenth-Century Literature (1972; reprint, Pittsburgh: Duquesne University Press, 1998).

The Living Temple: George Herbert and Catechizing. Berkeley and Los Angeles: University of California Press, 1978.

Is There a Text in This Class? The Authority of Interpretive Communities. Cambridge: Harvard University Press, 1980.

Doing What Comes Naturally: Change, Rhetoric, and the Practice of Theory in Literary and Legal Studies. Durham, N.C.: Duke University Press, 1989.

There's No Such Thing as Free Speech, and It's a Good Thing, Too. Oxford: Oxford University Press, 1994.

Professional Correctness: Literary Studies and Political Change. Oxford: Oxford University Press, 1995.

Surprised by Sin: The Reader in "Paradise Lost." Thirtieth anniversary edition with an extensive new preface. Cambridge, Mass.: Harvard University Press, 1997.

The Trouble with Principle. Cambridge, Mass.: Harvard University Press, 1999.

How Milton Works. Cambridge, Mass.: Harvard University Press, 2001.

Articles

"*The Nun's Priest's Tale* and Its Analogues." *College Language Association Journal* 5, no. 3 (March 1962): 223–28.

"Aspects of Rhetorical Analysis: Skelton's *Philip Sparrow.*" *Studia Neophilologica* 34, no. 2 (1962): 223–28.

"Nature as Concept and Character in the *Mutabilitie Cantos.*" *College Language Association Journal* 6, no. 3 (March 1963): 210–15.

"The Harassed Reader in *Paradise Lost.*" *Critical Quarterly* (Autumn 1965): 162–82.

"Further Thoughts on Milton's Christian Reader." *Critical Quarterly* (Autumn 1965): 279–84.

"Milton's God: Two Defences and a Qualification." *Southern Review* 11, no. 2 (1966): 116–36.

"Standing Only: Christian Heroism in *Paradise Lost.*" *Critical Quarterly* (Summer 1967): 162–78.

" 'Not So Much a Teaching as an Intangling': Milton's Method in *Paradise Lost.*" In *Milton: Modern Judgments,* edited by Alan Rudrum, 104–35. London: Macmillan, 1968.

"Question and Answer in *Samson Agonistes*." *Critical Quarterly* 11, no. 3 (Autumn 1969), 237–64.

"Discovery as Form in *Paradise Lost*." In *New Essays on Milton*, edited by Thomas Kranidas. Berkeley and Los Angeles: University of California Press, 1969.

"Literature in the Reader: Affective Stylistics." *New Literary History* 2 (Autumn 1970): 123–62.

"Letting Go: The Reader in Herbert's Poetry." *English Literary History* 37 (December 1970): 475–94.

"Reasons That Imply Themselves: Imagery, Argument and the Reader in Milton's *The Reason of Church Government*." In *Seventeenth-Century Imagery: Essays on Uses of Figurative Language from Donne to Farquhar*, edited by Earl Miner, 83–102. Berkeley and Los Angeles: University of California Press, 1971.

"Problem-Solving in *Comus*." In *Illustrious Evidence: Approaches to English Literature of the Early Seventeenth Century*, edited by Earl Miner, 115–31. Berkeley and Los Angeles: University of California Press, 1975.

"Interpreting the *Variorum*." *Critical Inquiry* 2 (Spring 1975): 465–85.

"*Lycidas*: A Poem Finally Anonymous." *Glyph* 8 (1981): 1–18.

"The Temptation to Action in Milton's Poetry." *English Literary History* 48, no. 3 (Fall 1981): 516–31.

"Things and Actions Indifferent: The Temptation of Plot in *Paradise Regained*." In *Milton Studies* 17, *Composite Orders: The Genres of Milton's Last Poems*, edited by Richard S. Ide and Joseph Wittreich Jr. (Pittsburgh: University of Pittsburgh Press, 1983), 163–85.

"Authors-Readers: Jonson's Community of the Same." Reprinted in *Representations* 7 (1984): 26–58.

"Transmuting the Lump: *Paradise Lost*, 1942–1982." In *Literature and History: Theoretical Problems and Russian Case Studies*, edited by Gary Saul Morson, 33–56. Stanford: Stanford University Press, 1986.

"Unger and Milton," Part I. *Raritan Review* (Fall 1987): 1–20; "Unger and Milton," Part 2. *Raritan Review* (Winter 1988): 1–24.

"Driving from the Letter: Truth and Indeterminacy in *Areopagitica*." In *Re-Membering Milton: Essays on the Texts and Traditions*, edited by Mary Nyquist and Margaret W. Ferguson. New York: Methuen, 1988.

"Spectacle and Evidence in *Samson Agonistes*." *Critical Inquiry* 15 (Spring 1989): 556–86.

"Masculine Persuasive Force: Donne and Verbal Power." *Soliciting Interpretations: Literary Theory and Seventeenth-Century English Poetry*, edited by Elizabeth Di Harvey and Katherine Eisaman Maus, 223–52. Chicago: University of Chicago Press, 1990.

"Wanting a Supplement: The Question of Interpretation in Milton's Early Prose." In *Politics, Poetics, and Hermeneutics in Milton's Prose*, edited by David Loewenstein and James Grantham Turner, 41–68. Cambridge: Cambridge University Press, 1990.

"With Mortal Voice: Milton Defends against the Muse." *English Literary History* 62 (Fall 1995): 509–27.

"What It Means to Do a Job of Work." *English Literary Renaissance* 25, no. 3 (Autumn 1995): 354–71.

"Mission Impossible: Settling the Just Bounds between Church and State." *Columbia Law Review* 97, no. 8 (Winter 1997): 2255–2333.

"Masculine Persuasive Force: Donne and Verbal Power." Reprinted in *John Donne*, edited by Andrew Mousley. London: Macmillan Press, 1999.

"'Void of Storie': The Struggle for Insincerity in Herbert's Prose and Poetry." In *Writing and Political Engagement in Seventeenth-Century England*, edited by Derek Hirst and Richard Strier, 31–51. Cambridge: Cambridge University Press, 1999.

"Marvell and the Art of Disappearance." In *Revenge of the Aesthetic: The Place of Literature in Theory Today*, edited by Michael P. Clark. Berkeley and Los Angeles: University of California Press, 2000.

"Holocaust Denial and Academic Freedom." *Valparaiso University Law Review* 35 (Summer 2001): 499–524.

"Truth but No Consequences: Why Philosophy Doesn't Matter." *Critical Inquiry* 29 (Spring 2003): 389–417.

About the Contributors

JOAN S. BENNETT, professor of English at the University of Delaware, is the author of *Reviving Liberty: Radical Christian Humanism in Milton's Great Poems* (1989) and other works on Milton.

LANA CABLE teaches in the Department of English at the University at Albany, SUNY. Her book *Carnal Rhetoric: Milton's Iconoclasm and the Poetics of Desire* (1995) received the James Holly Hanford Award. She is currently working on a study of popular secularism and the free conscience debate in early modern England.

STANLEY FISH is the Davidson-Kahn Distinguished University Professor and a professor of law at Florida International University, in Miami, and dean emeritus of the College of Liberal Arts and Sciences at the University of Illinois at Chicago.

MARSHALL GROSSMAN teaches at the University of Maryland. His publications include *"Authors to themselves": Milton and the Revelation of History* and *The Story of All Things: Writing the Self in English Renaissance Lyric Poetry*, as well as two edited collections of essays: *Aemilia Lanyer: Gender, Genre and the Canon* and *Reading Renaissance Ethic.*

ALBERT C. LABRIOLA, professor of English and Distinguished University Professor at Duquesne University, has been secretary of the Milton Society of America since 1974 and editor of *Milton Studies* since 1992. In 2000, he was named Honored Scholar of the Milton Society. He is general editor of *A Variorum Commentary on the Poems of John Milton.* He received the James Holly Hanford Award of the Milton Society for the most distinguished essay on Milton in 1981, and he has received three Irene Samuel Memorial Awards of the Milton Society for the most distinguished multiauthor collections on Milton, which he has edited or coedited.

BARBARA K. LEWALSKI is William R. Kenan Professor of History and Literature and of English Literature at Harvard University. Her Milton books include *The Life of John Milton: A Critical Biography* (2000, 2003), *"Paradise Lost" and the Rhetoric of Literary Forms* (1985), *Milton's Brief Epic: The Genre, Meaning, and Art of "Paradise Regained"* (1956), and an original language edition of *Paradise Lost* (2006).

MICHAEL LIEB is Professor of English and Research Professor of Humanities at the University of Illinois at Chicago. His most recent book is *Theological Milton: Deity, Discourse and Heresy in the Miltonic Canon* (2006). Lieb is Honored Scholar of the Milton Society of America (1992). He is currently working on a study of Milton and Galileo.

DAVID LOEWENSTEIN is Marjorie and Lorin Tiefenthaler Professor of English at the University of Wisconsin-Madison. His book *Representing Revolution in Milton and His Contemporaries: Religion, Politics, and Polemics in Radical Puritanism* (2001) won the Milton Society of America's James Holly Hanford Award. He is coeditor (with Janel Mueller) of *The Cambridge*

History of Early Modern English Literature (2002; revised paperback edition, 2006).

ANNABEL PATTERSON is Sterling Professor Emeritus at Yale University. For the last 30 years she has nibbled away at John Milton, especially his sonnets and divorce tracts, but she still has not written a whole book on the man and his works. The essay in this volume is the closest she has come to that goal.

STELLA P. REVARD is professor emeritus of Southern Illinois Uni-versity at Edwardsville, an Honored Scholar of the Milton Society of America, and past president of the International Association for Neo-Latin Studies. She has published more than 70 articles on Renaissance, classical, and other studies, and three books — *The War in Heaven, Milton and the Tangles of Neaera's Hair* (both winners of the Hanford Award), and *Pindar and the Renaissance Hymn-Ode*. A fourth book is forthcoming — *Politics, Poetics, and the Pindaric Ode: 1450–1700*.

JOSEPH WITTREICH, Distinguished Professor of English, The Graduate Center of The City University of New York, is the author of numerous books, the most recent of them, *Why Milton Matters*, was published by Palgrave Macmillan.

Index

311